Between Norteño and
Tejano Conjunto

Music, Culture, and Identity in Latin America

Series Editor: Pablo Vila, Temple University, and Héctor Fernández L'Hoeste, Georgia State University

Music is one of the most distinctive cultural characteristics of Latin American countries. But, while many people in the United States and Europe are familiar with musical genres such as salsa, merengue, and reggaetón, the musical manifestations that people listen to in most Latin American countries are much more varied than these commercially successful ones that have entered the American and European markets. *Music, Culture, and Identity in Latin America* series examines the ways in which music is used to advance identity claims in different Latin American countries and among Latinos in the US. The series sheds new light on the complex ways in which music provides people from Latin American countries with both enjoyment and tools for understanding who they are in terms of nationality, region, race, ethnicity, class, gender, age, sexuality and migration status (among other identitarian markers). *Music, Culture, and Identity in Latin America* seeks to be truly interdisciplinary by including authors from all the social sciences and humanities: political science, sociology, psychology, musicology, cultural studies, literature, history, religious studies, and the like.

Recent Titles in This Series

Between Norteño and Tejano Conjunto: Music, Tradition, and Culture at the U.S.-Mexico Border by Luis Díaz-Santana Garza

Modernity and Colombian Identity in the Work of Carlos Vives and La Provincia by Manuel Sevilla, Juan Sebastián Ochoa, Carolina Santamaría-Delgado, and Carlos Eduardo Cataño Arango

Decentering the Nation: Music, Mexicanidad, and Globalization edited by Jesús A. Ramos-Kittrell

The Latin American Songbook in the Twentieth Century: From Folklore to Militancy by Tânia Costa Garcia

Music, Dance, Affect, and Emotions in Latin America edited by Pablo Vila

Argentine Queer Tango: Dance and Sexuality Politics in Buenos Aires by Mercedes Liska

The Chilean New Song and the "Cultural Issue" during the Popular Unity: Voices for a Revolution by Natália Ayo Schmiedecke

Between Norteño and Tejano Conjunto

Music, Tradition, and Culture at the U.S.-Mexico Border

Luis Díaz-Santana Garza

Foreword by
Walter Aaron Clark

LEXINGTON BOOKS
Lanham • Boulder • New York • London

Published by Lexington Books
An imprint of The Rowman & Littlefield Publishing Group, Inc.
4501 Forbes Boulevard, Suite 200, Lanham, Maryland 20706
www.rowman.com

6 Tinworth Street, London SE11 5AL, United Kingdom

Copyright © 2021 The Rowman & Littlefield Publishing Group, Inc.

All rights reserved. No part of this book may be reproduced in any form or by any electronic or mechanical means, including information storage and retrieval systems, without written permission from the publisher, except by a reviewer who may quote passages in a review.

British Library Cataloguing in Publication Information Available

Library of Congress Cataloging-in-Publication Data

Names: Díaz-Santana Garza, Luis author.
Title: Between norteño and tejano conjunto : music, tradition, and culture at the U.S.-Mexico border / Luis Díaz-Santana Garza ; foreword by Walter Aaron Clark.
Description: Lanham : Lexington Books, 2021. | Series: Music, culture, and identity in Latin America | Includes bibliographical references and index.
    Identifiers: LCCN 2021014931 (print) | LCCN 2021014932 (ebook) | ISBN 9781793639004 (cloth) | ISBN 9781793638991 (epub)
Subjects: LCSH: Popular music—Mexican-American Border Region—History and criticism. | Music—Social aspects—Mexican-American Border Region. | Conjunto music—History and criticism. | Tejano music—History and criticism.
Classification: LCC ML3476 .D53 2021 (print) | LCC ML3476 (ebook) | DDC 781.64097—dc23
LC record available at https://lccn.loc.gov/2021014931
LC ebook record available at https://lccn.loc.gov/2021014932

Contents

Foreword		vii
Acknowledgments		ix
Introduction		1
1	Border Territory: Nuevo León and Texas from Colonial Times to the Nineteenth Century	21
2	Precursors to Conjunto: Culture, Migration, and Border Identity	39
3	The First Epoch of Conjunto: Instruments, Musical Forms, and Media	57
4	Conjunto: From Subaltern Mexican Culture to American Cultural Treasure	85
5	Transformation and Recent Trends in Conjunto	103
Conclusions		123
Glossary of Musical Terms		129
A Selection of Recorded Music		131
A Selection of Norteño/Tejano Performers		135
Interviews		137
Newspapers		139
Archives		141

Bibliography 143

Index 157

About the Author 161

Foreword

The space age dawned in the late 1950s and soon provided humanity with a new way of viewing its place in the cosmos. The famous photo of Earth taken from an Apollo spacecraft orbiting the moon in 1968, at a time at least as troublous as our own, revealed that the world does not look very much like the maps we have made of it. There are no boundaries, no borders, no walls. There are large expanses of green, brown, white, and blue, which correspond to forests, deserts, mountain ranges, and oceans, but the national delimitations of which we are inordinately fond are nowhere to be seen. Homo sapiens is but one species living on one planet, which itself is merely "a mote of dust suspended in a sunbeam," as Carl Sagan put it.

Clearly, this new planetary consciousness has had a transformative effect on our civilization, though it is distressing to see that many people are still obsessed with erecting walls to reinforce divisions. However, there is an irony lurking here. Though we may condemn territoriality and a fixation on borders and barriers, without them, there would be nothing to cross or transgress. This in turn would deprive us of one of the principal engines of hybridization, a process central to all types of creativity.

Although the author focuses on music, tradition, and culture at the U.S.-Mexico border, what this study makes clear is that there are many kinds of boundaries, not just geopolitical ones. The dichotomies we confront in our daily lives include those between past and present; tradition and modernity; upper and lower classes; assorted ethnic, racial, and national identities; classical, traditional, and popular musics; languages; genders; and sexual. The differences between a *bajo sexto* and an electric guitar may not seem significant to the casual observer, but in fact they raise crucial issues in the realms not only of musical technology but also society and culture—issues that the author skillfully and helpfully unpacks for us.

Indeed, the liminal space occupied by *norteño* and *Tejano* is replete with all of these confrontations, which are the source not only of conflict but also creativity. The Tex-Mex borderlands were originally inhabited by various Native peoples and later settled by Spaniards, Anglos, Germans, Poles, and Czechs. All of these groups have contributed in some way to this musical heritage, a heritage that thus coaxes unity out of diversity. In the author's words, "In this context, norteño conjunto, as well as its expansion into *Tejano* conjunto, can be considered a form of opposition to discrimination."

Prof. Díaz-Santana Garza speaks with the authority of personal experience, as he grew up in northern Mexico and spent a good deal of his youth on the U.S. side of the border. From his point of view, "People who are not born into this territory seldom know its history, and therefore will find it difficult to comprehend border culture." He is on intimate terms with this territory and writes about it with a familiarity tempered by scholarly detachment. As his narrative makes clear, it is precisely such border regions that are the metaphorical soil in which the seedlings of culture take deep root and sprout into life-affirming crops of literature, art, and music. The cross-fertilization of various styles then "enriches the traditions with which they merged." Such is the immemorial way of all things cultural.

This remarkable book provides not only a cornucopia of information at once valuable and fascinating, but it also imparts to the reader something even more important: food for thought. Without becoming abstruse, the author breaks down barriers to interrogating the borders we erect, and he does so in a language that though well informed from the standpoint of contemporary cultural theory never descends into jargon-impacted obscurantism. Indeed, his prose style is remarkably engaging, especially given that English is not his native language.

In light of the manifold challenges our world currently faces, the theme of this book is a timely one. As the author deftly notes, "norteño and *Tejano* conjunto, as a living heritage and a cultural tradition shared by Mexico and the United States, are two sides of the same coin." They thus hold out not only the hope but also the promise of helping to free us from the prison of our prejudices. Just as the fabled walls of Jericho came tumbling down when assailed by the sound of Israelite trumpets, so any walls we attempt to construct between the United States and Mexico will never withstand the force of music, tradition, and culture presented by the irresistible charms of *conjunto*. For that we can be truly grateful.

Walter Aaron Clark
Distinguished Professor of Musicology
Director, Center for Iberian and Latin American Music
University of California, Riverside

Acknowledgments

This book is the result of a grant from the National Council of Science and Technology (CONACYT, in Spanish) and another from the Autonomous University of Zacatecas (UAZ). Research that began in 2011 has led me to meet people who have supported me in various ways. First, I wish to acknowledge the encouragement and time of my teachers, in particular José Francisco Román and Genaro Zalpa. Eloy Cruz Soto also aided me in all our consultations.

The English-language books on this subject can, for the most part, be acquired easily on the internet, including some in digital format, except for the books published in Mexico, whose print runs are normally small and often sell out. For this reason, I would like to thank Juan Alanís Tamez and Alfonso Ayala Duarte for providing me with their texts for a pittance, while Guillermo Berrones flatly refused to accept money for his books and even had them sent to my house. José Juan Olvera Gudiño did the same with several digital files.

Similarly, some musicians opened the doors of their homes to talk for hours, and legendary *Tejano* composer Mingo Saldívar even invited us to eat at his favorite bar near San Antonio. In addition, I cannot fail to thank the staff of the libraries and archives that I visited, since I always encountered friendly treatment and unconditional support. The generosity that characterizes such people were an inspiration for the writing of this book on the history of northeast Mexico and South Texas.

Finally, the patience of my family made the days of reading and writing gratifying, and so I dedicate this book to my wife, Sonia Medrano, and my son, Javier, as well as my grandfather, Américo Garza Elizondo, who died in 2013 and was a wonderful companion on the many unforgettable trips that we made together through the municipalities of Nuevo León, Tamaulipas, and the Lower Rio Grande Valley, Texas.

Introduction

Some years ago, when I developed research on music from the Mexican state of Zacatecas during the *Porfiriato* (the era related to the government of Mexican president Porfirio Díaz, 1876–1910), I did a series of interviews with elderly musicians and the recurrent theme was migration to the United States. Many inhabitants of Zacatecas who lived through the problematic postrevolutionary years were forced by circumstances to relocate, either temporarily or permanently, to the United States. But they were not isolated cases: historically, a large number of citizens from various regions of México have sought a better life in the U.S., carrying their symbolic capital along, and among the most important thing to them was the music that they had known since childhood.

The U.S. Bureau of Immigration began operations in the 1820s, but for many years, the 2,000 miles of border that separated the United States from Mexico made it impossible to count the number of people who crossed into U.S. territory. But we know, for example, that for over 150 years Mexicans have been part of the community of the American Midwest: in an 1850 census, at least fifty Mexicans resided in the state of Illinois (Arias Jirazek 2001, 8). Additionally, Sánchez (1995, 18) estimated that over 20,000 specialized miners from Zacatecas and Sonora moved to northern California during the gold rush, although it is in the first decades of the twentieth century that we see the process of formation of regions, of origin and destination, between the two nations (Durand 2007, 55). It was after the Mexican Revolution that the first "substantial and permanent" migration toward the north commenced, and according to Grebler, Moore, and Guzman (1970, 63), in Texas the recently arrived had come from Coahuila, Nuevo León, and Tamaulipas.

Originally, my purpose was to write a manuscript about the impact of Mexican musicians in the United States, yet given the huge variety of musical forms and the extent to which they are spread over the great Mexican-American frontier, the topic of musicians and migration was too broad. It would be almost impossible to encompass in one project the mariachi and brass bands, the *gruperos* (groups), and the tropical, rap, rock, and electronic music that inhabit this area. Therefore, in this book I concentrate on *norteño* (northern) conjunto (the word *conjunto* in Spanish means group, or musical ensemble) and its relation to *Tejano* conjunto—also called Texas-Mexican conjunto, Tex-Mex conjunto, or simply *conjunto*—because I consider it erroneous to study them separately, due to their common origin and transnational nature, and because even today both remain to some extent relegated cultural traditions, deemed by some academics to be unworthy of serious consideration. There has even been an attempted ban on some norteño groups: a few years ago, the Mexican Secretary of the Interior declared his support to the government of the state of Sinaloa in relation to a law that prohibits *narcocorrido* (songs about drug trafficking) there.

However, being that the art of sound is one of the most significant manifestations of human society, we cannot ignore the importance of its study in the humanities, in particular in our area: history, informed by ethnography. To highlight its hierarchy, English ethnomusicologist Simon Frith (mentioned in Simonett 2001, 18) suggested that we should look to popular music in terms of how it can articulate meanings, organize our sense of time and memory, and contribute to the social construction of individual identities. As Watermann and Erlmann (cited in Simonett 2001, 20) have shown, popular music can provide a system for the presentation and public negotiation of identity, as well as for building alternative sources of power and meaning. In addition, Bourdieu (2002, 16) claims "there is nothing that allows one to assert her/his [social] class so strongly as tastes in music."

The so-called new cultural history (not so new, in fact) has fluctuated between a definition of popular culture as a "coherent symbolic system" that cannot be subdued by literate culture, on one hand, and, on the other hand, as something understood in terms of "its dependencies and shortcomings with regard to the culture of the dominant" (Chartier 2005, 30). For my part, I want to reach a middle point where it is possible to speak of popular culture as a system with principles of its own, but in constant dialogue and exchange with "official" culture, and with other marginalized cultural expressions.

The overall objective of this book is to analyze the origin, evolution, and dissemination of norteño and *Tejano* conjunto, a group that represents, historically, a marginalized local identity that was transformed primarily into an identity of the northeast, then gave way to the whole of northern México and the American Southwest, and later was assimilated internationally as a mainstream genre. My purpose is to give a long-term historic vision of conjunto and the various musical forms it uses, such as polka, corrido, or *canción* (song), and, more recently, bolero and cumbia, as well as its transformations and contributions to other musical cultures. Throughout this book there are places where I refer to both norteño and *Tejano* conjunto, for which I will use the word conjunto indiscriminately.

Among my specific goals are the following: (a) to identify the geographic region where norteño music was originally popularized; (b) to analyze the weight of economic and technological influence in the development of this musical style in the states of Nuevo León and Tamaulipas (México) and in Texas (USA); (c) to explain how the norteño and *Tejano* conjunto has been modified, detailing the musical forms used, the musical instruments employed, and their lyrics, to try to unfold their meanings; (d) to examine the means and places of dissemination of norteño and *Tejano* music; (e) to outline the features of cultural identity between migration and norteño music; and (f) to characterize the relationship between norteño music and narcoculture.

My aim is to re-evaluate the popular manifestations of Nuevo León, Tamaulipas, and Texas, especially in the area where conjunto music features as a cultural expression, which, by combining emotion and intellect, becomes moving to people, first becoming meaningful to a social group in northeastern México and the southern United States, and currently in various countries around the world. Along with its inherent value as artistic testimony, the value of this music resides in the sense of identity—and differentiation—that it embodies, and because it is part of a broader culture of resistance to assimilation and discrimination among migrant workers, contemptuously called *mojados* (wetbacks).

From its early years, the music of conjunto has been linked to *fiestas* (parties). The sphere in which it unfolds is that of the streets, of markets, bars and squares, of weddings and any kind of family celebration where people normally dance (Ayala Duarte 2000, 82–87). It is thus understandable that these places served as a form of advertising: they offered the most convenient moment in which to secure the next show. As we shall see later, the music of both norteño and *Tejano* conjunto shares a literary and musical syncretism: in both artistic manifestations they sing in Spanish, while reaffirming language as one of the most powerful ingredients of identity: "The principal means by which culture is brought within reach is language . . . it is the most meaningful way" (Halliday 1998, 278). In addition, in both conjuntos, there are influences and adaptations from various European and American musical cultures, as well as other folk music of the region, such as Cajun and country. As an example, Tony de la Rosa, one of the most prominent *Tejano* conjunto accordionists, loved Cajun music and made sure that when he played the accordion he imitated the sound of Western country and Cajun violin, as he said in an interview (Ragland 2009, 69).

Another issue to be discussed is whether norteño music reflects the identity of second and third-generation Mexicans in the United States. In this regard, the reaction of Lupe Sáenz, director of the South Texas Conjunto Association, is quite illustrative. When listening to *Tejano* conjunto, Sáenz says, people ask whether it is Mexican music and that disappoints Sáenz, as he told Elbein (2011): "Maybe it's Spanish music; maybe it's German music; maybe it's rock 'n' roll music. But it's sure not Mexican music." As norteño music is currently enjoying more time on the Texan airwaves and higher sales in record stores than the local conjunto, we should not be surprised that Sáenz declares he is "anti-norteño."

With more moderate ideas, the director of the organization Texas Folklife, Cristina Balli, regrets that, in spite of the music having common roots and styles, there are discussions and distinctions regarding the differences between norteño and *Tejano* conjunto, which only brings out a lot of "intra-ethnic tension" (Elbein 2011), while to an outsider, both seem to be exactly the same thing. Currently, *Tejano* conjunto has a stream of artists performing daring musical fusions with harmonies from jazz and rock, and occasionally singing in English, distancing them somewhat from norteño conjunto, which despite innovations has been comparatively faithful to its origins. However, the pioneers of *Tejano* conjunto did not separate *their* music from Mexican music; by way of example, we can cite the blind accordionist Bruno Villarreal, whose early recordings included *La cucaracha* (The Cockroach), *La Adelita* (The Woman Soldier), and *La rielera* (The Railroad Worker) (Shorkey 2001, 305); or Santiago Jiménez, father of Grammy winner Leonardo "Flaco" Jiménez, who claimed to be "one of the first to play *música norteña* here in San Antonio" (Tejeda 2001, 255).

Until the mid-twentieth century, it was very easy to cross the border between Mexico and the United States. Now, when referring to this space, we think in terms of two different cultures, but historically, the vast northern part of Mexico (*el Gran Norte*, the Great North) was a region that included the current southwestern United States. The territory to the north and south of the present dividing line was thus developed through Mexican and *novohispanas* (Neo-Hispanic or Mexican viceregal) traditions. Various historians have pointed out the unique characteristics of this area, especially its isolation and remoteness from major population centers: it is an independent zone, with a strong affinity among its communities, and cultural continuity. Américo Paredes, one of the fathers of border folklore, described the contours of the Rio Bravo/Grande as a country different from the United States as well as Mexico.

This area has, without a doubt, a strong cultural identity, not only in its music but also in its personalities, to the point that the image of the Texan cowboy has become a stereotype, as in Mexico has *Don Matías* or *Piporro*, those mustachioed chatterboxes dressed in traditional Tamaulipas leather, boots, and hats. It is no coincidence that the traditions we study here are from a region of great industrial development, but also with constant migration from the countryside to the city, where ambivalence about identity and a search for culture prevail. As an emblem of this territory, norteña music represents, and over time changes, a specific worldview, which participates in the building of a reality: we must speak of outsourcing, the objectification and internalization of such music. The very term "norteño music" is a social construct, whose significance has changed over time. We thus extend our study to the ideas of sociologists of knowledge such as Peter Berger and Thomas Luckman (1995) regarding the powerful relationship between the individual and society.

But what do we mean when we talk about this music? Norteño and *Tejano* conjunto developed as a musical expression of the border between Mexico and the United States (Chew Sánchez 2006, 35). Its basic musical instruments are the diatonic button accordion and *bajo sexto* (a Mexican 12-string folk guitar), later joined by the *tololoche* (a sort of upright bass), electric bass, and drums, and sometimes saxophone. It was born in the early decades of the twentieth century in the rural area of Nuevo León and from there spread to the *cantina* (canteen) and neighborhoods of Monterrey through migration (Ayala Duarte 2000, 83). One should note that at the beginning of the twentieth century, because the city of Monterrey was one of the most prosperous industrial centers in Mexico, its economic and cultural influence in the region, its *hinterland*, stretched toward the neighboring states of Tamaulipas and Coahuila, and also included southern Texas. In music, and as we will see later, the *neoleoneses* (people of Nuevo León), who were instructors and performers of the most varied musical instruments, had great influence in the region, particularly in Texas, where them enjoyed a reputation for being orchestral performers with excellent training (Peña 1985, 28).

Mainly due to migration, norteño conjunto was soon common in other latitudes. It flourished almost simultaneously in South Texas and northern Tamaulipas, and by the 1960s, we find groups pumping the accordion and strumming the bajo sexto throughout northern Mexico: Baja California, Sinaloa, Sonora, Chihuahua, and Durango (García Flores 2006, 235). Today, one of its most prominent representatives—Los Tigres del Norte (The Tigers of the North)—is a group from northwestern Mexico based in California, whose music is played by groups all over Mexico and the United States, and even in Central and South American countries, and their recordings and concerts have generated a multimillion-dollar industry.

Among the musical instruments that enjoyed great popularity in the region of the current study, the diatonic button accordion became representative. The German company Hohner, founded in 1857, exported its accordions to

Mexico and the United States at the end of the nineteenth century, probably entering the continent through the port of Matamoros in Tamaulipas. Because the area was regarded as one of the best for distribution, a representative of the German company opened, in 1908, a branch in Mexico City, although it closed doors three years later due to the outbreak of the Revolution. Of acceptable quality, sonorous, lightweight, and much cheaper than the piano accordion (Ragland 2009, 49), the instrument saw unquestionable success. In 1906, one could buy a two-row instrument in the Rio Grande Valley for only three dollars (Goodwyn 2011). Two decades later, the virtuoso Antonio Tanguma, from China, Nuevo León, acquired a similar accordion in the town of La Feria, Texas, for ten pesos. At that time, Tanguma earned 50 cents a day working in the fields (see "Polka, roots of accordion playing in South Texas part 4 of 7," n.d.). Although these instruments were not costly, Mexicans from the interior of the country viewed them as a sign of economic prosperity, probably due to the complexity of their production, involving a large number of moving parts of various materials, which evoked the modernity of the factories in which they were made.

Along with the accordion and, later, the bajo sexto, a cardinal event in the spread of conjunto was the emergence of radio. A pioneer in the transmission of Hertzian waves in Latin America was engineer Constantino de Tárnava (Ayala Duarte 2000, 69), who in 1921 founded the first organized radio station in Mexico, although he already had been broadcasting sporadically from the living room of his home in downtown Monterrey since 1919 (Vizcaya Canales 2006, 147). It is notable that this broadcaster officially began to transmit almost a year and a half before the first commercial broadcast in Texas, which originated in Houston, in March 1922 (Ragland 2009, 76).

Even before radio, the music of the accordion and *tambora de rancho* (ranch drum, a traditional big drum) that had existed since the end of the nineteenth century in sparsely populated communities to the east and northeast of Nuevo León was being replaced by accordion and guitar, and later by accordion and bajo sexto. This, however, remained marginal because it was linked largely to *zonas de tolerancia* (red-light districts) (Ragland 2009, 54). It was for these reasons, coupled with migration and a lack of technology, that conjuntos norteños had to travel to Texas to record. In a sense, the appearance of record albums was equivalent to the birth of the book: both helped spread a form of expression. Indeed, just as important as radio was the fact that, thanks to new portable recording technology, the first commercial records produced in Texas and other states in the American southwest were manufactured by large U.S. companies, including RCA/Victor's subsidiary Bluebird. This brand was created to cover rural and regional markets, to record what was known as "regional roots music" or "race records" (Ragland 2009, 50).

An inspection of the most influential recordings of which we are aware allows us to say that at the dawn of conjunto, in the 1920s and 1930s, these small musical groups recorded instrumental pieces exclusively, in particular polkas—almost 40 percent of the music recorded by conjuntos before 1941 consisted of polkas (San Miguel Jr. 2002, 10)—and the repertoire was very similar in Texas and Nuevo León. In Mexico, before the appearance of the group Los Alegres de Terán during the 1940s, it was very rare to hear songs accompanied by bajo sexto and accordion. Just a few years later, we can appreciate the great importance of language as creator of affinity in a particular social group, because, on both sides of the border, people were singing in Spanish.

In this way, we can observe that Mexican migrants have contributed to many areas of American society: Beyond working in the fields, they also promoted the cultural development of their own communities in the north. We know not only the complexity of the migration of cultural goods that it takes but also how it enriches the traditions with which they merged. This process continues today, and is what American ethnomusicologist Steve Loza (2001, 52) has called *transethnicity*, an example of how to reconfigure and update identities and traditions. In this context, norteño conjunto, as well as its expansion into *Tejano* conjunto, can be considered a form of opposition to discrimination: the music becomes an act of "expressive-cultural resistance" (Peña 1999, 21). In this regard, at the end of the 1960s, the trend of ethnic pride among Mexican Americans known as the Chicano Movement transformed the status of conjunto in the United States from "cantina trash to cultural treasure" (Peña 1999, 115).

The music of conjunto would be stigmatized initially, but as the 1960s drew near, it was transformed into a mass phenomenon. Following Theodor Adorno, sociologists Joseph Kotraba and Phillip Vannini (2009, 74–75) argue that mass culture is one in which the tastes of the people have been "standardized by a culture industry" anxious to preserve the political and economic status quo. But the music of conjunto is a culture that seeks to pose an alternative to power, or at least centralized power. In addition, if we agree with theorists who, in speaking of popular music, identify a conservative ideology, protected by groups that wield political and economic dominance in a capitalist society, we can say that over the period of this study, and prior to the era of mass accessibility, the music of conjunto was dispersed to the margins of a power that supported it only in subtle ways, such as when, during election periods, it was used to promote candidates.

At present, the conjunto, especially norteño, is located in the field of mass culture. Interpreters usually do not see themselves as special or different from the rest of society, and they do not fit into the dominant stereotypes of some other musical genres: the eccentric singer and drug addict, the drunkard or womanizer. In spite of the fact that its origins are considered to lie in rural *cantina* music, the truth is that conjunto musicians are known to be exemplary parents, exceptional workers, and leading figures in their communities. Among the characteristics I found when interviewing various musicians, both in the United States and in Mexico, were humility and generosity. Pioneers like Narciso Martínez, Pedro Ayala, or Benny Layton, for instance, performed at no cost for their respective churches until the last days of their lives (Martinez 2011, 90). Every year at Christmas, accordionist Ramón Ayala organizes a large *posada* in the town where he lives, Hidalgo, Texas, during which he gives away thousands of toys to the children of the Rio Grande Valley and northern Tamaulipas. In a similar manner, and with the aim of digitizing old recordings, in 2000, the University of California at Los Angeles received the largest donation ever made by a civil organization to promote traditions when it received half a million dollars from the Los Tigres del Norte Foundation (Gurza, Clark, and Strachwitz 2012, 10).

I find the topic of regional-transnational music significant, especially because the few books published on this topic tend to be written from the perspective of researchers based to the north of the Rio Bravo/Grande, as a result of which some cannot avoid falling into stereotypes of an exotic and wild Mexico. Despite the fact that Mexico is a country with a high human development index, journalist Elijah Wald (2001), for example, while traveling through both rural and industrialized areas of México, gave the impression of a land of ingenious musicians, but also of a land that was sparsely populated and awash in corruption and ignorance, with poor, archaic services and means of communication.

In the Mexican academic world, we can find remarkable publications linked to the border, detailing its economy, society, culture, and issues of migration. There are various books on the subject, among which we can find *Migración México-Estados Unidos: Implicaciones y retos para ambos países* (U.S.-Mexico Migration: Implications and Challenges for Both Countries), edited by Elena Zúñiga and Jesús Arroyo; *Mitos en las relaciones México-Estados Unidos* (Myths in U.S.-Mexico Relations), compiled by Mary E. Schumacher; and *El país transnacional: Migración mexicana y cambio social a través de la frontera* (The Transnational Country: Mexican Migration and Social Change across the Border), coordinated by Marina Ariza and Alejandro Portes.

Other publications offer opportunities to develop one of the fundamental discussions of this book: the center-periphery conflict. In fact, after having consulted the research of experts from the United States and northern México, a very peculiar perspective and various prejudices regarding the border region are evident in various volumes published in Mexico City. American historian Philip Wayne Powell (1997, 348), observing from north of the current border, stresses that the American West became a universal symbol, attracted great public interest, and spawned a huge number of movies and other artistic expressions. But he also regrets that, despite its profound and lasting influence in shaping the destiny of Mexico, that country did not develop a norteño imaginary similar to that of the cowboy, and that "the [Mexican] northern border . . . is an almost forgotten historical world."

On the other hand, we have Mexican historian Josefina Zoraida Vázquez alluding to the crisis of 1840 (discussed later) in the book *Historia general de México* (General History of Mexico) (2002, 545), claiming "the rebels of the Rio Bravo fled to Texas and hired mercenaries, which inspired Texans to promote the idea that the federalist revolt should become a separatist movement, supposedly to establish the Republic of the Rio Grande." It is true that some citizens of Texas gave financial support to the movement started in Laredo, but we must place the facts in their historical context. Texas had a large number of internal problems. Texans wanted, before anything else, recognition of their independence, the ability to organize their internal elections, their city halls, and state congress; supporting armed movements with uncertain outcomes was not a priority. The author also attributes very little initiative to the military and political leaders of the movement—some of them very prominent, like Antonio Zapata or the governors from the north—and even presents them as easily manipulated by the Texans.

It is clear that the *General History of Mexico* is addressed to students and a wide audience, but it is also true that a prominent historian like Vázquez cannot afford to fall into reductionism, attributing a problem to a single cause, when the historical facts she disdains could well explain the origin of a new country, or at least a state in the American union. It is likely that bias generated by a Mexico City perspective influences her opinions, since around the same time as the uprising of the Republic of the Rio Grande, the state of Yucatán also declared independence from México and sought incorporation into the United States; this event, however, draws no commentary from the author.

In any case, we should attribute these remote regions' attempts at emancipation from central government to a feeling of isolation—which also, of course, necessarily strengthens autonomy—as well as to the insignificant federal support they received in times of difficulty. Fortunately, in the same book, Enrique Florescano and Margarita Menegus (2002, 392) draw a very different picture, recognizing regional differences and asserting that, at the distant border

> The human groups interned in these lands, and the human conditions that they found in them, helped to shape a different society from that of the center and

south. Prospectors and adventurers . . . soldiers and ambitious captains . . . friars consumed by an evangelizing faith . . . those were the agents of this latest colonizing wave. They were joined by a few dozen Spanish farmers and ranchers, several hundred Tlaxcaltecas and Tarascan Indians brought north as civilizers of the Chichimecas, and Indians native to the place. . . . Isolated, few in number, in a land of war and faced by hostile nature, these men became accustomed to building and defending continually the *socavón* [mine], the church . . . and the society they wanted.

But if we find insufficient historical research on the region, there is even less material focused exclusively on the art of sound along the border. Although in later editions of the book she discarded this statement, in *Historia de la música popular mexicana* (History of Mexican Popular Music), Yolanda Moreno (1989a) originally argued that singer and bajo sexto player Cornelio Reyna was the only artist and composer of norteña music who had been acclaimed by a large audience, but she specifies this acclaim was "only by immigrants," which reveals prejudices that scholars of folk music have toward the genre. Prominent composers and interpreters of norteño music, like Ramón Ayala or Julián Garza, have expressed their desire to see more academic work devoted to their art, citing a shortage of the same in comparison to publications on its *Tejano* counterpart (Ragland 2009, viii). We can, however, cite the summaries of anecdotes and historical data gathered by architect Juan Alanís Tamez in *Los Montañeses del Álamo*; the work of professor Guillermo Berrones on corrido norteño and the life and times of norteño duo *El Palomo y el Gorrión* (the Pigeon and the Sparrow); or the research of sociologist Alfonso Ayala Duarte in relation to the history of music in Monterrey and popular musicians.

Award-winning research was conducted by José Manuel Valenzuela (2002, 17–25) in *Jefe de jefes, corridos y narcocultura en México* (Boss of Bosses: Ballads and Narcoculture in Mexico), in which the author explores the language of the drug world. He picks up on other authors' ideas, saying that the corrido is an example and a symbol and was used as a form of resistance to assimilation by Mexican settlers in the United States, as American ethnomusicologist Manuel Peña had proposed years earlier. However, Valenzuela's book focuses on a sociological examination of lyrics, ignoring the fact that studying these songs solely through their words means studying only a very small part of them; the analysis of lyrics reveals nothing about the music that accompanies them, or about the social practices associated with the genre, or about the contexts in which music is present (Frith 1996). In desiring to know the reason why individuals join gangs, the author seems to justify the role of the drug trafficker, insisting on two consecutive paragraphs that "poverty frightens" (Valenzuela, 2002, 104–105).

North of the Rio Bravo/Grande, the most prominent researcher on *Tejano* conjunto, the aforementioned Manuel Peña, has narrated in detail the history of the ensemble from its genesis. Nevertheless, in his books *The Texas-Mexican Conjunto: History of a Working-Class Music* and *Música Tejana: The Cultural Economy of Artistic Transformation*, his gaze barely moves south of the border, highlighting only the economic and sociocultural prominence of the city of Monterrey in the region.

One of the most recent contributions to the construction of norteño conjunto history has been Catherine Ragland's book *Música Norteña: Mexican Migrants Creating a Nation between Nations*. This evocative research revolves around corrido, referring only sporadically to other musical forms, in addition to focusing on the problem of migration, emphasizing the reception of norteño music by Mexicans living in the United States. Last but not least. *Music in Mexico: Experiencing Music, Expressing Culture*, by Mexican-American cultural theorist Alejandro L. Madrid, dedicates one of its chapters to "norteño music and its history of hybridization." In modern Mexico, it is common to talk of Latin American nations in terms of "sister republics," but not regarding the United States, which is usually considered an oppressor country that struggles to impose its patterns of behavior and culture on other nations. However, Madrid (2013b, 8) recognizes Mexico exceeds the United States in many aspects as an invader of those "sister republics," developing into a true "cultural imperialist." As an example, he mentions the Mexican television show *Siempre en domingo* (*Always on Sunday*), broadcasted in Spain and Latin America between 1969 and 1998, which reached audiences of 420 million viewers. This kind of assessment can only be forged from an acute knowledge of Mexican and American musical culture: Madrid enjoys a privileged point of view, as he was simultaneously inside and away from his object of study, due to the fact that he lived in Mexico during his childhood and youth, and was then educated in the United States. Unlike traditional historiography, Madrid's book contemplates a Mexican popular music the development of which was influenced from abroad, both culturally and economically. This is one of the author's most provocative notions, because he affirms that the musical genres propagated by the mass media in Mexico have been modified by the growing economic power of millions of Mexican workers who crossed the northern border (Madrid, 2013b, 6–7) and who constantly pursue their own cultural tastes.

Finally, returning to Mexican editions, the collection *Testimonio musical de México* (Mexico's Musical Testimony), published by the Music Library of the National Institute of Anthropology and History, introduced in 2013 the book-record number 59, *¡Arriba el norte! Música de acordeón y bajo sexto*. Through its two volumes, it provides an overview ranging from the gestation to the transnationalization of norteño music. I was invited to contribute two articles, though only one was published and the other was modified. The two CDs included are dominated by norteño and South American conjuntos, but the substantial contributions of *Tejano* conjunto or the early norteño accordionists are absent. In addition, most of the seventeen chapters included were written by researchers from central and western Mexico, quite distant from the region under examination. They argue that norteño conjunto was influenced by musical traditions from various regions of the nation, with Guanajuato and Michoacán being the main contributors. Due to the alteration of sources, and the geographical mistakes present in some articles, the conclusions are rather questionable, but it is an inescapable fact that, as discussed in this book, the musicians who synthesized all those sound ideas—that is, the first accordionists and performers of bajo sexto that we know of—were born in rural Nuevo León and Tamaulipas. Due to little interest in their art in their native areas, many were forced to migrate to Texas. All these publications on norteño and *Tejano* are relevant to my study because they provide elements for dialogue or discussion.

I have explored newspaper libraries and archives in Nuevo León and Texas, where I found more accurate and unpublished data on the beginnings of norteño and *Tejano* conjunto. In addition to a varied literature, there are recordings of major historical significance. While it is true that historians usually give greater significance to documents, paying scant attention to the objects of the past, recordings are of priceless importance, since they allow us to inspect viva voce forms of interpretation produced since the 1920s. Chris Strachwitz, founder and president of Arhoolie Records, has in his catalogue various historical records of norteño and *Tejano* music, accompanied by useful historical data on the performers and pieces. His productions include records by Narciso Martínez, Santiago and Leonardo Jiménez, and the Conjunto Bernal. Similarly, I have included discography of norteña music that ranges from the 1930s to the present (see "A selection of recorded music" at the end of the book). Complementing the recordings, there are some photos and films on the theme of music and migration that enriched this book. Lastly, I want to comment briefly on the methodology of my fieldwork. Because of the violence generated by drug trafficking in rural areas of northeastern Mexico, it was a tad dangerous to do interviews in small villages, so I worked only in the large urban centers of the region: Monterrey, Nuevo Laredo and Reynosa. Every concert I attended, and many parts of the interviews I conducted with norteño and *Tejano* musicians, were carried out in south Texas: the Lower Valley, Corpus Christi, and San Antonio. I conducted ethnographic interviews to learn what participants thought about their activities, and I also watched, listened, participated, and recorded.

As far as I know, this book is the first one to study conjunto on both sides of the border, and my research aims to answer some of the following questions: How was the extraordinary spread of *Tejano* and norteño music achieved, when it was considered the exclusive possession of the working class, and often linked to cantinas and other immoral places? Was the dissemination of norteño music in the 1930s and 1940s connected to the development of the recording industry, radio broadcasting, and phonographs? Why did the Mexican government not support this music? Is it still considered an inappropriate representative of Mexican culture because it deals with drug trafficking and illegal immigrants? I want to know how—and when—this music, originally associated with marginalized areas and poor people, became synonymous with identity and media popularity.

My hypothesis is that, despite not having been spread directly by either of the two nation-states where it proliferated, the regional-transnational music of accordion and bajo sexto has been one of the leading symbols of Mexican and Chicano identity since the mid-twentieth century, today even displacing mariachi, because Mexican migrants demanded their music. Meanwhile, to the south, the economic power of the northeast of Mexico has sought to impose a cultural hegemony by means of popular harmonic sounds. Currently, we can hear broadcasts, walk through the markets of Mexico and the southern United States, find CDs, and hear norteño music groups appropriating the visual and auditory horizon. This music becomes an alternative identity, contesting the power created by the Church or the State.

In this sense, this book is intended to make a contribution to the issue of the conflict between the center and the periphery, both in the United States and Mexico, but also to discussions of migration and the relationship between Mexico and its diaspora in terms of culture, in the middle of a debate situated "disproportionately within the fields of political science, diplomatic history, and sociology" (Hernández 2012, 7). Of particular interest is the field of cosmoaudition, understood as a cognitive system of perceiving the world through sound, which has been ignored until recently, neglecting the fact that the overwhelming majority of reality is perceived through hearing and not just sight (Anderson 2006, 23)

I have divided this book into chapters in which I look at the comprehensive, dynamic, and complex social and cultural phenomenon that is popular music. The field of study is so large that some researchers, like Mark Slobin (2011, 1–3), assert that the term "folk music" has changed so much over time and space that it cannot be explained in a single sentence. But he daringly proposes that perhaps the best definition might be "restless creativity."

CULTURE, POPULAR CULTURE, AND POPULAR MUSIC

Our subject is the music, but we must not forget its context. Fearlessly, Peter Burke (1996, 198–199) raises the complexity of the issue:

> We're going to start with the problems. . . . In the first place, we could say that we, historians, as a group, do not know what we mean when we say *popular*. Secondly, we do not know what we say when we speak of culture. . . . One can be honest and build one's own definition from the start and keep it, but the problem is that there are always good reasons against it and factors that accept virtually any definition that we can choose.

Mexican cultural studies scholar Genaro Zalpa (2011) provides an extensive tour of the conceptual development of the term "culture" in the social sciences, from its appearance in Europe during the eighteenth century to contemporary theories. In its origin, the word "culture" has in the French language virtually the same meaning as in Latin—that is to say, a cultivated land (*culture*), and the action of cultivation (*cultiver*). The ruling class grabbed up the term, and initially culture was interconnected "with the fine arts, with the academic institution, and with cultural heritage" (Zalpa 2011, 24–25). In the same way, there was the cultivated spirit, as opposed to the ignorant spirit.

Various thinkers have proposed many definitions of culture, but for our purposes, my definition is closest to two hypotheses that complement each other. The first is from sociologist Talcott Parsons (cited in Geertz 2001, 215), who developed a concept of culture understood as a system of symbols by virtue of which man gives significance to his own experience. For his part, American anthropologist Clifford Geertz (2001, 20) goes farther, and, relying on Max Weber, says:

> Believing . . . that man is an animal inserted into frames of *significance* that he himself has woven, I believe that culture is the warp and that the analysis of culture therefore has to be not an experimental science in search of laws, but an interpretative science in search of meanings.

I can now suggest my own approach: I find that culture serves, in the first place, to guide human beings in all scenarios of their daily lives, in any society in which they are located. Culture is produced by the person and at the same time shapes that person, and music is an essential element of this process:

> Music informs our sense of place . . . the musical event, from collective dances to the act of putting . . . a CD into a machine, evokes and organizes collective

memories and present experiences of place with an intensity, power and simplicity unmatched by any other social activity. The "places" constructed through music involve notions of difference and social boundary. They also organize hierarchies of a moral and political order. (Stokes 1997, 3)

I must also draw attention to another central element of this book: popular culture. At the end of the eighteenth century, especially in Germany, intellectual interest emerged in the working classes, in rural people and their traditions, and especially in those songs and stories handed down through oral tradition (Burke 2009, 23–24). The Marxist vision of the working class encouraged the establishment of a myth: the hungry and degraded were those with whom we should sympathize, because they had the remnants of the "noble savage" in them, and we should feel nostalgia for the art they produced: "rural folk-art or genuinely popular urban art" (Hoggart 1958, 5). However, for the middle and higher classes, considering these forms of expression the "best of all art forms" was often no more than simple exoticism or a way to pretend to be a person of "open mind" and "modern ideas."

Some pioneering anthropologists, like the American Robert Redfield, have divided the traditions into two major sections, and although they tend to minimize popular customs by referring to them as the "small tradition," they recognize in them a plasticity and autonomy not found elsewhere: "The 'great' tradition is cultivated in schools and temples; the 'small' tradition operates on its own and remains active in the lives of illiterate people in their villages. . . . The two traditions are independent of each other. The great tradition and the small tradition have influenced each other for a long time and continue to do so" (mentioned in Burke 2009, 50). Eventually, with the arrival of the Industrial Revolution, popular culture became synonymous with urban culture, in such a way that it is now identified with the "universal" symbols manufactured by cinema and radio, the recording industry and television, as well as by large companies that produce various goods, from cars to cereals and cigars (Betts 2004, 9–20).

The above may be partly valid for the American southwest, but to the northeast of Mexico I believe that we can go farther, applying the definition of Intangible Cultural Heritage provided by UNESCO in 2003, such heritage encompasses "The uses, representations, expressions, knowledge and techniques—along with the instruments . . . that communities . . . recognize as part of their cultural heritage" (Amescua 2011, 103–127). In short, popular culture will be cited here as a synonym for living heritage.

But what, specifically, do we mean when we talk about popular music and what is its relationship to classical or academic music? Between 1774 and 1778, J. G. Harder collected a series of songs under the title *Volkslieder* (in English, folk songs) and published them. Since then, the different languages of the world have forged their own names to designate such popular songs. The definition of popular music is very tricky, and in our day, many researchers tend to link it to the market: "we are talking about music that is commercially oriented" (Shuker 2005, 204). For practical purposes, throughout this work, popular music will refer to urban or rural music that has no connection to "academic" music, regardless of whether or not the former is disseminated by the mass media.

Simon Frith (1996, 26) declares that currently, and in the developed societies all over the world, we hear music within three "overlapping and contradictory networks . . . the art discourse, the folk discourse, and the pop discourse." The equivalents in the region examined here would be, respectively, classical music (to which we apply older-fashioned value judgments such as "concert music," "elitist," "academic," "scholarly," "cultured," or "legitimate"); rural folk music (also called "traditional" or "folk"); and urban popular music (of the "working class," or also now simply called "pop," which has become meaningful for all social classes). We locate the birth of *Tejano* and norteño conjunto in the second category, that is, as rural music that with time joined the third category, popular urban, without losing much of its rural base.

The paradigm of high culture and low culture, and consequently of a classical music separated from popular music, was established during the nineteenth century and is associated with the establishment of social classes. Nineteenth-century music vividly reflected social stratification: it was at this time that demand grew for the professional conservatory training of musicians who personified "high culture," while "amateurs" and music meant for entertainment (heard in cafes, parks, and ballrooms) were seen as ordinary, and, eventually, even vulgar. In this way, in the imaginary of the growing middle class, the chants of the unfortunate became a spectre from which it was necessary to escape, while symphonic and chamber music, or solo concerts, were transfigured into luxurious entities of desire. This categorical division was part of this process, but, on the other hand, it led to a growing market for musicians: as teachers, interpreters, or publishers (Weber 1975, 19–21).

We have seen that, even today, popular music is still considered by some researchers as an unworthy object of analysis, and we certainly see this in the prejudices that dominated music education during much of the twentieth century, which tended to mix personal tastes with value judgments (see Sammartino 2011, 65–70). One of the most important musicians of that century, the Hungarian Bela Bartok, spent years collecting traditional songs in various Balkan countries, along with writing articles justifying his labor, and an example of this is the article "The Importance of Popular Music." In Mexico, Rubén M. Campos, Manuel M. Ponce, and Concha Michel were the first collectors of ethnic and traditional songs and pieces and, like Bartok, they felt the need to provide a series of arguments to convince specialists and the public of the importance of their work. Later, I will discuss "official" post-revolutionary nationalism, but we can reveal that in an essay entitled *La música y la canción mexicana* (Mexican Music and Song), Manuel M. Ponce expressed the belief that the "indigenous" music of Mexico was ignoble and unfinished, and only a scholarly composer might, or should, dignify it: "I consider that it is the duty of every Mexican composer to ennoble the music of his homeland, giving it artistic form, covering it in the clothing of polyphony and lovingly conserving the sorts of popular music that are an expression of the national soul" (cited in Moreno Rivas, 1989b, 102). In this way, popular music was considered a sort of half art, a product of the unhappiness of the "dispossessed," of the "peasant hapless and dusty." In the end, the chauvinistic "ennobled" music had little in common with what it purported to represent (see Stokes 1997, 15).

There is progress around this paradigm of traditional music, but even in our time, some writers still feel the weight of the idea of the composer born in Fresnillo, Zacatecas. Yolanda Moreno (1989b, 112), for example, commenting on a part of Ponce's "mexicanista" work—that is, his arrangements of popular songs—believes that the author accomplished his mission, because he was able to escape "the vulgar expression of feeling [and] adopts a clarity and *good taste* that should be exemplary in the *translation* of the Mexican as a melodic model that is expressed with all simplicity."

But if popular music has generally been sidelined, the space of norteño conjunto has had an even cloudier horizon. In her *Historia de la música popular mexicana* (History of Mexican Popular Music), Moreno Rivas (1989a) devotes only two pages to norteño music, and she links it more to migrants and Texas than to the northeast of Mexico. In addition, although she offers in her book a good number of biographies of composers, the sole author cited as representative of conjunto is the singer, actor, bajo sexto player, and composer Cornelio Reyna. It is likely that Moreno Rivas included this musician in her book because his fame transcends the region, as he participated in more than thirty films, and was often accompanied by a mariachi. For its part, *Tejano* conjunto began with very similar marginalization, and even a recently published book on the history of the squeezebox (Jacobson 2012) makes scant mention of accordion players from Texas.

In the last few decades, norteño and *Tejano* conjunto have enjoyed a greater presence in the mass media, being internationally distributed by major record companies like WEA, Sony, Capitol-EMI, and Arista (Peña 1999a, 107). As well, prominent intellectuals like Manuel Peña (1985, 1999 a,b) have published research on the history and social value of conjunto. Despite the progress that norteño and *Tejano* music have made, however, it cannot be said that knowledge of conjunto is on a par with its current impact in the social and economic sphere. Is this because, in both México and the United States, this music celebrates otherness, which is still disturbing in the context of both nations' discourses?

In the first chapter, "Border Territory: Nuevo León and Texas from Colonial Times to the Nineteenth Century," I propose an overview of the history of my region of research, which includes Texas and Nuevo León, as well as parts of Tamaulipas and Coahuila, with commentary on migration, as well as on ethnic, economic, and political conflict. I describe how the inhabitants began to build a regional concept of belonging and identity, with expressive culture as a key element in this process.

In the second chapter, "Precursors to Conjunto: Culture, Migration, and Border Identity," I review the various musical groups of the nineteenth and early twentieth centuries that began to disseminate the musical forms that ultimately would become the *Tejano* and norteño conjunto. This chapter explores the impact of migration on culture and the way in which the inhabitants of the area of our research constructed their reality and how they defined it against other realities. I also analyze the links among music and borders, war, and trade. A brief paragraph stresses the importance of language in the construction of identity.

The third chapter, "The First Epoch of Conjunto: The Instruments, Musical Forms, and the Media," trace the early development of conjunto, in particular the proximity between performers to the north and south of the Rio Bravo/Grande. This section covers the years of World War II, when the new possibilities for amplifying the volume of musical instruments represented a watershed in musical development. In addition, after World War I, there had been a significant transformation in the standard of living of Mexican-American people, which partially distanced them from the traditions of northern Mexico.

The fourth chapter, "Conjunto: From Mexican Subaltern Culture to American Cultural Treasure," shows the panorama of the post-war era, when, gradually, the music starts to be heard beyond *cantinas* and parochial weddings, eventually to become a mass phenomenon. This chapter outlines the problem between popular culture and dominant or "official" culture, stressing the importance of the Chicano movement and the ups and downs of conjunto in Mexico. Technology, cultural movements, assessments of the political situation, and aspects of identity are part of this section.

Chapter 5, "Transformation and Recent Trends in Conjunto," presents the latest trends in conjunto in Texas and northern Mexico—above all the weight of the mass media on both sides of the border—and the influence of rock, country, and jazz. A section is devoted to the phenomenon of the narcocorrido.

I must emphasize that the investigation of conjunto has not been easy. My personal history does not differ much from that of thousands of inhabitants of the northern Mexican border: on the one hand, having grown up middle-class in Monterrey, Nuevo León, during the 1970s, my childhood was closely linked to South Texas, with frequent trips to supermarkets in Laredo and McAllen, holidays on South Padre Island, and summers with my grandparents in Houston. Visits to malls included an inspection of the latest LPs and cassettes, mainly of the music that I much later learned to recognize as mainstream pop. I remember, in particular, the extraordinary influence of the soundtrack of the film *Saturday Night Fever* (1977). In spite of the fact that various songs from this album include violins, the sounds of electrical and electronic instruments were dominant. They were nothing like the *rancheros* and *mariacheros* groups presented on the TV show *Siempre en domingo*, enjoyed by adults and detested by children.

In a location such as the one where I lived, conjunto norteño was played sporadically, usually by an elderly duo from a rural municipality, who, loading up their accordion and saxophone, and not forgetting their best Stetson hats and leather jackets, sang at the doors of our homes for a few coins. While the sounds of conjunto did not have the impact on me that, say, the Swedish quartet ABBA did, neither were they unpleasant, probably because they brought back memories of school festivals, especially polkas like *El Cerro de la Silla* and *Evangelina*. However, declaring a taste for conjunto norteño, in this context, would have been little less than shocking: "educated" people simply did not listen to "rustic" compositions. Rock was preferred in high school, and during my years of study at university, I turned away from any type of composition that was not "classical," since there was an obligation for a student of music to patronize the "universal" repertoire of the "great masters." Fortunately, after obtaining my degree, I was again able to enjoy all kinds of music, but always at home; the first conjunto concert that I attended was at the Pharr West Club, at the Rio Grande Valley, Texas, *fiesta* organized by Radio Papalote, where I heard norteño and *Tejano* conjuntos a few months after starting this research.

The above is relevant since I know the region of research very well, but in spite of the fact that I enjoy the music, I could be considered an outsider to the world of conjunto, putting me at "obvious risk of misrepresentation," as put by British cultural studies scholar Richard Hoggart (1958, 6). Nevertheless, this lack of "emotional involvement" also keeps me away from other "considerable dangers." Part stranger, part expert: individuals who belong to a particular group and those who do not produce "different interpretations, both valid" (Nettl 2005, 153).

I have created the following site for this book, with videos of songs and more information about the groups mentioned here: https://www.facebook.com/Between-Norte%C3%B1o-and-*Tejano*-conjunto-Music-tradition-and-culture-1629591487315650/.

Chapter 1

Border Territory

Nuevo León and Texas from Colonial Times to the Nineteenth Century

"The inhabitants of northeastern Mexico tend to be entrepreneurs and sincere. For the rest of the Mexicans, with whom nature has been generous, it is not easy to understand their tendency to frugality." This is how the English photographer Michael Calderwood—who has lived in Mexico for over thirty-five years—and writer Gabriel Breña (1992, 134) described the attitudes of Mexican citizens living along the northeast border in their book *México: Una visión de altura* (*Mexico: A Higher Vision*). In many ways, northerners are unknown to, and even seen as foreigners by, other Mexicans, and something similar can be said of *Tejanos* in their country. People who were not born in this territory seldom know its history, and therefore will find it difficult to comprehend border culture. Because of this, and in order to understand the traditions and culture of the studied region and its various manifestations, such as norteño and *Tejano* conjunto, it is necessary to know the lengthy history of the current northeastern border between Mexico and the United States. This chapter gives an overview of the region covered by this research, from the perspective of some of the geographical, economic, historical, and cultural forces that shaped it.

Thinking about, imagining, and building our border, which historically has been a fluctuating one, depends on the geographic and temporal point of view of the observer. The representation of a person who lives in a border space is very different from that of an inhabitant of the interior. The starting point is identity, which in the case of the border citizen is negotiated every day, depending on opportunity, fantasy, or mere speculation. Meanwhile, as we move away from that zone, identity is seldom questioned.

Let me start by recalling that the current border between the two countries is purely a political and administrative one. Geographically, there is a natural continuity manifested by, among other things, the Chihuahuan Desert, whose northern half covers parts of New Mexico and Texas, and also by Zacatecas and San Luis Potosí in the south (Morgenthaler 2004, 11). Culturally, we can also speak of continuity, because, while it is true that today the two heterogeneous cultures compete, even with different languages, it is also true that the centuries of Hispanic and Mexican presence carry a very heavy weight. And let me clarify some other issues: when talking about a *border,* we refer to a concept that has been modified over time; during the viceroyalty period, it designated remote regions from the center of power, but after the formation of modern nation-states it became a line, one that divided, but also a meeting point. Alejandro L. Madrid (2008, 3–4) defines borders "as fluid give-and-take areas where complexity, negotiation, and hybridity are everyday constants." On the other hand, *border zone* refers to an indeterminate area extending to the north and south of the border. Furthermore, just as we currently see a mutual agreement among several cities to be considered an area, here we will consider Texas and the Mexican states of the northeast a dynamic economic and cultural region. Proof of this is the music that this research will examine, in addition to the pairing of cities across the border, with the following being of interest to us: Eagle Pass-Piedras Negras, Laredo-Nuevo Laredo, McAllen-Reynosa, and Brownsville-Matamoros.

Regardless of the current economic differences between the two nations, if there is now a shared culture, it is thanks to the fact that Mexican-Americans, who suddenly became unwelcome guests in their own land during the nineteenth century, have maintained the traditions of their southern ancestors and a whole network of exchanges of symbolic and material goods that continues today. The cultural hybridization observed in this territory includes the Anglo community, which has adopted various words from Mexican society. The first Anglo settlers, for instance, not being able to pronounce the word *vaquero*, transformed it into *buckaroo*, and afterward it was converted into *cowboy*, a symbol of the American southwest that owes much to its Mexican counterpart. To this respect, throughout the following chapters, some terms will be used that should be clarified here: "Anglo" is used to indicate an English-speaking person of European origin who is not Mexican-American (McKenzie 2004, 3). "*Tejano*" refers to Mexican residents of Texas, regardless of whether they were born in Mexico or in the United States, while "Texan" refers to Anglo citizens of the Lone Star State (De León 1983, xiii).

Lastly, in his recent research, published as *Imaginary Maps of Mexico*, whose intention was to discern perceptions of Mexico's northern border, psychologist Alfredo Guerrero administered surveys to postsecondary students in various places in the Mexican Republic. While the country's southern border is perceived by young people as a continuity of the nation, open and practically devoid of meaning, the northern dividing line is related to drugs, violence, and walls: it is a closed and conflicting border. Questioning students about their responses revealed that the most common reason for this feeling was "Because that is what we see every day in the news, books, magazines, reports, and comments" (Giménez 2007, 28–31). We can see this negative image, formed by the mass media, in Mexican public opinion. However, the northern border is a lot more than this hollow cliché: in economic terms, historian Mario Cerutti (2000. 28) expresses that, rather than a divide, the Rio Bravo/Grande serves as a hinge: It is the unifying axis of the region. Each day, millions of dollars change hands on both sides of the border due to the informal economy, but also through established trade, and this book's intention is to demonstrate an equally dynamic cultural exchange in the area of study.

PRE-COLUMBIAN TIMES AND THE FIRST EUROPEAN SETTLERS

In 1943, anthropologist Paul Kirchhoff coined the term *Aridoamerica* (arid America) to refer to the region that currently occupies the southwestern United States and north-central Mexico. The purpose was to distinguish a territory that had possessed, since very distant times, a strong, natural affinity among its communities and that extended to the north of the area that he had recently termed *Mesoamerica* (Kirchhoff 1943). In *Aridoamerica,* the climate is mainly dry, the vegetation is comprised of various shrubs, and among the few animals that may be found are the armadillo, rabbit, and opossum (Cavazos Garza and Morado Macias 2006, 25).

Because of the enormous archaeological wealth of the Aztecs and Mayans, archeologists paid very little attention to the inhabitants of the Gran Norte of Mexico. However, since the 1960s, a group of anthropologists from the University of Texas in Austin, coordinated by Jeremiah F. Epstein, launched an ambitious exploration project in the area. The value of this research was justified by the leader of the group: "In central and southern Mexico there are spectacular ruins; it was only natural that the region of Coahuila, Nuevo León, and Tamaulipas . . . which forms a unity with south Texas, might be forgotten" (Cavazos Garza and Ortega Ridaura 2010, 19–22). It was generally believed that human groups established in *Aridoamerica* before the arrival of the Spanish were nomads, although recent research suggests that these communities were settled definitively near places where they had access to water and spent dry seasons elsewhere when water became scarce (Cavazos Garza and Morado Macias 2006, 27). There is also an old prejudice that labels the various Native American groups as savage and lacking in culture. Indeed, such racial groups maintained habits that were unimaginable to the first Europeans who came in contact with them, but they lived together in a society and managed to preserve a part of their culture, as we can verify when we look at the nearly thousands of etched stones at *Boca de Potrerillos* in Nuevo León; farther to the west, we find the architectural complexes of *La Quemada-Tuitlan* in Zacatecas, the ancient city of *Paquime* in Chihuahua, and *Canyon Chaco* in New Mexico (Weigand 2002, 74).

In the region researched, which includes the states of Nuevo León and Texas, and was inhabited by a large number of Native American groups, such as the Comanche and Apache, what seems most likely is that the hostile attitude of these groups was triggered by the invasion of their lands. For example, during the early decades of the nineteenth century, the Caddo of Texas inevitably became diplomats, when they were forced to live first between the Spanish and the French, then among *novohispanos* and Anglos, and were later flanked by Mexicans and Americans (Anteo 2010, 50). We just cannot imagine how the dozens of tribes were socially and culturally transformed by such associations. At the same time, their presence also transfigured their new neighbors.

Before pointing out the cultural matches and clashes, it is worthwhile to focus briefly on the origin of Texas and Nuevo León. Having already discussed the Pre-Hispanic human groups, it is imperative to mention the outsiders who arrived to settle the region, significantly altering local ways of life. The first Europeans most likely to have explored both states were Alvar Núñez Cabeza de Vaca and his companions in an expedition of the 1530s (Del Hoyo 2005, 25). However, there was no permanent settlement in the region until 1577, when Alberto del Canto discovered the Extremadura Valley, calling it Santa Lucía, where the city of Monterrey is currently located. The site did not flourish; neither did the instrument that Luis de Carvajal signed with king Felipe II in Toledo, on May 1579, in which he agreed to pacify and settle what would be called the New Kingdom of León, consisting of about 200 leagues per side, covering most of the current states of Tamaulipas and Texas (Cavazos Garza and Ortega Ridaura 2010, 97). The third and final settler establishment would take place on September 20, 1596, when a lieutenant commander of Carvajal, Diego de Montemayor, established the Metropolitan City of Our Lady of Monterrey, which would remain the only village in the kingdom for more than thirty years. Known for its isolation, the trip to the capital of New Spain featured dangers and discomforts and lasted at least a month (Cavazos Garza and Ortega Ridaura 2010, 26–93).

Gradually, the east and northeast of the territory were occupied through the founding of missions in the towns of Cerralvo (1630), Boca de Leones (1687), and Lampazos (1698). According to Cavazos Garza and Ortega Ridaura (2010, 40–43), these missions, as well as those founded in the first decades of the eighteenth century, would provide a layover for preachers on their way to Texas toward the middle of the century. The ambitious lieutenant of the viceroy Revillagigedo, José de Escandón, obtained permission to settle the Nuevo Santander (now Tamaulipas and part of Texas), as a result of which he escorted dozens of families from Nuevo León to their new lands (Cavazos Garza and Ortega Ridaura 2010, 97–105). In such enterprises, the Franciscans of the Apostolic College of Guadalupe, Zacatecas, played a central role.

For these Franciscans, the exploration of Texas would take place at the end of the seventeenth century. In this case, the original motivations were not mining or evangelization, but to try to contain French raids, the one most dangerous to the Spanish crown being that led by Robert de La Salle. The Marquis of San Miguel de Aguayo, at that time governor of the Nuevo Reino de León, ordered two expeditions to apprehend the foreigners, in 1686 and 1688, each of which had little success. The following year, the viceroy, the Count of Gálvez, sent General Alonso de León out again to apprehend the reckless French. The use of force was not necessary, however, because the colony, located close to San Bernardo Lake, was abandoned: the residents had been killed by epidemics or Native American attacks (Cavazos Garza and Ortega Ridaura 2010, 78–80).

The Texas territory had problems of isolation and marginalization very similar to those of the New Kingdom of León. In fact, the outskirts of the Gran Norte of New Spain remained on the sidelines in terms of greater development, not just because of the insecurity of the roads but also because of laws that did not favor their progress. During the colonial era, despite the proximity of the Gulf of Mexico, all goods from Spain going to Nuevo León or Texas were supposed to go to Veracruz first. It is clear that, when the merchandise reached its destination, its value was several times higher than it would be in Mexico City (Weber 2000, 254). The expedition of the governor of the state of Coahuila, General Alonso de León, succeeded in establishing the first mission in Texas in 1690, called San Francisco of Texas, but it was abandoned three years later. Texas remained uninhabited for another twenty years, in the absence of any new foreign threat in the territory (Quirarte 2002, 17). In 1716, one of the main Texan settlements, Los Adaes, was founded, which served to contain French traders attempting to enter New Spain through Louisiana. The village ceased to serve as the capital of the territory in 1770, when a military presence was no longer needed in the area, due to the fact that the town had developed around a wooden *presidio*, a fortified military fort (Weber 2000, 280). The first town founded by civilians was established in 1718 and was named Villa de Bexar, its location taking advantage of the San Antonio River (De la Teja 1995, 32). The town would expand very modestly: In 1750, the Hispanic population was around 580 people (Weber 2000, 250–252).

TRANSFORMATION AND ADAPTATION TO THE ENVIRONMENT

For the most part, the *villas* (towns) of the far north were plotted in grids, following the royal regulations of 1573. This fact, together with the introduction of non-native animals to the region, profoundly altered the local environment. Even before the settlement of Texas, cattle and horses had already found refuge in the territory. Hispanic residents also attempted to replicate the institutions of their homeland, although in the north this attempt was made in a simplified or hybrid manner. As the Spanish and Mexicans were transforming their new space, isolation and solitude were beginning to change *them*. Very few people managed to build luxurious housing; most homes were small and functional, with interchangeable rooms in which the residents cooked, ate, and slept (Weber 2000, 432–456). In the 1820s, Stephen Austin said that the houses of San Antonio had small, dark rooms containing few or no pieces of furniture (Weber 2005, 299). The Spanish initially tried to preserve their culinary traditions; they favored the farming of wheat, olives, and grapes, but being unable to obtain such gifts from their desert-like surroundings, they adapted to native ways, devouring corn, pumpkin, chilis, and beans. Even the few wealthy inhabitants of the north ate *tortillas* and drank chocolate and *atole* frequently. At the end of the day, the sacrifices were worth it, because the inhabitants of the north usually sat at the pinnacle of the social scale (Weber 2000, 442–457). The best-known case is that of families from the Canary Islands who, at the request of the local Franciscans, arrived in 1731 to settle in San Antonio. The Spanish crown paid for their relocation and granted them the title of *hidalgos* (noblemen), thus, despite their lack of wealth, the *canarios* refused to build a *villa* or work in the fields (Fehrenbach 2000, 54–55).

These transformations in the way of life also affected the various Native groups of the region. The Caddo of Nacogdoches, for instance, adopted European attire and used European tools since the first decades of the nineteenth century (Weber 2000, 427). Eventually, the Anglos who came from farther north also took advantage of the knowledge and skills of the Mexicans and Spaniards: In mining, they practiced panning for gold in a *gamella*, while the cowboy benefitted from the vaquero's techniques of livestock organization, clothing, and utensils (Weber 2005, 321). All these adaptations and assimilations resulted in the establishment of new practices: A collective imaginary and a popular culture developed that differed from the various traditions that nourished them, with the future norteño and *Tejano* conjunto becoming heirs to such traditions.

BETWEEN MYSTICISM AND WEAPONS

The Gran Norte was the reason various religious orders undertook a new wave of evangelization during the seventeenth and eighteenth centuries. This new devotion was stimulated by unusual spiritual events that occurred in the region. In 1630, fray Alonso de Benavides, a Franciscan who had served in the missions of Santa Fe, published a report in Madrid on the progress of the disciples of Saint Francis of Assisi in New Mexico. The friar stated that they had been able to baptize some 86,000 natives from among the Apache, Comanche, and Pueblo. However, the most notable part of his story is the "miracles." Benavides claimed that the baptismal waters had resurrected an Acoma child, that a cross restored the eyesight of a Hopi boy, that a lightning strike killed a sorceress in the town of Taos, and that a priest became invisible to a group of residents who tried to assassinate him. The Franciscan also recalled that the Apache and Jumano described a woman dressed as a nun who appeared to them and preached in their language (Weber 2000, 144–145).

As mentioned previously, the founding of missions in the northeast was slow and arduous. An example is the mission of Most Holy Mary of Guadalupe, established in 1714, in what is now Sabinas Hidalgo, Nuevo León, by Father Antonio Margil de Jesús (Figure 1.1), a Franciscan from the College of Our Lady of Guadalupe, Zacatecas. As was usual, clergy were accompanied to their mission site by a military escort. The mission was constructed in the old-fashioned way, with wood and straw that offered very little resistance to the elements, and the structures were called *jacales* (huts or shacks) (Alcocer 1958, 117–119). When he realized that robberies and murders had no end, however, Father Margil abandoned the mission. It is important to note that the Franciscan spread the Western music tradition in Nuevo León and Texas: He sang a touching *alabado* (praise) every time he arrived at a house and at the end of a chat or confession (Felis de Espinosa 1737, 117).

The faith of the Franciscans did not weaken. In 1716, an escort and some missionaries from Zacatecas and Querétaro were already in the land of the Hasinai, who called them *texas*, meaning "friend" in their dialect. At this time, the friars suffered many hardships: sometimes all they had to eat was crow cooked in unsalted water, and they spent vigilant days watching out not only for the various local Native groups but also for the French, who in 1719 ransacked the mission of San Miguel de los Adays. At the time of the pillage, the attackers took all the inhabitants of the mission prisoner: a missionary and a soldier. The news of the raid dampened the spirits of the Spanish captain Domingo Ramón because of the twenty-five soldiers who had arrived in the region with him, several had died, others had deserted, and those remaining were mere boys on foot and without weapons (Alcocer 1958, 123–128).

Figure 1.1   Fray Antonio Margil de Jesús, from fray Isidro Félix de Espinoza, Valencia, 1742.

The misfortunes of the Franciscans in the Gran Norte continued throughout the colonial period. In 1756, by decree of the viceroy, the Marquis of Amarillas, two friars from Zacatecas departed for Texas with the order to found a mission adjacent to the presidio of Lampe, near the Trinity River. The monks reported to superiors that the place was "unfit for human habitation, and had so many pests and discomforts, that not even the Native Americans wanted to live in it" (Alcocer 1958, 141). Although the missions were a key institution in extending the northern border, by the late eighteenth century their decline had begun, with complete collapse coming under independent Mexico. Between 1820 and 1825, when Texas was part of the diocese of Nuevo León, just one Franciscan was taking care of the four San Antonio missions, and the bishop of Monterrey allowed him to stay in place simply because he could not find priests to replace him. One reason for the failure of the northern missions was that they isolated Native American tribes from the rest of society, and the missionaries often compared Native people to children, thinking that they were inferior and unable to change (Weber 2005, 81–95).

A SENSITIVE ISSUE: NATIVE AMERICANS

We know that the Spanish called the inhabitants of the newly discovered lands "Indians" because they thought that they had docked in "the Indies." Throughout the viceregal period, and because of the confusion caused by the large number of Native groups, the Spanish used the terms *Chichimeca, Toboso,* and *Apache* to label, generically, the Native Americans of the north (Guidicelli 2009, 57). Generally, settlers described Native Americans as "barbarians," which had a derogatory meaning since it was the lowest rank on their grading scale, while in the Gran Norte they were also referred to as "gentiles," thanks to the influence of the Judeo-Christian tradition (Jimenez 2009, 367). The conquest of the New World represented a demographic catastrophe of extensive and enduring impact. Peter Gerhard (1996, 39), a specialist in Novo-Hispanic history, has estimated the approximate number of Native people inhabiting North America when the Spanish arrived and the dramatic decrease after contact. If we look at the New Kingdom of León in 1521, we find around one million Native American inhabitants. However, by the mid-eighteenth century, at the lowest point, this number barely reached 2,000. In Texas, as in the rest of New Spain, something similar happened: Of the 20,000 individuals who had wandered the plains in the sixteenth century, only about 700 people would remain by the year 1800.

Such a decline in the population was due, among other things, to wars of extermination. As mentioned earlier, throughout the colonial period and well into the nineteenth century, one of the central conflicts experienced by the communities of northern New Spain was with Native American tribes. Due to the clashes between settlers and "barbarians," the region came to be known as the "land of living war" (Cavazos Garza and Ortega Ridaura 2010, 140), although it is probable that historian Santiago Roel (1948, 192) exaggerated the gravity of the problem when he declared that people "fought to live and lived to fight." It is likely that northern inhabitants may have overstated the problem of attacks, because in letters sent to the viceroy of New Spain, they often played up this problem when they were requesting exemption from taxation. Various researchers have highlighted the marked differences between testimonies sent to the king or the Council of the Indies and the letters of various travelers. In the first case, descriptors applied to Native Americans are very harsh, while the travelers seldom qualify their encounters (Jimenez 2009, 368).

Similarly, the exaggeration of the problem could have been used as an excuse for killing Native people and for the lack of progress in the conquest in the north after its rapid beginning in central Mexico. In carefully reviewing southern Texas newspapers published since the region's independence from Mexico at the San Antonio Central Library, it became plain that reporting on the theft and slaughter of livestock, as murders committed by the "demons with red faces," was very rare. In one situation in which there were deaths, the newspaper *El Bejareño* (1856) clarified that, despite rumors of pillage and robbery, at the ranch of a Mr. Hill, near Austin, Native Americans had killed a "defenseless" man and a "negrito" (Black man) who were working in the orchard. In this way, the newspaper justified advocating that all the companies of riflemen camped around San Antonio be called into action because "the blood of the victims clamors for vengeance."

To the south, the United States did not respect the Treaty of Guadalupe Hidalgo, whose chapter XI established a commitment to contain the incursions of Native tribes and to compensate Mexicans affected by them (Anteo 2010, 40). Thus, the attacks became more frequent in Nuevo León in the early decades of the nineteenth century, to the point where Anglos occupied formidable territorial extensions in the southwestern United States, pushing the Apache and Comanche further south (Cavazos Garza and Ortega Ridaura 2010, 140–141). There are also records that "the fierce savage showed his knife" in places as far south as Zacatecas, and on at least one occasion in Querétaro (Weber 2005, 132). In the aforementioned territory of Zacatecas, in the municipality of Pánuco, an attack involving about forty Native Americans was reported in 1853. The invasion left a total of two dead and one wounded, as well as about 440 pesos' worth of property damage, not to mention the fact that the women of the community were left "flogged and battered". What is striking is that the interior minister stated that when aggression of this nature occurred it should be proven before the appropriate authority, because "fortunately we are protected from the incursions of the tribes by the Peace Treaties of Guadalupe Hidalgo," which, as we have seen, was not true.

A Texan historian who spent most of his life in Monterrey, Isidro Vizcaya Canales, produced a considerable number of publications on the topic, highlighting *La invasión de los indios bárbaros al Noreste de México en los años de 1840–1841* (*The Invasion of the Barbarian Indians into the Northeast of Mexico in the Years 1840–1841*), *El fin de los indios lipanes* (*The End of the Lipanes Indians*), *Incursiones de indios al noreste en el México independiente 1821–1855* (*Indian Incursions into the Northeast of Independent Mexico 1821–1855*), and *Tierra de Guerra Viva: invasión de los indios bárbaros al noreste de México 1821–1885* (*Land of Living War: Invasion of the Barbarian Indians into the Northeast of Mexico 1821–1885*). One must point out that most of this "classical" literature, as well as many colonial and nineteenth-century reports on Native Americans, categorized them as "savages," while observers, of course, were assumed to be "civilized." In the end, the black legend prevailed, as the "civilized" wrote the history and annihilated the "barbarian." Mexican historian Luis Aboites Aguilar (1993, 304) characterizes the war between Native tribes and settlers as "the confrontation between two forms of occupying, possessing, and using space."

Both old stories and Mexican and American films have left a deep impression on their audiences, forging a dark and biased idea of Native Americans. Fortunately, in recent decades, various publications have tried to put an end to many myths, such as the one presented by archaeologist Jesús Ramírez Almaraz (2009, 13) who, before going into detail, clarifies some points:

> Each culture has to be understood on its own terms, and cannot be compared with value judgments. . . . We must forget the ethnocentrism, the tendency to believe that our own way of life is preferable to all the others . . . there is zero or little presence of an archaeological discourse on indigenous peoples who inhabited Nuevo León, and in the absence of an explanation from an anthropological perspective of the modes of life of these groups, the only way to get to know them has been through the written sources and regional historiography that, to a large extent, has reflected a prejudiced view.

If, in truth, the natives of America became increasingly violent, it was surely due to religious persecution, as well as the abusive demands made on their labor and land, to say nothing of the disenchantment effected by the systematic violation of conventions established with both Anglos and Hispanics. In terms of work, even the Franciscan missions depended almost entirely on Native workforce (Weber 2000, 182–198). But in his diary, Lieutenant José María Sánchez, a soldier who lived with the Comanche, provided quite a different image of the black legend. The Comanche protected and raised children from other Native groups until they were integrated, in addition to accepting any individual into their camp who wished to settle in it. Nevertheless, we should not think that before the arrival of the Spanish the northern region was one of brotherly love: there were, of course, conflicts when one tribe wanted to occupy the domains or take the natural resources of another (Anteo 2010, 27–30). Contact with the invaders of their land had devastating effects on various traditional communities of the Gran Norte: By the end of the eighteenth century, the Caddo had almost disappeared and the number of Karankawa was rapidly declining. The Coahuiltecan, a people of extremely gentle spirit who once resided in the missions, were beginning to die. Disease and epidemics were one cause, but it is likely that a good many of the deaths had their origins in spirits broken by the destruction of traditions, the exhausting work to which they were subjected and the impossibility of escape (Fehrenbach 2000, 50–54).

The topic of the Native peoples of the north is very complex, and even the Westerners who lived with them in the nineteenth century did not know what to expect, since there are reports that speak of various categories of "Indians" in relation to their belligerence: peaceful, semi-peaceful, and "those who are always up in arms, defending themselves and offending [against others], and who do not want to embrace either subjection or the faith" (Guidicelli 2009, 56). Regardless, contemporary historiography is gradually achieving a balance that distances Native peoples from the traditional idea of the "savage." One of these new voices noted that "the Spanish in the vicinity daily encountered an Indian, not always good, not always bad, but alive, unpredictable" (Jiménez 2009, 389). In the end, the union of various northern villages against the Native peoples generated a sense of pride, as well as of independence and membership, contributing to the development of a regional identity (Valerio-Jiménez 2013, 46).

To complete this section and support the hypothesis that the issue of trouble with Native tribes might have been overstated by border residents to obtain exemptions from taxes or other benefits, one must refer to the case of a town in the region: Refugio, subsequently known as Matamoros, in the current state of Tamaulipas. In that village, in the ten years between 1830 and 1840 alone, a dozen newspapers were published whose main theme was politics and in which "the idea of nationalism . . . succumbed to regionalist realities" (Valerio-Jimenez 2013, 106). Some decades later, and while Native Americans were being persecuted, an idea of culture was being promoted that had to do with the creation of theaters, markets, and public squares, based on the French model. In our research area, it is evident that in Matamoros there was sufficient artistic activity to eradicate the idea that the north was a cultural desert. For example, the newspaper *La Revista del Norte* (1887) applauds the fact that audiences are growing at performances in the "small but elegant Teatro de la Reforma" and is particularly pleased that these feature "artists who are both Mexican and accomplished, which proves that it is not entirely accurate that we deny any protection to our compatriots, always supporting foreign ventures." The article emphasizes that the local public did favor Mexican theater companies, probably as a response to the prejudices of people observing the region from afar, and who since the nineteenth century had considered citizens of the Mexican frontier to be not very loyal to "national" culture. *La Revista del Norte* also gives an account of the regional taste in reading; the same issue includes advertisements from merchants dedicated exclusively to the publication and sale of books, such as Irineo de la Peña, who also "is responsible for placing orders for books from the capital." If this were not enough, the magazine published serialized novels, which readers could later bind, among which was Emilio Castelar's *Historia de un corazón* (*History of a Heart*).

But if theater and literature fascinated the inhabitants of Tamaulipas during the nineteenth century, it is clear that they were big fans of music too, as can be seen by the frequent serenades and concerts offered by both local groups and outsiders, such as the Orquesta Italo-Mexicana, and the ensemble directed by "the clever Mr. Quirino González." All of the above shows that, if conflicts with Native Americans had caused problems in the area, by the 1880s those had subsided, and it was a fact that the lives of the people revolved around many other things, among which was a good number of artistic and cultural activities that had not developed overnight.

FROM PROVINCES TO INDEPENDENT STATES

The affinity among the communities of our research's target area has been recognized since colonial times. The idea of granting some independence to the Gran Norte was not new: Juan Picado Pacheco, the Spanish crown's representative, had proposed in 1719 the establishment of another viceroyalty in the region (Cavazos Garza and Ortega Ridaura 2010, 91). It is interesting to note that the Inspector General of New Spain, José de Gálvez, saw the great potential of the provinces of the interior, declaring in a bill of 1768 that these territories were "abundant and rich in nature and that in a few years they could form a new empire, equal to or better than Mexico" (Weber 2000, 340).

In 1776, at the time of the Bourbon reforms, the General Command of the Internal Provinces of Northern New Spain was created. Now, the north would depend on a Commander General, who reported directly to the king through the Council of the Indies. The territory would undergo various changes, one of the most important in 1787, which divided the Internal Provinces into two parts: west and east. Coahuila, Texas, Nuevo León, and Nuevo Santander were grouped into the latter (Jiménez Núñez 2006, 133–134). After Mexico's independence, and in accordance with the Constitution of 1824, almost all the provinces of the new republic became states. Nuevo León was designated as a free and sovereign state, and subsequently established its own congress (Ortega Ridaura and Márquez Rodríguez 2005, 48). At the same time, Coahuila and Texas joined to form another state (Alessio Robles 1978, 12).

I must point out that, according to a report from the Congress, Coahuila and Texas were the poorest states in the nation. If Texas agreed to join Coahuila, it was only because the influential father of Mexican federalism, Miguel Ramos Arizpe, urged them to do so, warning the city council of San Antonio that if they refused, Texas would be converted into a territory whose public lands would become property of the federal government, as had occurred in Alta California and New Mexico. However, a feeling soon spread among the populace that Coahuila and Texas should indeed be separated because of their very different conditions and the remoteness of the capital: Saltillo. It was not until 1836 that conservatives raised the status of Texas to a department, but by then it was too late, as the Lone Star State had already proclaimed its independence from Mexico. Texas was labeled rebellious by the new Mexican republic and continued to be until 1845, when its separation from Mexico and subsequent accession to the United States was finally recognized (Weber 2005, 54–67). The northern governors continued to believe that the union would strengthen them, which is why in 1856 Coahuila and Nuevo León merged to form a state. President Benito Juárez ended this alliance in 1864, however, likely as a punishment for the support that the state's governor, Santiago Vidaurri, had given to the emperor Maximilian.

THE SHORT-LIVED REPUBLICS OF THE NORTH

Before and after joining the American Union, Texas suffered years of perpetual shock and agitation generated by separatist motivations, among other things, which would involve Mexican states and would ultimately fail. For example, in December 1826, Anglos allied with a group of Comanches, to which Mexico had denied land concession, revolted and proclaimed the Free Republic of Fredonia with its capital in Nacogdoches (Anteo 2010, 78). This would not be the only separatist project. Because of its precarious situation, in 1840, the Texas government supported (although only morally) the creation of the Republic of the Rio Grande—also called República Norte-Mexicana—which would serve as a "buffer" between the future U.S. state and Mexico (Van Wagenen 2002, 10). A delegation headed by federalist leaders from the states of Coahuila, Nuevo León, and Tamaulipas met in Laredo, Texas, on January 17, 1840, announcing their separation from Mexico and claiming the territory of northeastern Mexico up to the Medina and Nueces rivers, as well as New Mexico, Durango, Chihuahua, and Zacatecas, for the new republic.

Despite the attempts of the leaders of the movement, the Republic of the Rio Grande could not consolidate its power, due to lost battles against centralist militias. The few remaining memories of this adventure reside in the Museum of the Republic of the Rio Grande in Laredo, Texas, in the same building that served as their capitol, as well as in the name of the nearby county and village of Zapata, named in honor of Antonio Zapata, a colonel from Tamaulipas and one of the leaders of the movement, accused of treason and executed by centralist forces (Adams 2008, 68). Years later, another unsuccessful separatist attempt was made when the Texan José María

Carvajal announced in Brownsville the creation of the Republic of the Seven Northern States of the Sierra Madre. Carvajal attacked Matamoros in 1851, but was repelled, and the following year attempted to capture Reynosa. In the end, the troublemaker would become governor of Tamaulipas and then Mexican President Benito Juárez's financial agent to the government of the United States (Anteo 2010, 84–87).

THE BORDER: FROM CELLULOID TO THE NATIONAL IMAGINARY

The border between the two young republics captivated the attention of the popular imagination in the years after the treaty of Guadalupe-Hidalgo, and it is no coincidence that some of the first film productions were set in the Old West, perhaps as a way to justify the seizing of land and the massacre of Native Americans. Short films shot in the 1890s include titles such as *Buffalo Bill* and *Sioux Ghost Dance*.

In the 1920s, an actor who would become synonymous with the *western* appeared. Marion Morrison, with the stage name of John Wayne, was a young man from Iowa who attracted the attention of Californian film producers. From his earliest films, we can observe various constants that directors wanted: impressive natural open spaces, typically treeless and with sunny skies, as well as sparsely populated villages. The western also perpetually exploits the border conflict. There are fistfights, gunfights, and risky pursuits on horseback, showing the boldness inherited from Mexican and Comanche riders. These are violent times and places, in which one must be wary of any outsider entering the village. There is usually an attempt to establish law and order, but there are many obstacles, which make it necessary to request assistance from the U.S. Marshall, or even from Mexicans and Native Americans. The titles of several John Wayne films allude to the border: *The Lawless Frontier, Rio Grande, Rio Bravo*. In a 1971 television documentary, *The American West of John Ford*, Wayne, in paying tribute to the famous film director, asserted that westerns are "the most colorful part of our American heritage, the way we keep in touch with our past," and concluded by explaining that not having westerns would be like "not having a soul."

In the case of Mexican cinema, the frontier persona appeared very late, was generally not historical in nature, and, nationally speaking, appeared in the middle of the twentieth century. Among its most prominent representatives was Eulalio González, known as Piporro. We can appreciate his work on the film *El bracero del año* (*Laborer of the Year*), in which he plays Natalio Reyes Colás, who, after crossing illegally into the United States to work as a field hand, changes his name to Nat King Cole, at the same time as he must stay hidden from the border patrol, the "migra." While working from sunrise to sunset, Natalio discovers an enormous solidarity among the Mexicans who have recently migrated, but also with Mexican-Americans and other Latin Americans. The film starts with a dedication from the production company: "Sotomayor Productions. . . . Dedicates the cheerful message of this film to all the Mexican *braceros* (laborers) who, outside of their homeland and in the friendly country of the United States of North America, identify the name Mexico with the work, effort, and the dignity of man."

In spite of this tribute to migrant workers, in the end, after winning a Laborer of the Year contest and acquiring a small fortune, Natalio Reyes Colás loses all his money and, missing his girlfriend in Tamaulipas, returns to Reynosa. At this point, we can distinguish the centralist "official" line, which neither supports nor understands the cultural and economic relationship of northern Mexico to its region, which extends beyond the border. Piporro gives an undeniable message to his countrymen who plan to migrate: "I went to the United States, yes, swimming. Got all the way to New York because I worked hard. . . . But I discovered one thing: that the land is the same here as there, so why don't we work our own land?"

ECONOMIC AND INDUSTRIAL DEVELOPMENT IN THE NINETEENTH AND TWENTIETH CENTURIES

The National Bank of Texas was established by governor Jose Félix Trespalacios in San Antonio on October 21, 1822. Although it closed its doors after only a short time, it showed that Texans realized rather quickly that a banking institution would give momentum to their economy. There would not be a bank in Monterrey until 1890, when a branch of the National Bank of Mexico opened; and in February 1892, the Banco de Nuevo León was founded, the first with regional capital. These institutions emerged out of necessity with the budding heavy industry of the so-called first industrialization, which lasted from 1890 to 1910, when the capital of Nuevo León saw the beginning of several companies that would provide a livelihood for many other, smaller factories; the former included Cervecería Cuauhtémoc (Cuauhtémoc Brewery), Fundidora de Hierro y Acero de Monterrey (Monterrey Iron and Steel Foundry), Vidriera Monterrey (Monterrey Glassware), and Cementos Hidalgo (Hildalgo Cement) (Vizcaya Canales 2006, 82–96).

But Monterrey had a commercial vocation since the 1820s, when the opening of the port of Matamoros and the refounding of Tampico had made it into a natural stop between the Sierra Madre mountain range and the interior (Cavazos Garza and Ortega Ridaura 2010, 178). By 1855, Monterrey had already been transformed into the hub of a regional economic system that included South Texas. In fact, with the annexation of Coahuila and its powerful influence in northern Tamaulipas, the city became the "political, administrative, military, and commercial axis of a wide area" (Cerutti 2000, 32–42). Added to this, the American Civil War (1861–1865) gave a boost to the local economy, as the blockade of Texan ports by the navy of the North meant that all products moving between Texas and Europe had to pay tariffs at customs controlled by the government of Nuevo León (Vizcaya Canales 2006, 9).

This regional-transnational interaction is evidenced by the fact that, in 1867, the first stagecoach service between Mexico and the United States began operations, and it is no surprise that it connected the already influential cities of Monterrey and San Antonio (Vizcaya Canales 2006, 16). Another indicator of the unity between northeast Mexico and South Texas is the area's newspapers. For a foreigner, it would be disconcerting to read, in Spanish, a newspaper printed in Texas with news from Monterrey, such as *El Progresista* (1903) of El Paso. rebuking the "*porfiriadas* [supporters of the government of Porfirio Díaz] in Monterrey," and *La Libertad* (1902) of San Diego, a hamlet in Duval County, bitterly criticizing both the "unconstitutional governor" of Nuevo León, calling him a "mannequin," and the "libertine" mayor of Monterrey. In a similar manner, to the south of the border, *The Monterey News* (1903), published in English and sometimes in Spanish, featured details on various businesses in the area, a high percentage of which were headed by foreigners.

Citizens of the United States began to establish lasting trade ties with the city of Monterrey. The Ladrillera Monterrey (the Monterrey Brick company), for example, was founded in 1890 by three dynamic Americans, and soon was shipping millions of bricks to the interior of Mexico and to the United States (Vizcaya Canales 2006, 91). The twentieth century would see the entire region flourish economically.

Thus far, I have attempted to provide a general overview of the history, complex migrations, relationships, and changes in our region of research, based on economy and politics. We have outlined the difficulties of strengthening the border in the north, as well as the isolation and difficult living conditions endured by soldiers, religious figures, and citizens. The next chapter delves into cultural aspects and the way in which tradition helped people endure hardship.

Chapter 2

Precursors to Conjunto

Culture, Migration, and Border Identity

The unusual features of our region (its remoteness from the centers of power, its isolation, and its independence) would forge specific lifestyles and artistic expressions, such as those of the norteño and *Tejano* conjunto. From a historical perspective, it is possible to highlight the diverse musical traditions of various social strata, because they contributed to the origins of conjunto. This enables us to delve deeper into the impact of migratory movements on culture and traditions, the ways in which settlers created their reality and how they defined it against other realities. In this process, the importance of language in the construction of identity is highlighted, and it is possible, by general reference, to find its expression in groups that preceded conjunto, as well as in the instruments and musical forms that we shall explore in greater detail in the third chapter. But here we are witnessing the birth of a new identity: To what extent did conjunto become an expression identifiable by northeastern Mexicans and Texans? Working from Benedict Anderson's (2006) concept of "cultural artifacts," words like *nationality* and *nationalism* refer to a wide range of processes, but with definite limits, because the nation is "an imagined political community, and imagined as both inherently limited and sovereign." Here the text will favor the cultural rather than political definition of nation.

MEXICAN ACOUSTIC TRADITIONS

A few years ago, in a publication (Díaz-Santana 2009), I plunged into the Mexican music of the nineteenth century at a historic moment in which there was no noticeable division among the melodic predilections of heterogeneous social strata. This cultural proximity was a constant, and it is no coincidence that during the colonial era, on Mondays and Thursdays, there were, in the

Gran Teatro Coliseo de México, "free performances as a gift to the working class . . . the same as those held on the outskirts of the city" (Olavarría y Ferrari 1961, 15). We should recognize this generosity on the part of the viceregal regime as a form of control, designed to disseminate the ideas of the group in power and to achieve their recognition, acceptance, and assimilation on the part of the impoverished. We can see an example of this practice on a summer night in 1790, when the Compañía de Bolatines, performing in the above-mentioned Teatro Coliseo, featured a clown dressed as a woman, dancing the *jarabe*. What seemed like a naive show was in fact a burlesque, ridiculing one of the better-known and most rebellious of Mexican dances, which represented the music of the ragged, of "the dirty and half-naked people" (Prieto 1996, 48), frequent visitors to taverns or open-air eateries.

Of course, in the nineteenth century, one could already find both aristocratic venues and the most obscure *pulquerías* (a type of cantina). The music of the elite, of Italian or French influence, considered acceptable in parlors and concert halls, could be seen to represent an amalgamation of their values and to be a "symbol of modernity, freedom, status, moral, refinement, patriotism, art, and education" (Diaz-Santana 2009, 140). But the access to music that the country's posh inhabitants enjoyed was not envied by the more humble, who could brighten their days at any time with a guitar or mandolin: "Many played and sang for their own delight, in doorways or in the square, at the end . . . of days spent on the commons or the ranch" (Diaz-Santana 2009, 76).

Shortly before Mexican independence, a difference between the perceptions of elitist and popular music was that the former was associated with foreigners, while the latter was perceived as an element of the new nationalism under construction. Here, in speaking of popular music, I am not referring only to "certain poorly styled lyrics" about which Father Juan de Torquemada had complained in the seventeenth century (Saldívar 1934, 249) or the many songs that sailors, peasants, and small merchants brought with them on their long transatlantic journeys to New Spain throughout the colonial period. I am speaking here above all of the era in which "official" recognition was given to a whole range of "subaltern" popular music: the 1770s, when those *sonecitos* and *jarabitos* (dances and songs) from the "country"—like "Los Enanos" ("The Dwarfs") or "El Perico" ("The Parrot")—that for decades delighted marginalized groups, were presented for the first time in the Gran Teatro Coliseo of Mexico (Castellanos 1969, 6). Not all of society accepted those cheerful songs, however, as once entirely innocent civil and religious authorities started to become aware of their satirical verses against the clergy or their open attacks on the government. A notable example, and one that is still popular today in the streets of Veracruz, is the *chuchumbé*: "En la esquina está parado/ un fraile de la Merced/ con los abitos [*sic*] alzados/ enceñando [*sic*] el chuchumbé" (Standing on the corner/ there's a friar from the Merced/ with his robe raised/ showing his *chuchumbé*)."

People not only mocked priests; some scathing couplets from the seventeenth century addressed the saints, and even God Himself. If the Almighty was unable to escape the jokes, Mexican presidents of the nineteenth century, like the tyrant Antonio López de Santa Anna (Table 2.1), had much to worry about:

With the nationalist fever that spread after Mexico's independence, people also sang to heroes Miguel Hidalgo and Jose María Morelos. The following verses (Table 2.2) were collected by historian Cuauhtémoc Esparza Sánchez (1976) in Zacatecas:

These examples, whose author is unknown, attest to a long creative and critical tradition at the grassroots level and can be considered an antecedent to the Mexican *corrido*. Although still nascent, these verses show us a nationalist sentiment under construction, as well as a means by which the marginalized classes made themselves visible.

THE BORDER: REGIONAL IDENTITY VS. NATIONAL IDENTITY

The first chapter demonstrates that, historically, there has been a great cultural and economic affinity between northern Mexico and the American Southwest. Just as today we consider the union of several cities to be a region, this text will consider Texas and Nuevo León as a dynamic economic and cultural area. We need only recall that in 1867 the first international stagecoach service between Monterrey and San Antonio had begun and that in 1882 a railway line joined Monterrey with Laredo, six years before trains would arrive from Mexico City (Vizcaya Canales 2006, 16–19). The first chapter also considers the ideas of American folklorist Américo Paredes, who identified the contours of the Rio Bravo/Grande as those of a different country from the United States and Mexico. It also notes the isolation that prevailed throughout the colonial period until the Porfiriato, at which point factors, such as industrialization, the extensive introduction of livestock, and other elements, turned the Northeast from a peripheral area into an economy much more complex than that of the rest of Mexico (Mora-Torres 2001, 1–3); a similar situation developed in Texas.

Table 2.1 Juan Cervera Sanchís, "Santa Anna, generador de versos satíricos," *Semanario La Voz del Norte* (April 3, 2011)

¡Ave María Purísima!	Hail, Blessed Virgin Mary!
Las cuatro y sereno.	Four o'clock, and serene.
¿No hay quien de veneno	Is there no one to poison
a su Alteza Serenísima?	his Serene Highness?

Table 2.2   Cuauhtémoc Esparza Sánchez, *El corrido zacatecano* (México: INAH, 1976), 11–12

A las seis, a Guadalupe,	At six, in Guadeloupe [a town in Zacatecas],
por la casa de Cifuentes,	by the house of Cifuentes,
llegaron el Cura Hidalgo	arrived Father Hidalgo
y su tropa de insurgentes.	and his troop of insurgents.

But if, on the one hand, culture and "Mexican folklore . . . know no borders" (Paredes 1995, 8), the new dividing line and economic development brought major alterations that are also found in other complex boundary zones. Because Mexicans in Texas were a minority, and they saw their identity as threatened, some of these changes were positive, such as when there was an "intensification" of nationalism. Paredes (1995, 9–10) claims Mexican nationalism can be observed until the last third of the nineteenth century, encouraged by the arrival of the Second Empire, while in the northern border areas, and in the territories that would soon be ceded to the United States, one can detect an early nationalism in the 1830s, largely due to conflicts with Anglos. Moreover, a writer, in 1932, thought that more Mexican music had been made north of the Rio Bravo/Grande than in Mexico (Sánchez 1995, 179).

Another interrelated aspect is the musical tradition, which is a fundamental part of identity negotiation that border residents must carry out daily to survive between the powerful cultural influences of two nations. Alejandro L. Madrid (2008, 193–194) notes that the boundaries of the country are perceived by central Mexicans as lying at the edge of the nation: it is a limit, not only in geographical terms but also cultural, a conflicting territory where "the coherence of the hegemonic national identity discourse collapses." When he talks about the border, Madrid asserts that the population on the Mexican side refers to it as *bordo*, a *Spanglish* term derived from the word *border*. He mentions that scholars from the center of Mexico believe that *bordo* is equivalent to *edge*, and says that this confusion reveals a rejection of the cultural particularities of the northern region. At this border, listening to conjunto, and discussing the lyrics of the songs and corridos, are ways to establish a norteño—and *Tejano*—identity, different from a centralist identity, and therefore different from the national *myth*. Here, an outsider could hardly follow the thread of the conversation because, as Peter Van Der Merwe suggests (mentioned in Frith 1996, 10), "Aesthetic arguments are possible only when they take place within a shared critical discourse." Therefore, when we talk about the border, we usually refer to the center-periphery conflict, which manifests itself broadly in popular music. Everyone recognizes that the "national" sounds of Mexico are those performed by the mariachi band, as this music originally belonged to a particular geographic region—the Mexican west—and was considered rough music of the poor and the cantinas: "En algunos pueblos de poca importancia, haciendas y ranchos del estado . . . se verifican bailes que denominan *mariaches*, y en otros lugares *fandangos*, a los que generalmente concurren personas de costumbres que nada tienen de morigeradas" ("In some insignificant towns, government estates, and ranches . . . they organize dances that are called *mariaches*, and in other places *fandangos*, to which people of immoderate habits usually go.") (mentioned in Ochoa Serrano 2008, 104). However, other regional music of equally modest origin, like conjunto or the music of brass bands, was not promoted in the same way. Various authors have drawn attention to the way in which a "Mexican identity" was "built" from the nation's capital after the Mexican Revolution. In this context, the traditions closer to the center of power—closer to the west of the *charro* (horseman), and to the east of the traditional *china poblana* costume and its exotic origins—merged with the sound of the traditional dance of jarabe (see Pérez Montfort 2003).

At the end of the Revolution, and through the arts, the Mexican government sought to establish an identity that would embody all citizens of the nation as a way to legitimize itself. Since the legendary Russian ballerina Anna Pavlova had performed the *jarabe tapatío* in classical ballet pointe work in 1919, it had become an obligation for Mexican theatrical entrepreneurs to include a nationalist subject in their programs (Parga 2004, 45). Members of the Orquesta Típica del Centenario (Typical Centenary Orchestra) were obligated to wear the traditional charro costume, including the large ornate hat. Such attire would later become inseparable from the mariachi; the first rural groups of this type were dressed in white. Another important change undergone by mariachi bands during the 1930s concerned their original instrumentation, with a preference developing for the trumpet and excluding the *tambora* (big drum) and large harp (Ochoa Serrano 2008, 109).

Mexico's first Secretary of Public Education, José Vasconcelos, promoted a nationalism that sought to dissolve ethnic and class differences through the implementation of myths. During the inauguration of the National Stadium, in 1924, 1,000 couples dressed in "national costume" attended and danced a jarabe. Amparo Sevilla (1990) notes that this dance "was not a product of the expressive needs of the Mexican people, but rather was a creation that responded initially to theatrical performance, and ended up being . . . one of the official symbols of a supposed national culture built by the Mexican State." The jarabe and its dancers were cultural manifestations close to the center of power, but northern traditions did not please Vasconcelos, and oral tradition ascribes to him the infamous assertion: "Culture ends where grilled meat begins." For him, the northeast would not have been an example to follow, since there was no such thing there as an "indigenous" musical tradition: Nuevo León had no ethnic groups like those that still reside in Jalisco,

Nayarit, or Veracruz, and whose music, after passing through a process of miscegenation, would be the basis for the post-revolutionary nationalism of composers like Manuel M. Ponce and Carlos Chávez. In addition—and contrary to the assertions of Cathy Ragland (2009, 102), who claims that "since the nineteenth century, Mexicans have both idolized and fantasized about the valiant and humble "norteño" peasant cowboy"—the similarity of the northern *vaquero* to the American cowboy made the *vaquero* a dangerous interloper into the national imaginary. Vasconcelos thus needed to promote western Mexico's *jarabe,* because it had already been constructed as a symbol that by then was significant in various social spheres.

On top of that, the creation of a *mariachera* identity would have the support of the president and of the new national cinema. At the end of 1933, Lázaro Cardenas launched his campaign for the presidency, being accompanied from then on by a mariachi band. Once he became president, the chief of the executive branch continued to promote this music group, and also attended presentations at the Palacio de Bellas Artes (Palace of Fine Arts) put on by the actor Roberto "El Panzón" (Potbelly) Soto, with nationalist performances from the popular theater (Parga 2004, 91–93). Similarly, the *ranchera* (country) comedy *Allá en el Rancho Grande (There on the Big Ranch),* released in 1936, opened doors to Spanish-language markets for Mexican cinema (Torres 2008, 188) with tremendous acceptance in the United States as well. Mexican anthropologist Jesús Jáuregui (2007, 148–150) argues that to establish the "national music group," the Mexican State used the archetype of Jalisco, based on a "cultural-racial argument": With a population more similar to the European ethnic type than to the indigenous or black, the state of Jalisco was the perfect *mestizo* (i.e., the mixing of different races) prototype. Supporting this theory, the protagonist of *Allá en el Rancho Grande,* singer and actor Tito Guízar, the first Mexican charro to appear on the big screen, was of fair complexion, had blue eyes, and was almost six feet tall. The region's economic and cultural importance also meant that there were other "historical, geographical, and political reasons for . . . the imposition of the *jalisciense* model as the ideal of Mexico." Even today, the word *mariachi* continues to be attributed to a mythical French origin, as, in some places in west Mexico, *mariache* or *mariachi* had been used as a synonym for *fandango* (public outdoor dance) at least since the 1850s (Meyer 1984, 257–268). With the passage of time, the mariachi band would become a Mexican stereotype, becoming what Hobsbawm and Ranger (2012) called "invented tradition": when history is used to legitimize actions and as a foundation for social cohesion.

Through cinema, and at the same time as they were seeking to form a concept of nation, both the Mexican and American imaginary portrayed a border zone where it was not recommended to dwell, a lawless frontier, belligerent and rough. The films of John Wayne, discussed in the first chapter, are prominent examples of this, as is the Mexican film *El padre pistolas* (*Father Guns*). In this movie, when the character played by Eulalio González "Piporro" must leave his land to live in the north, he is forced to cross a great deal of desert just to get to a dusty village dominated by a *cacique* (chieftain), where there is no political authority, or even a priest to take care of the abandoned church.

WARS AND TRADE AS A PRETEXT
FOR MIGRANT MUSIC

Expatriates from different European countries were responsible for disseminating dance music in Nuevo León and Texas, popularizing the waltz and polka, the schottische and mazurka. During the 1820s, some French-speaking Alsatians, as well as Germans and Swiss, settled in Texas, although it was not until 1844 that they founded a village of non-English speakers: Castroville (Fehrenbach 2000, 292). Envisioning immense open spaces and the promise of free land, the Society for the Protection of German Immigrants introduced more than 7,000 people to the state in 1848. Many were farmers, but there were also some educated professionals, among them Adolf Fuchs, music teacher at the Baylor Female College, and Wilhelm Thielepape, who worked as an engineer and surveyor and was also director of the San Antonio *Männergesangverein* (San Antonio Men's Singing Club) (Hartman 2008, 103).

A decade after Texas had been incorporated into the United States, its population of Texan-born Anglos exceeded 400,000, while approximately 32,000 residents were from Eastern Europe (Fehrenbach 2000, 296); the latter had relatively little economic and cultural influence, and therefore their music was the music of the minority. The number of inhabitants and local European migrants to Texas grew throughout the nineteenth century, and by the 1930s, the Czech community alone peaked at about 300,000 souls (Strachwitz 1993, 4). At the same time, Mexican migrants arrived in the state in quantity, their numbers increasing significantly around the time of the Revolution, from 71,000 residents in 1903 to about 250,000 in 1920 (Paredes 1995, 11). Most of these people had traveled from central and border states (Durand 2007, 55–81). The history of Mexican migration to the United States is extraordinarily complex, and we will see later the changes, over time, in places of origin and destination.

In the capital of Nuevo León, a similar migratory phenomenon occurred, although it never reached Texan proportions. One of the main drivers of migration into Monterrey was armed conflict. At the time of the U.S. invasion launched in 1846, at the beginning of the Mexican-American War, the city was already one of the most important settlements in the region. A soldier involved in the Battle of Monterrey wrote that before reaching their destination, the invading force noticed a charming shift in the area of the Rio Grande: after having crossed deserts and mud, they were amazed to find well-laid roads surrounding the capital of Nuevo León, as well as cultivated fields where figs and pomegranates flourished (Eisenhower 2000, 118). One of the few good things brought about by this invasion was one of the first references we have to that magical instrument that will appear again and again throughout this book: the accordion. According to American historian Justin Harvey Smith (1919, 213), in 1847, an American soldier "used to sit cross-legged in the square of Monterrey and play his rickety accordion for the benefit of the crowd." Less than two decades later, the invasion known as the Second Mexican Empire brought about 6,000 foreigners to the city—Arabs, Turks, Germans, Irish, and Belgians—and after the death of emperor Maximilian, some deserters settled in rural cities like Arteaga in Coahuila. There were also a few dozen prisoners of war, Hungarian, Austrian, and Bohemian, who, when released in 1867, asked to stay in the region (Garza Gutiérrez 2006, 81–91).

In addition to migratory movements caused by hostilities, various other immigrants, with local entrepreneurs as partners, had recognized an opportunity to consolidate their productive visions in Nuevo León since the mid-nineteenth century. Founded in 1854, the great textile factory La Fama had among its developers four Spanish citizens, one American and one Dane. Clearly, these men were wealthy—as were some of the founders of the Compañia Minera, Fundidora y Afinadora Monterrey, a mining/smelting/refining concern, in 1890—among them the Italian Vicente Ferrara and the Irishman Patricio Milmo (Rojas Sandoval 1997, 61–103). Similarly, in 1903, the Fabrica de Vidrios y Cristales de Monterrey (Monterrey Glass and Crystal Factory) signed two managers and bought two smelters and two annealers from Germany, but forty-eight glassblowers also traveled to the capital of Nuevo León (Garza Sada 1981, 47).

These new neighbors came from different social strata, and thus the variety of their traditional music was substantial, and it would be enriched still further, as we will see. As Monterrey offered the best salaries in the area, and needed a large workforce, the city attracted not only foreigners but also residents of other cities in Nuevo León and several Mexican states. San Luis Potosí made the biggest contribution to this population growth, followed by Guanajuato, Coahuila, Tamaulipas, Jalisco, and Zacatecas. During the Porfiriato, in the years 1877 to 1910, the population of Monterrey grew 460 percent; the famous neighborhood of San Luisito alone had about 9,000 inhabitants, most of whom came from the state of San Luis Potosí (Mora-Torres 2001, 100–103; and Cerutti 2006, 119–122).

I will briefly provide details of the musical forms used by conjunto, but I could anticipate the possibility that the newcomers from San Luis Potosí would have brought with them to Nuevo León their style of *huapango*, which is different from the huapango found in other regions of the Huasteca (a Mexican region that includes the states of Veracruz, Tamaulipas, San Luis Potosí, and Hidalgo): its rhythm is "more vigorous, strong, and forceful . . . developed and complex, intense and impetuous" (Hernández Azuara 2003, 102–103). Its syncopated structure, contrasting with the rhythm of *son* (another Latin-American music genre), would be woven into the future conjunto. Finally, both in Texas and in Nuevo León, the majority of outsiders came to stay permanently. Many established bonds of blood, assimilated local customs, and set up dynamic networks of economic and cultural exchange in central and northern Mexico, as well as in the United States (Fehrenbach 2000, 295; and Cerutti 2006, 6–8).

MILITARY AND RURAL BANDS, THE *TÍPICA* ORCHESTRAS, AND OTHER GROUPS

In the newspaper *La Gaceta* (1864), published in Monterrey on September 7, 1864, a statement appeared that informs us of the predilections and musical tastes of the elite:

> We are informed that the very illustrious City Hall and the most notable people of this city have agreed to hold a vibrant dance as a gift to H. E. General De Castagny and the officer corps of the first division of the French-Mexican army. The judicious selection of the people who make up the various committees responsible for preparing this event guarantees that there will be nothing left to be desired with regard to the good tone and elegance that this kind of event requires in order to be pleasant to good society.

This chronicle brings us back to the period of the Second Mexican Empire, when the country was occupied by European forces. But, as we have seen, this invasion brought not only weapons but also a culture that would leave a deep impression, in this case, an artistic culture. The "Belgian Music of the Empress's Regiment" was devoted to inculcating ideology and education to the lower classes of the empire governed by Maximilian of Habsburg. This band had the opportunity to make a lot of noise in Monterrey, playing pieces by Donizetti and Dervit, among other fine composers. The above-mentioned General Armand Alexandre Casigny, the first high-ranking French military officer to set foot in the capital of Nuevo León, without the aid of any musical subtlety, had issued a proclamation, now in a private collection:

I have come among you to recognize Emperor Maximilian I of Mexico; that is, to bring you peace, order, tranquility, and free you of the conspirators who, under different titles, have not ceased to plunder in order to enrich themselves. . . . Men of good will from all parties who desire the glory of your country surround the Mexican Imperial throne that the disinterested hand of France has just restored. Inhabitants of Nuevo León, follow the example of other regions, and may the sons of the Border repeat in turn the cry that resounds in all corners of Mexico. Long Live the Emperor Maximilian!

In traditional historiography, the Habsburg Empire is perpetuated in the Mexican national memory as a dark period of sad memory. However, no one can deny that Maximilian was a great promoter of the arts: He arrived with highly disciplined musical groups and supported various Mexican artists, a highlight being the appointment of the soprano Angela Peralta, in 1866, as "Chamber Singer of the Empire" (Orta Velázquez 1985, 337). During the almost two years that the European armies occupied Monterrey, music became a central element in trying to pacify the city and restore the torn social fabric. In that period, at least three high-quality military bands (Banda del Regimiento Belga, Banda del Regimiento de Cazadores, and Banda del Regimiento Extranjero) offered performances as often as hostilities permitted, alternating between Saltillo and Monterrey (Garza Gutiérrez 2006, 83–87). Once it became *The Imperial Gazette*, the former *Official Newspaper of Nuevo León* continuously encouraged lavish musical entertainments, at which bands invariably played a polka, some *chotis* (a form of the schottische), and a *redowa*, musical forms that would influence conjunto. All the European bands, which continued their musical lives during the second empire, transmitted to the Mexican instrumentalists an exceptional discipline and respect for the musical vocation. Clarinetist Esteban Pérez, for instance, tells us that by the year 1864 the Belgian Band needed a performer of his instrument, for which the band convened an open competition to select a clarinetist from among the best Mexican bands. The winner was Feliciano Ramos, from the Band of Supreme Powers, who had to play at first sight an improvised piece, with variations, from Verdi's *Il Trovatore* (Campos 1928, 200). These bands also brought with them the innovative instruments created by Adolphe Sax, which enriched traditional village bands. Mexican folklorist Rubén M. Campos (1928) believed that there were three classes of bands: popular bands, in rural areas; city bands, "prostituted" by playing American *fox trots* and British *schottisch*; and military bands, which emerged "to ennoble the popular band, in imitation of the great bands brought by the French army . . . and the imperial guard of Maximilian."

During the same century, the Baca Band of Fayetteville was regarded as the first musical ensemble of its kind in Texas. The Baca family came from

Moravia in 1860, and very soon after organized its band, recording their first album in 1929 (Strachwitz 1993, 4–5). This disc appeared in the record company's catalog of bohemian music, that is to say, it was considered *ethnic music*. We have news of musicians from the Baca family as late as the 1970s, more than 100 years after their predecessors started to spread their melodies in Texas; they would not have been the only music group with such longevity, and we are thus certain that this continuity is an example of cultural resistance aimed at maintaining an identity.

I have indicated on several occasions that Nuevo León and Texas were part of the same region, and north of the current border we find very similar musical influences during the nineteenth century. Just as the *fandango* was a beloved form of entertainment all over Mexico, a visitor to San Antonio at the end of the 1830s commented that "there are seldom fewer than three or four [fandangos] during the night in different parts of the city." Originally, the term *fandango* was applied to a public dance, but by the 1830s, it referred to functions held by the lower strata of Mexican society (Peña 1999a, 27–29).

In the early nineteenth century, *típica* orchestras were disseminated widely throughout Mexico and South Texas, featuring instruments like the violin and the flute; they also used Mexican folk instruments: the *bandolón* and *jaranita*, the *salterio* and the *bajo de cuerda* (Campos 1930, 144). Later, because they were intended to build a national icon in the local and international collective imaginary, some *típicas* had sponsorship from the Mexican government. But the truth was that these groups were not favored by the Mexican public: several news reports reveal that their performances in Mexico drew very small audiences. They did, however, make lengthy and applauded tours in the United States and South America. Such groups were seen as exotic abroad, but the poorly attended concerts in Mexico seem to suggest that, initially, Mexican spectators considered shocking the presentation of musicians dressed like charros, playing European instrumental music—almost always opera overtures mixed with a *sonecito del país* (Mexican folk song)—with musical instruments taken from peasant communities.

With the support of the government, many *típicas* proliferated throughout the country and traveled to the American southwest with the migrants, but perhaps most notable was the Orquesta Típica de la Ciudad de México ("Typical Orchestra of Mexico City"), a group that continues to perform today and that was founded by the Italian-Mexican director Carlos Curti in 1884. Originally calling his group Orquesta Típica Mexicana (Typical Mexican Orchestra), Curti had the idea to adopt charro attire as a uniform for all orchestra members (Jáuregui 2007, 52). Within a short time, típicas appeared in Querétaro, Puebla, and Campeche. In its first performances, the Orquesta Típica Mexicana featured a harp, two violins, a viola, two violoncellos, a flute, seven *bandolones*, two *salterios*, and two *bajos de cuerda*, which

Enrique de Olavarría and Ferrari (1961, 1112) called *guitarras-bajos* (bass guitars), making clear that the two terms were interchangeable at that time. The year after its formation, the orchestra embarked on an extensive tour of the United States, appearing at the World's Industrial and Cotton Centennial Exposition in New Orleans, where a journalistic report gave an account of the *bajos-dobles* (basses with double the normal number of strings) proudly shown off by the group (Dickson 2009). If, during their debut in front of Mexican president Porfirio Díaz, in 1884, the bass notes was relegated to the *bajos de cuerda*, for their international tour, the group used *bajos-dobles*, as we can see in a photograph taken in Ohio, now in the Harry Ransom Center of the University of Texas at Austin, in which one of the instruments on the floor clearly has double strings, unlike the single-stringed *bajo de cuerda*. Shortly after, the ensemble added *bandurrias* (another traditional Mexican instrument) and guitars to its lineup. The then director of the Conservatorio Nacional de Música (National Conservatory of Music), Alfredo Bablot, was one of the organizers of the Orquesta Típica Mexicana, and it is worth reproducing part of a letter that he sent to the newspaper *El Siglo Diez y Nueve* (*The Nineteenth Century*) (September 19, 1884), in which he reveals the reasons for founding the group:

> As a member of the Mexican Commission of Fine Arts for the exposition in New Orleans, I began the organization of a typical Mexican orchestra that might give, in that international context, an idea of the particular character of several instruments cultivated with intelligence and skill in the country . . . among the performers were true artists . . . of indisputable merit. . . . All of them possess the extraordinary musical intuition that distinguishes Mexicans of all social classes. . . . As you can clearly observe, the bandolón does not figure in the modern orchestras; this is because it is an instrument of its own, almost exclusively from Mexico and Central America, and it is not well-known in Europe. . . . If Mont [illegible] and his immediate successors wrote, with great success, orchestra parts for guitars, our composers can do the same for the bandolones, whose sonorous power and varied resources exceed the instrument of Aguado and Carulli.

Taking into account both the fact that the first references we have to the bajo sexto are subsequent to this date and also Bablot's passionate defense of the use of Mexican folk instruments in the orchestra, it is not illogical to think that such an instrument, which will become inseparable from conjunto, would have seemed a necessity for the modern *típica* orchestras. In the north of Mexico, the distinguished composer and bajo sexto player, Ramiro Cavazos, born on the Garza Ayala ranch in Los Ramones, Nuevo León, in 1927, recalled that his maternal relatives were musicians "of the violin," and played "in those large, beautiful, and perfect orchestras" (personal communication, July 11, 2011).

The basic occupation of the various instrumental ensembles listed was to accompany dances, and their proliferation could give a misleading picture, since it is possible to think that there was no place for the song and the human voice. In fact, the Spanish operatic tradition was introduced in New Spain during the early colonial period, and any theatrical performance always included *romances*, *boleras*, and *seguidillas*, accompanied regularly by two guitars. After the war of independence, the influence of these verses, as well as of Italian opera songs, was received and adapted in the farthest points of the country's capital, transformed by the temperament of rural residents (Mendoza 1998, 31). By the end of the nineteenth century, we can distinguish in Mexico between the *romantic* and the *typical* song, which, toward the 1920s, would be called *ranchera* (country) (Peña 1999a, 50–51). During these years, Mexican songs enjoyed huge popularity in various parts of the world. In the United States, for example: "there is no theater of fashion or music hall where they do not dedicate the interval to the Mexican song, [and it is] the same in California and in New York or Louisiana" (mentioned in Campos 1928, 78). Also, some of the first recordings of Mexican music in California and Texas included hundreds of songs and corridos, performed by vocal duos and guitar.

Even in our day, it is still possible to listen to another ensemble that contributed to the repertoire of conjunto: the *tamborileros* (the drummers), also called *picota*, a traditional ensemble of the Nuevo León and Tamaulipas sierra, consisting of one or two clarinets and a *tambora*. This type of group flourished from the middle of the nineteenth century in the cities of Nuevo León, including Linares (Esquer 1997, 23–26), Montemorelos, and General Terán, and in Tamaulipas in the Sierra de San Carlos (García Flores 1997, 19–22). All these vocal and instrumental groups popularized a musical culture derived from the various European social classes, and a good part of their repertoire, such as polkas and waltzes, would prove well-suited to the marginalized classes in the border region, played by groups, such as Los Montañeses del Álamo (the Álamo Mountaineers) and then through norteño and *Tejano* conjunto.

THE MONTAÑESES DEL ÁLAMO: HERALDS OF NORTEÑO CONJUNTO

Tejano singer Lydia Mendoza, known as *la Alondra de la Frontera* (the Lark of the Border), recalled that during her childhood in Monterrey in the 1920s, she began to collect song lyrics, printed on the little pieces of paper in which a chewing gum company was wrapping its product. But there was one problem: she did not know the melody to the lyrics. Fortunately, Mendoza was able to learn the songs, thanks to the fact that every Saturday afternoon a quartet of elderly musicians came from a nearby ranch, with flute, violin, bajo sexto, and bass, and played any song people requested (Broyles-González 2001, 104–106). Certainly, these types of musical ensembles were heirs of the *típica* orchestras that were so prominent at the end of the nineteenth century throughout the nation. Probably due to the economic crisis generated by the Mexican Revolution, musicians began to form smaller groups in order to stay competitive, as it was cheaper to pay for a quartet than a larger band. That is surely why the flowering of various orchestras in South Texas was nourished by Mexican migrants: ensembles unable to find work in the northeast of the country decided to seek their fortune in the United States. It is not a coincidence that in 1928 the Orquesta Mexicana Calvillo, one of the many Texan orchestras, recorded for Vocalion the two-step "Monterrey alegre" ("Cheerful Monterrey") and the waltz "México bello" ("Beautiful Mexico") (Peña 1999a, 123). Incidentally, Beto Villa, considered the father of *orquesta tejana*, had a parent who had emigrated from Monterrey (Peña 1985, 28).

Of all the groups of their era, Los Montañeses del Álamo stands out as one of the first to gain fame in Nuevo León and, as we have seen, they reflected a regional musical tradition of several decades. The founder of the group, Pedro Mier, began to receive lessons from his neighbor Isidoro Leija in 1925, and shortly after, they formed a duet with violin and bajo sexto. Brightening up ranch parties in the city of Cadereyta Jiménez, their reputation grew, and after studying the flute Mier decided to form, in 1931, an ensemble with violin, flute, bass, and bajo sexto, naming it the *Orquesta de las Abras* (Alanís Tamez 1994, 22–25).

In 1936, Leija, who had also taught music to Pedro's sons, decided to move to Tamaulipas, where he died shortly afterward. But Pedro Mier was determined to continue with his group, at least in whatever free time farming left him, so, along with his children, he traveled to the region's various *cantinas*. The group went through difficult times, but their perseverance paid off when the then-president of the municipality of Villa de Santiago, Alfonso Salazar, supported their efforts to tour and introduce them on radio, making their first recordings, always promoting the music as a source of regional pride (Alanís Tamez 1994, 25–30). Pedro Mier's sons and grandsons stated that the group completed its first recording in 1938, but American producer and folklore researcher Chris Strachwitz affirms the first Mexican recording took place in 1940, and the first one in the United States in 1946 (Berrones 2002, 8). The sweet music of Los Montañeses del Álamo consisted of instrumental waltzes, polkas, and *chotises*, as well as romantic songs and corridos; their performances always rooted in nineteenth-century folk traditions. Pedro

Mier composed, recorded, and published the scores of various pieces and was particularly famous for his polka "La mosca" ("The Fly"), which has become part of the traditional nursery rhyme repertoire in several countries. In northeastern Mexico, until just a few years ago, it was common to hear a game in which the children sang "La mosca" ("The Fly") several times, using a single vowel in each repetition.

Over time, Los Montañeses added other musical instruments, such as the guitar and saxophone, and, ultimately, in 1959, the accordion. The golden age of the group was in the 1950s and 1960s, when they had to form a second lineup to keep up with the large number of national and international tours; they called this group Nuevo Conjunto del Álamo (Alanís Tamez 1994, 47–52). At present, Pedro Mier's grandchildren and great-grandchildren still play under the group's original name and continue to make recordings and public appearances, while safeguarding one of the oldest musical traditions of the Mexican republic. Los Montañeses del Álamo left an indelible mark on the north of Mexico, as well as in many Mexican-American communities in the United States, and its influence on conjunto is undeniable. Some musical groups, such as the Conjunto Río Grande, from Zacatecas, continue to play instrumental pieces in the manner of Los Montañeses.

WE SING IN SPANISH (AND IN ENGLISH!): LANGUAGE AS A GENERATOR OF IDENTITY

I had mentioned in the preface that language is one of the most important elements in disseminating a specific culture. In many places in the United States, the Spanish language has a very prominent public presence in the media, even in places where historically there were no Spanish-speaking migrants. Some of the terms often heard in the United States, and which identify *Tejanos* and Chicanos, are *bordo*, referring to the frontier (from the English *border*); *troca*, when speaking of a *truck*; or *puchar*, relating to *push*. These words are a mixture of Spanish and English, known as Spanglish, a "language" born of particular contact between languages. In linguistics, this phenomenon is called *cambio de código* (code switching) (Roca 2000).

Generally, members of the first Mexican-American generation in the United States speak their ancestral language, while their children tend to be bilingual and their grandchildren speak only English. Any type of generalization is risky, but we appreciate that for the third generation, the official language of their country is a source of identity, and there is an appropriation and transformation: "words, phrases, rhythms, intonations, and specific sounds that Hispanic speakers used to symbolize their identity" (Amastae 2010, 293–301). Of course, there are exceptions to this "rule," such as when even the fourth generation of a Mexican family in the United States speaks fluent English and Spanish, as in the case of a Juan Tejeda, accordionist and promoter of *Tejano* conjunto from San Antonio. Born in the early 1950s, he mentions that, both at home and in elementary school, he was punished for speaking Spanish. Chicano students were made to feel ashamed of their culture. He also talks about an "institutional racism" that still exists today. To the question of whether things changed after the Chicano movement, he refers to an American saying: "The more things change, the more they stay the same" (personal communication, July 11, 2011). The way in which musicians continue to encourage the use of the ancestral language by means of conjunto songs is thus quite representative.

In the case of norteño and *Tejano* conjunto, and after reviewing more than 100 compact discs, as well as vintage 1978s and 1945s, it is evident that the pioneers of this tradition began with purely instrumental music, and later, when they started to introduce songs and corridos, they invariably sang in Spanish (see "A selection of recorded music"). Even today, it is astonishing that to the north of the Rio Bravo/Grande some singing forms have persisted, including *glissandos*, as well as vocabulary that was in daily use in Mexico a century ago, but today would be archaic. The song *Soy Tejano*, by Oscar Argumedo (Table 2.3), shows the dichotomy faced by Mexican-American people.

Despite proudly claiming their "Mexican origin," we perceive that some musicians born out of Mexico must learn, or at least practice, Spanish when approaching conjunto. A typical example is the Dutch accordionist Dwayne Verheyden, who had no roots in the region and who, for years, did not understand what he was singing, and so chose to absorb the language of Cervantes in order to understand and "feel" the music more acutely (personal communication, May 17, 2013). And speaking of the similarities between norteño and *Tejano* conjunto, in Mexico, people think that Verheyden is a norteño singer and accordionist, while in Texas, they say he plays *Tejano* music.

These days, Mexicans and Chicanos exercise increasing influence in all U.S. public spaces, so it is not a mere euphemism when a music producer from the Texas coast—who preferred to remain anonymous—states that "the Mexicans are going to win the Alamo in a peaceful manner" (personal

Table 2.3 Lorenzo Luera y su Conjunto, "Soy texano," by Oscar Argumedo, 45 rpm (Fort Worth, TX: Gabe Records Inc., n.d.)

Es mi orgullo ser *Tejano*	It is my pride to be *Tejano*,
y de origen mexicano,	And of Mexican origin,
pero soy americano	But I am American,
de purito corazón.	From the heart.

communication, July 12, 2011). Of course, one of the "weapons" with which they will win that battle is the music of conjunto. Lyrics are discussed at greater length in the next chapter. For now, I can say that, although the vast majority of their songs remain Spanish, over the last few decades, a few *Tejano* conjuntos, influenced by country, jazz, and rock, have opted to record in English or bilingually, while the norteño conjunto has remained faithful to Spanish. In the following paragraphs, I will focus on the development of conjunto from the dawn of the twentieth century to the 1950s, its main exponents, and technological innovations that, by means of radio, film, and the recording industry, radically transformed the sociocultural life of the border after World War II.

Chapter 3

The First Epoch of Conjunto
Instruments, Musical Forms, and Media

While the United States of America has become a world power since the last quarter of the nineteenth century (Felix 2009, ix), in Mexico there were setbacks that did not allow sustained development until the 1930s (Ramos Sánchez 2000, 40). In addition, at the beginning of the twentieth century, south of the Rio Bravo/Grande there was a certain self-absorption and hyper-focus on the big city: "Everything that is not the capital is ignored" (Taibo I 1988, 7). This section will look in detail at the history of conjunto from the early twentieth century to the period of World War II, providing an overview of the various musical forms it originally promoted, and the way in which society, economy, and technological advances had an impact on its development. It will reveal the difficulties faced by early musicians in finding spaces in which to practice their art, mainly because of conjunto's bad reputation, especially in Mexico. Throughout this chapter, we will see that various types of European music were assimilated on both sides of the border, but the greatest dissemination was in southern Texas, thanks to three particular factors: recording technology and radio; the migration from northeastern Mexico of musicians fleeing post-revolution misery; and the emerging identity of Mexican-Americans, who found in the new music a source of ethnic and cultural pride.

EUROPEAN MUSIC IN AMERICA

The previous chapter identified some aspects of the migration of Germans, Poles, and Czechs to Texas and Nuevo León. These ethnic minorities built community centers where dances and concerts were offered; between 1897 and 1980, the Texan Czech community in particular, through the Slavonic

Benevolent Order of the State of Texas (Polish acronym SPJST), built 200 of these centers in the region that functioned as points of meeting and recreation. For their part, the Germans also erected ballrooms throughout the state, which eventually were open to all kinds of music, including blues, rock, *Tejano*, and conjunto (Hartman 2008, 110–117).

One of the dances known in those halls since the nineteenth century, and that we still enjoy today, is the polka. Originally part of the music of the lower classes of Bohemia, little attention was paid to its precise origin at the time; it is known that it was a rural community dance dating from no earlier than the 1830s (Cernusak, Lamb and Tyrrell 1980, 34–36). The Czechs claim they invented the polka, while the Poles say their neighbors adopted it after seeing young Polish women dancing, because the literal translation of the word *polka* is "Polish woman" (Rivard and Jasinski 2012, 479–481). To expand the discussion, some German writers have asserted that the polka is just a schottische with a new name (Cernusak et al. 1980, 34).

In the middle of the nineteenth century, and probably as a result of the wars of independence and the anti-Spanish climate they engendered, Iberian dances dropped in popularity very quickly, at the same time as the polka and other music of Eastern Europe were being adapted across the entire American continent. We can find a good example of this in Argentina, where the oldest available reference to the polka was in a newspaper of 1845 and involved a dancing master who promised to teach the "elegant national dance of the polka," describing it as "the rage of Europe" (Plesch, Cragnolini and Ilarraza 1999). A year earlier, in Mexico, there is the first mention of a "new *jota* called the Polka" in a note in the *Diario del Gobierno de Veracruz (Newspaper of the Government of Veracruz)*, reprinted shortly after in *El Siglo Diez y Nueve (The Nineteenth Century)* (September 12, 1844) in Mexico City:

> Who has not heard of the Polka? The old people talk about it, young people and the mature are dedicated to learning it, and all with the exception of the crippled or blind are trying to dance it. From the most aristocratic lounge to the most humble room . . . we are learning the polka. . . . The polka has spread like a contagion from the depths of Poland to St. Petersburg, from there to Vienna, from Vienna to Paris, from Paris to London; and there is no doubt that soon it will be jumping across the great Atlantic. . . . Music teachers are making fortunes with the tunes they're composing for the Polka.

The report confirms that the furor caused by the polka in Europe was real, offers details of its dissemination from one country to another, and reveals that the publication of sheet music for this dance was making composers and editors wealthy. This is one of the first occasions in history when we can recognize that, without the support of the Church or the aristocracy, music was becoming a lucrative profession. The polka was so popular in Mexico that, by the end of the 1840s, it had become a fashionable word with varied meanings, such as, for example, a certain type of garment for men known as "polka trousers," which was "simply a small stripe or cord on the sides that ran down to the *pialera*" (Revista Científica y Literaria 1845). In fact, at one time, "everything strange and extravagant" was called *polkos*, such as, for instance, a certain type of small black silk hat. As if that were not enough, on January 11, 1847, there was a revolt known at the time as the *Revolution of the Polkos*, when a group of young soldiers from wealthy families, lovers of the polka, rebelled against president Valentín Gómez Farías (Quiroz Zamora 1997, 83). This insurrection, which reveals the proximity of this memorable dance to the elites, was promoted by the clergy, stirring up the reluctant snobs who had originally been called to fight in the war against the United States (Orozco Linares 2005, 178).

But it was not only the big cities or wealthy classes that enjoyed fashionable European music; very soon it extended to all social strata. The predilection for certain variants of *contradanza* (contredanse) and *cuadrillas* (square dance), for example, produced exchanges among various spheres of society, to the point where they became the predominant music of the nineteenth century: they were the "common cultural medium" in the islands of the Caribbean Basin (Manuel 2009, 1). The polka, usually in 2/4 time, was so famous everywhere that we can find a large number of regional variants: *zäpperlpolka*, polka-mazurka, French polka, *polka tremblante*, lounge polka, military polka, correntina polka, Russian polka, rural polka, *polka canaria*, Paraguayan polka, and *polka criolla*, among many others (Cernusak et al. 1980, 34; Plesch et al. 1999); and then, of course, there is its appropriation by the conjunto: *polka norteña* (which, despite sharing similarities, should not be confused with the northern Nicaraguan polka). If that were not enough, Manuel Peña (1985, 83) argues that ranchero music played by conjunto is nothing other than a polka—or a waltz—to which has been attached a melody with lyrics.

In the early twentieth century, there were so many polkas in the area of the current study that even the accordionists did not know their names, as mentioned by norteño composer Antonio Tanguma. In Monterrey, according to newspaper *El Porvenir* (June 26, 1930), the polka even reached the local Masonic Lodge, which, to celebrate its 25th anniversary, momentarily forgot hymns and the music of its Masonic brothers Mozart and Haydn, preparing instead an artistic program for the Independencia Theater, at which was performed, among other things, the concert polka "Castles in the Air."

If we accept the Polish origin of the polka, it is remarkable that the community usually interpreted it on violin, while the Czechs and Germans put the accordion in the place of honor (Rivard and Jasinski 2012, 480), as a result of which one can say with certainty that both the *polka norteña* and the *American polka* show marked German and Czech influence. In Texas and Nuevo León, the polka is danced with vigor and strength, because folk-dance teachers recommend that dancers execute the steps with as much lift in each step as their skill and the tempo permit (Duggan, Schlottmann and Rutledge 1948, 58).

If in the seventeenth and eighteenth centuries dances in Mexico reflected a division between the wealthy and the underprivileged, by the nineteenth century the membrane between traditions was quite permeable. We have already mentioned the contra dance and the *cuadrillas*, which dominated the social dance landscape for more than a century in Western Europe, where "as social phenomena they were particularly important as vehicles for collective recreation and self-definition on the part of the rising middle classes, in contrast to the courtly . . . minuet". The contra dance and *cuadrillas* performers ranged from the uneducated peasant who played the violin, to Mozart himself (Manuel 2009, 3).

In the middle of the nineteenth century, there was a weakening of the strict social norms that had previously prevailed, as the aforementioned group dances eventually lost ground to couple dances like the polka and the *chotis*. The latter is a type of ballroom dance slower than the polka, which probably originated when somebody incorporated turns similar to the waltz into the schottische (Tilmouth and Lamb 1980, 635); initially, it was known as the German polka. Coming from Paris, it became fashionable in Spain in the 1840s and passed from the theater to lounges and public dances (Sobrino 1999, 868–871). By the middle of the nineteenth century, the *chotis* and polka already had deep roots in Mexico, both in "city dance halls and even on the *patios* of village houses" (Galindo 1933, 552).

For its part, the *redova*, or, as Texans call it, *redowa*, exemplifies the neglect and ignorance to which Mexican popular music forms have been subjected, because while there is agreement among scholars that this dance is of Czech origin and resembles the minuet, some question whether it appeared in New Granada toward the end of the eighteenth century (Yépez 1999, 73), was introduced to the halls of Prague in 1829 (Tyrrell 1980, 58–59), or was merely a variant of the polka in three-quarter time (Cernusak et al. 1980, 34). This confusion illustrates how, even before reaching the coast of America, these dances had already been through many influences. In the particular case of southern Texas and northeastern Mexico, the redova was transformed and stylized, and from the 1920s, it became known as the *vals bajito* (short or low waltz) (Peña 1999a, 90). It is an instrumental piece in 9/8 time, with accents on the first and third beats and requires great virtuosity on the part of an accordionist to interpret it (Ragland 2009, 210).

If European composers took advantage of the popularity of these dances to make money, the musicians of our study region were not far behind. From the second half of the nineteenth century, Mexican and American newspapers regularly published advertisements for new musical scores, usually for the piano or guitar. If the buyer of the piece happened to be part of a small band or orchestra, then he could make an arrangement for his group. An example of the dissemination of the works of composers across Mexico can be seen in an article in the newspaper *El Cronista* (June 24, 1888), from Matamoros, Tamaulipas, which trumpeted a function for the benefit of the "peerless Flute-Man," where the orchestra played the polka *Yo con mi negra*, composed by Sermeño, as well as the mazurka *Te amo*, by Martínez, and the waltz *El Tamaulipeco*.

The hierarchy that historically represented Mexican music in southern Texas is confirmed by figure 3.1, where we can see the "choicest Mexican

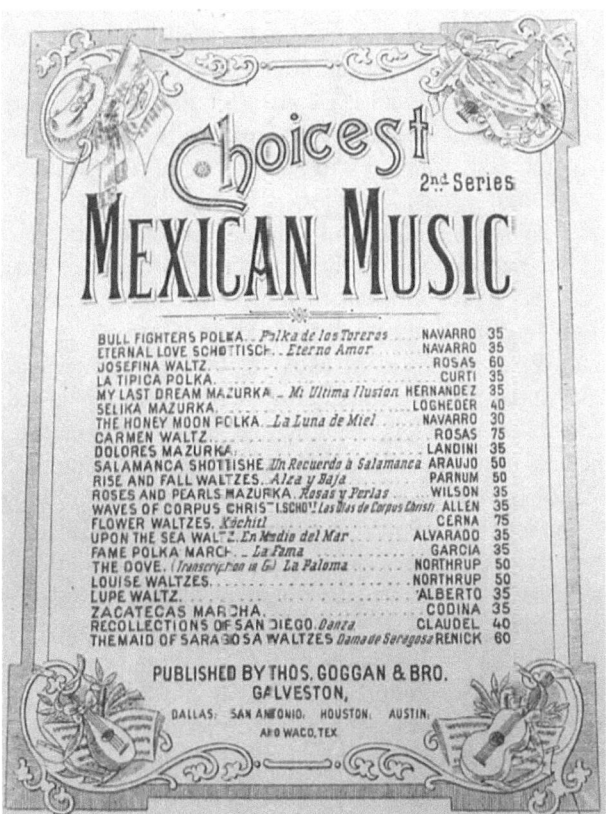

Figure 3.1 Score published by Thomas Goggan, personal collection.

music," dominated by polkas and mazurkas, published by Thomas Goggan and Brothers, from composers like Luis G. Araujo of Guanajuato, Genaro Codina of Zacatecas, or the famed Italian-Mexican director of *típica* orchestras and bands Carlos Curti. The publisher of this music was an Irish immigrant, who opened the first music store in Texas in 1866 (Gish and Jasinski 2012, 245–246).

All these European dances were assimilated and experienced an extraordinary boom, being banged out in the streets by *organilleros* in Spain and the Americas (Sobrino 1999). But a hundred years after their onset, by the late 1930s, they had become out-of-date in many cities, or at least were despised by some post-revolutionary Mexican citizens, to whom they were inseparable from the *ancien régime* of the *porfiriato*. This is confirmed by an item appearing in the Monterrey newspaper *El Porvenir*, dated July 5, 1931. On that occasion, students from Colegio La Luz danced at a festival in the Teatro Salon at the Mercantile Mutual Circle. The author tells us that a group of seven children presented a few "old dances" such as the polka, *chotis*, and contredanse. But these musical forms continued to predominate in the case of conjunto: in 1941, almost 40 percent of all the music recorded by such groups consisted of polkas (San Miguel 2002, 10). Small musical ensembles played instrumental pieces exclusively, and their repertoire, which, as we have seen, was not considered fashionable by the dominant culture, was very similar in both Nuevo León and Texas.

These days, the nineteenth-century dances are not interpreted regularly, but have not been entirely lost, as there are festivals devoted largely to polka in both the United States and Mexico. In the United States, these shows take place anywhere there are people of Polish, German, or Czech descent, from Texas to Wisconsin, and in Mexico we find them especially in the northern border states. Before concluding this section, it is key to recall how some scholars believe that "in the absence of a strong culture, the polka, the waltz, the mazurka, and the *chotis* acquired their naturalization papers without substantial modifications or *mestizajes*" (Tinajero Medina 2004, 87). Nevertheless, the musical forms that came from Europe were not simply imitated in our territory of research but experienced transformations and adaptations that altered them. I invoke here the ideas of English ethnomusicologist Martin Stokes (1997, 19), who states that Western popular music of the post-war period preserved, in essence, the "harmonic-melodic vocabulary" of the dominant European culture, specifically the Viennese tradition of the eighteenth and nineteenth centuries, but subverts it by means of repetition, tempo, or timbre. Stokes's impressions are valuable and can be applied in the case of conjunto because, indeed, its performers use repetition and very fast tempos, and the harsh timbre of the accordion and mestizo bajo sexto is fairly strident, never comparable to bel canto or the refined violin. And it does all this without becoming a parody of the European music that the Mexican upper classes worshipped. The coming chapter will discuss the changes conjunto repertoire underwent after World War II, relating not only to fashion but to the sociocultural needs of citizens of the border.

ACCORDION AND BAJO SEXTO: SYMBOLS AND CULTURAL UNIFIERS

Earlier, the second chapter mentioned that the music of the bands and *típica* orchestras, as well as the sound popularized by the *tambora de rancho* and clarinet, common since the end of the nineteenth century in the rural areas of Nuevo León, were gradually replaced by the button accordion and bajo sexto. Because of that, it was not until the early 1940s, around the time of the introduction of the Bracero Program, that the accordion appeared in the larger cities of northeastern Mexico (Ayala Duarte 2000, 40) and in South Texas (Broyles-González 2001, 104). Both the button accordion and the bajo sexto have become inseparable from the conjunto; they are inextricably linked to social groups and social practices and represent cultural hybridization, since the first one is truly a machine, symbolic of the modern European culture of the nineteenth century, while the bajo sexto is a noted mestizo and traditional instrument. Both instruments have become a symbol of conjunto; they are important cultural unifiers (La Rue 1997, 189–205). As mentioned by a *Tejano* composer and accordionist, "Here in the United States, if you don't have a bajo sexto and an accordion, it is not conjunto . . . (these instruments) formally identify conjunto" (personal communication, July 14, 2011). To these basic instruments were later added the electric bass and the drums.

In Texas, it is commonly said that "Germans do not like Mexicans very much"; however, it was mostly thanks to the Germans that Mexican-American people learned to play the accordion a century ago (Tejeda 2001c, 265), and the close contact between Czechs and Mexicans has enriched both musical traditions: the former have learned Mexican popular melodies, while the latter have adapted many Czech and Bohemian pieces to their repertoire (Cuéllar 2001, 142).

But it is worth clarifying the qualities that belong to each of the instruments that comprise our music. Although similar instruments had circulated in Europe since the 1810s, the first patent for an accordion was obtained by Austrian Cyril Demian around 1828. He called his machine *akkordeon*, based on the Italian word *accordare*, which means "sounding together," in reference to its capacity to produce several notes at the same time. Considered a handheld substitute for an orchestra, the Demian accordion soon had imitators all over Europe, as well as in the United States and Russia. But it was only at the beginning of the twentieth century that, thanks to developments in the plastics industry, accordions started to be mass-produced in Italy (Jacobson 2012, 15–16). The accordion belongs to the family of free-reed aerophones and is composed of two harmonic boxes of wood in which smaller boxes are placed, called *burros* (donkeys) or *voces* (voices), in Mexico. These smaller boxes contain the steel reeds—known as *pitos* (whistles)—that vibrate when air from the bellows moves them.

Technically, the main difference between the keyboard accordion and the button accordion lies in the fact that, with the former, we hear the same notes regardless of whether the bellows are opened or closed, while the latter produces different sounds depending on the direction of movement. Socially, the elitist view favors the keyboard accordion, which is even studied at conservatories, while the button accordion is considered to be characteristic of "ethnic music." Because of button accordions' capacity to play in only a few keys, they are not considered "complete instruments in their own right." Regardless, while the keyboard accordion presently enjoys great popularity, the diatonic button instrument, such as the one used in conjunto, has its admirers, and it was the favorite during the nineteenth century. Indeed, such was its fame that in 1902 one could buy this instrument through the Sears Roebuck catalogue (Jacobson 2012, 16–17).

As we saw in the previous chapter, the first news we have of the accordion in Mexico is around 1847, during the United States' invasion of Monterrey. Elsewhere in the nation, Mexican weeklies allude to the curious instrument a few years later: it appears on a list of items carried by the French vessel *Hippolite Adolphe*, which sailed from Bordeaux with a final destination of the state of Tabasco in October 1849. In the early years of conjunto, accordionists played the melody with the right hand, with the left providing bass notes and harmony. This practice has not been lost, although it has become increasingly rare since the introduction of the bajo sexto. The squeezebox is supported by two straps that hang from the player's shoulders, and many accordion players prefer to remove the *burros* for the left hand in order to make the instrument lighter, and thus avoid fatigue during performances that may last several hours. In addition, in removing the "voices," and thus their sound, the left-hand buttons may be used to remove air from the instrument, and thus open or close the bellows faster. In fact, some instruments are sold without any buttons for the left hand.

Some songs have been inspired by this leader of the instruments that make up the conjunto; one of the most representative is "Accordion," (Table 3.1) by norteño composer and singer Lalo Mora.

Turning now to the bajo sexto and its origins, it is clear that this instrument possesses distinctive features: it is similar to the guitar, but its sonority, body, and fingerboard are larger than those of the guitar. It has twelve metal

Table 3.1   Fragment of the song "Acordeón," by Lalo Mora

Tu sonido es el más claro sentimiento,	Your sound is the most clear feeling,
el espejo del amor y desamor,	the mirror of love and heartbreak,
y dibujas con tus notas tantos sueños,	and you sketch with your notes so many
convirtiendo en realidad una ilusión . . .	dreams, converting Ilusion to reality . . .
Acordeón, ladrón de mis suspiros,	Accordion, thief of my sighs,
acordeón, cupido enamorado y soñador.	accordion, besotted Cupid and dreamer,
alcánzame la estrella más lejana,	catch for me the most distant star,
y un poquito de su amor.	and a little of her love.

strings that are depressed in pairs and is usually played using a plectrum (pick). When accompanying the accordion, the bajo sexto can lead the bass line, and also play chords, while it is limited to harmony and marking the beat when played together with a *tololoche* or electric bass. Any person who has played the guitar and takes a bajo sexto in his or her hands for the first time will immediately discover that it is a very "generous" musical instrument. Once the performer has become accustomed to the double strings, it is very simple to play; with only two or three chord positions and a few rhythms, one is ready to accompany almost any song.

On the social side, the instrument has been subjected to the same prejudices that have weighed on many guitars that have not had the good fortune to be *classical*: "For many people, the 'classical' guitar is the only legitimate form of the instrument; the folk and electric [ones] are relegated as elements of an ephemeral popular culture. . . . The guitars of Latin American folklore are completely ignored" (Cruz 1993, 17). Due to a resulting lack of research into the instrument, the product of a marginalized culture, there is a great confusion among researchers regarding its origin. Manuel Peña (1999a, 46) asserts that the use of bajo sexto was conventional until the 1920s, and he believes that it started (or at least was popularized) in Guanajuato and Michoacán; although he admits that that information was obtained from a Mexican luthier in San Antonio (Peña 1985, 39). The Hungarian composer and ethnomusicologist Béla Bartók (1997, 49) notes that "it is not a good idea to [rely on the opinions of] people who have left their villages and have gone to live in other places . . . these individuals . . . unconsciously may have also have distanced themselves from their people's 'music community.'" For her part, without citing a single source, American ethnomusicologist Cathy Ragland (2009, 205) said that the bajo sexto "is found on the Texas-Mexican border region and is believed to be originally from the state of Durango in Mexico."

Some Mexican scholars have confused the bajo sexto with instruments of the *típica* orchestras, such as the *bajo de cuerda*, also called *bajo de armonía*. However, in a description by folklorist Rubén M. Campos (1930, 146), it is clear that the object he describes is like the mariachi's *guitarrón*: "The *bajo de cuerda* or *bajo de armonía* is a massive six-stringed *guitarrón* that is played with the thumb on the initial low notes of the accompaniment."

Among Mexican scholars, Luis Montoya (2013, 200) argues that the *bajo sexto* was born in the *Bajío* region (comprising the states of central Mexico: Guanajuato, Querétaro, Aguascalientes, Jalisco, and Michoacán). He believes that Campo's description of the *bajo de cuerda* is precisely that of a *bajo sexto*. Montoya, however, alters Campos's words and adds to them; in his text, the "massive guitarrón" now has "double" strings. These kinds of "modifications" are not new: in another article, he (2012) confuses the word *bass* (the musical instrument) with the color *beige*. Montoya refers to Mexican sociologist Gustavo López Castro, who, discussing the bajo sexto, wrote in his book *El río Bravo es charco* (*The Rio Bravo is a Puddle*) (1995, 14): "[I]t is unlikely that the origin of the bajo sexto was in the Mexican Bajío, unless it is a variant of the lute or some other colonial instrument." With great imagination, Montoya (2013, 201) alters and expands the above as follows: "The bajo sexto is a variant of the colonial lute, manufactured by some of the guitar or harp workshops of Michoacán or Guanajuato. Remember that the mandolin and guitar emerged from the lute, that instrument characteristic of the Renaissance." One cannot sustain a thesis with falsehoods, and this is one of the few occasions on which the lute is conjectured to be an antecedent of the bajo sexto, since it is unlikely that a pear- or almond-shaped instrument would have engendered another with cinched body and flat back.

Due to the fact that this instrument was originally popularized by the *típica* orchestras, which, as mentioned, had been ubiquitous throughout Mexico and the American southwest since the mid-1880s, it is impossible to speak of a specific birthplace for the bajo sexto. In spite of the fact that some musicians, like Miguel Lerdo de Tejada, tried to sustain the nationalist fashion represented by the *típica* orchestras, the truth is that by the end of the Mexican Revolution ensembles were dwindling, and very probably the bajo sexto would have also succumbed had it not been for norteña and *Tejano* music. In this regard, it is possible to identify a region where the instrument began to gain significance for conjunto: the border, specifically the Rio Grande Valley, Texas, and northern Tamaulipas.

I believe that bajo sexto is one of the many folk instruments that owe a particular debt to the five-course Spanish guitar, now known as the baroque guitar. This European instrument, in vogue from the sixteenth to the eighteenth centuries, left a great legacy across the length and breadth of the American continent, particularly in Mexico, where even in the first decades of the twentieth century it was possible to hear its descendants, among them seven- and six-strings guitars with double courses. This conviction is shared by Eloy Cruz Soto, a specialist in historical instruments of the guitar family, who thinks that bajo sexto is a variant of the six-string guitar with double courses, which was common at the end of the nineteenth century: "At that time, the 'Mexican guitar' (even the Germans used that name) had six, or more commonly, seven courses." He does not believe that there are any records on the origin of the instrument, but thinks it is probably derived from the baroque guitar, and he stresses that, prior to the nineteenth century, all folk instruments derived from it were known simply as "guitars" (personal communication, May 9, 2012).

The bajo sexto has great morphological similarity, for example, to another heir of the baroque guitar: the *huasteco* apparatus called *huapanguera*, known today as *guitarra quinta*, although a century ago its stringing consisted of five double courses (Hernández Azuara 2003, 68). It is no coincidence, then, that the Mexican ethnomusicologist Arturo Chamorro Escalante considers that the bajo sexto derives from the huapanguera (personal communication, April 2, 2014), which is supported by the fact that the Huasteca region of the state of San Luis Potosí contributed markedly to the population growth of Monterrey during the formative years of norteño conjunto. In the Huasteca we also find various towns where traditional musical instruments are manufactured using wood from the region, in particular Texquitote, a town in the municipality of Matlapa, San Luis Potosí, where about thirty families make their living as luthiers. For several generations, they have constructed guitars, violins, jaranas, harps, *huapangueras*, and bajo sextos (Frumencio Hernández Cándido, personal communication, July 25, 2007). This instrument is also close to the popular twelve-string folk guitar of our day, which appeared at the end of the nineteenth century in sparsely inhabited areas of the southern United States. To complicate its genealogy further, the way in which the bajo sexto is tuned, by intervals of fourths, follows the same pattern as the ancient Spanish *bandurria* (Rey and Navarro 1993, 114). In fact, if you put a capo on the second fret of the largest instrument of the Spanish lute family, the *laudón*, you will have the same tuning as the bajo sexto, simply without the octaves.

The second chapter mentions the founding, by Carlos Curti, of the Orquesta Típica Mexicana. At the beginning of the 1880s, a few years before the group was formed, the Italian-Mexican conductor had established an *estudiantina*—a group consisting of music students—that made an extensive tour of the United States; he dubbed it "Los verdaderos estudiantes españoles de Curti" ("Curti's True Spanish Students") (Dickson 2009, 63), and it consisted of mandolins, violins, and various instruments of the Spanish lute family. It is thus possible that the ingenious director integrated the tuning of the *laudón* into his *orquesta típica*, but using a form of the Mexican instrument that would later be known as bajo sexto. On the other hand, one of the most competent researchers of Mexican organology, Guillermo Contreras (1999, 67–69), includes the bajo sexto in the family of stringed instruments known as *bajo de espiga* ("pick bass"), due to the way in which the sound is produced with a plectrum. He claims that this family of instruments is composed of the *bajo quinto*, the *bajo sexto*, the *bajo sexto por séptima*, and the seven-string guitar; the inclusion of the last instrument is unlikely, since it could also be played without a pick. Contreras confirms that all these instruments have fallen into disuse, with the bajo sexto, which is "played across the country," as the only survivor, due to "its definitive adoption by northern groups, traditional ensembles of the northern border states of Mexico . . . and the southern United States."

During the early years of the conjunto, there was such demand for these instruments in the American southwest, especially in Texas and California, that very soon suppliers preferred to stop importing them from Mexico and began to build them in the United States. My research seems to corroborate that the instruments and musical forms of the conjunto first stirred enthusiasm in southern Texas and towns along the northeastern Mexican border. There is evidence of concerts in which bajo sexto was involved in Mexico and the American southwest from the final decades of the nineteenth century, but, as an artisanal object, the instrument's production was very limited. In the twilight of the nineteenth century, it was inextricably linked to the *típica* orchestras, and according to the scant surviving inventories of music stores, its form was a midpoint between the guitar and the *bajo de armonía*. Due to a shortage of music teachers, in one of the many catalogues from the end of the nineteenth century, the prominent Wagner & Levien music store published images and data from a booklet for bajo quinto and bajo sexto. It is notable that the "practical method for bajo 5th and 6th," by Francisco R. Del Prado, is presented as "the only method for this instrument in Spanish," which speaks of scanty interest in the bajo sexto. Another interesting fact is that in the same announcement they use the term *bajo de espiga* as a synonym for bajo sexto.

One must remember that music houses' catalogues were directed at a small number of people, those devoted to the art of music, and a small group of enthusiastic amateurs. These catalogues' existence is not an indication that the instrument was particularly popular. It is surely another example of that "intensification of nationalism" among Chicanos that the earliest information about the bajo sexto—by which time it was already being built on a production line and its music widely broadcast—appears in a San Antonio newspaper in the summer of 1918. In fact, from 1915 on, a set of bajo sexto strings could be purchased in the same city with "Mexican money, silver or bills" from T. Puente & Son (*La Revista de Taos*, 1915). Meanwhile, in Mexico, Wagner & Levien advertised their "Mexican models of German manufacturing" in newspapers until February 1922. It must be noted that this did not appear in newspapers in Durango, Michoacán, or Guanajuato, but in the local Monterrey newspaper *El Porvenir* (Figure 3.2). I will return to this matter in the fourth chapter.

Figure 3.2 Ad for bajo sexto, El Imparcial de Texas, San Antonio, August 8, 1918.

The saxophone has also played a prominent role in the conjunto ensemble, with some ups and downs. The second chapter mentions the importance of the great bands that had accompanied Emperor Maximilian, which possibly indicates that the regional use of this instrument may be traced back to that period. By the dawn of the twentieth century, the Montañeses del Álamo were already using the saxophone on a daily basis. However, the use of the instrument in conjunto norteño may in fact be a *Tejano* influence, according to saxophonist Guadalupe Quezada, of Linares, Nuevo León. Quezada had joined an accordion and bajo sexto duo at the beginning of the 1950s with the purpose of emulating the popular recordings that the father of the *orquesta tejana* and saxophonist, Beto Villa, made in conjunction with Narciso Martínez (Cuéllar 2001, 139). Finally, musical forms such as the polka and the redowa were transplanted by German immigrants and regionally adapted, but it is important to note that some musical instruments adopted by *Tejano* conjunto and conjunto norteño from the first decades of the twentieth century—the bajo sexto, and percussion instruments such as the *tambora* or the redoba—are unfamiliar to European musicians. Thus, these instruments can be a reference point for the appropriation and reinvention that the music undergoes here: we can pinpoint the construction of a new identity.

PIONEERS OF CONJUNTO

One of the reasons behind the spread of the predilection for the accordion and bajo sexto was the convenience of remunerating one or two musicians with a few coins (or with a meal) instead of hiring the old brass bands or *típica* orchestras. An example of such practice can be seen in the 1940s, in one of the red-light districts of Linares, Nuevo León, where both instruments were a success with patrons, and also pleased proprietors, because these duos drew larger audiences and were cheaper than the usual dance orchestras (Medina Montelongo and Quezada 1995). On the other hand, by the middle of that decade, Nuevo León was suffering from severe winters, with the consequent loss of crops, which forced the migration of hundreds of laborers to the United States who, upon returning to their villages in the south, liked to spend their money in bars and clubs, listening to their preferred regional music (Cuéllar 2001, 138).

If the money that can currently be made by *Tejano* musicians, and especially some norteños, is extraordinary, the initiators of the genre survived mainly by working in the fields, and the music served only to supplement their meager income. Composer and accordionist Antonio Tanguma, for example, worked exhausting days in the fields, and only sporadically performed "tours," such as one on which he played for a mobile cinema for several months, for which he was paid according to how well the cinema did. Fortunately, recognition did come for some promoters of conjunto, if late; others, however, died in abject poverty, as was the case of *Tejano* musician Bruno Villarreal, who made the first accordion recording in the region in 1928 (Peña 1985, 40).

I must emphasize that, despite the progress made in research into norteña and *tex-mex* conjunto, there will probably never be agreement about the exact point at which accordion music was introduced to the region. Manuel Peña (1985, 22–36) argues that the "logical origin" must have been Monterrey, via Matamoros. His arguments are based on the economic and cultural dominance of the city, known then as the Pittsburgh of Mexico thanks to the steel industry; Peña also believes that the accordion could not have been introduced by Anglo-Americans in Texas, because relations between them and Mexican-American people were violent, and cultural exchange was minimal until the 1920s. In favor of this theory, one can add that the parents, and even grandparents, of the first accordion players we know in the region had already been playing the instrument at least since the final decades of the nineteenth century; these people were from in and around Monterrey. Regardless, many musicians had preferred to move to south Texas because, aside from the poverty left behind by the Mexican Revolution, the inhabitants of Monterrey continued to disdain the local conjunto at least until the 1950s and the emergence of the first radio stations to play norteño music daily (Ayala Duarte 2000, 82).

Ramiro Cavazos, composer of more than 250 songs, and one of the pillars of the region's music, agrees with the above, and adds

The ranchers engaged us to sing them *corridos* and whatever you want, but in Monterrey, at the beginning, they didn't give much support to norteño music, they looked at it as very crude, cantina music; even some ranches did not want weddings to have norteño music because they said it was very common. . . . I came here [to South Texas] in 1945, . . . norteño music was always played in Reynosa (in Tamaulipas) and in the United States . . . before it was in Nuevo León, where you could find it, but it was still not very well recognized, because it wasn't being recorded. It was along the border where norteña music started to gain real strength. (Personal communication, July 24, 2013)

Indeed, the musicians who decided to stay south of the Rio Bravo/Grande experienced many predicaments. Antonio Tanguma, born around 1903 (his birth was not registered by his parents, so this date is approximate; Garza Guajardo 2015, 43), commented that in Nuevo León, from the earliest years of the twentieth century, there were one-row button accordions, which served only as toys for children (Ayala Duarte 2000, 41). It was difficult to get a good-quality instrument with two rows of buttons, so he had to travel to the town of La Feria, Texas—"sometimes on foot, sometimes by train"—to buy a used accordion for ten dollars. Other Mexican accordionists also had problems getting hold of instruments. Unfortunately, we know very little about the life of Tanguma's contemporaries, like Valentín Chapa, from the municipality of China, or Abelardo García, from Los Ramones, who by 1933 was already making a sporadic living from music. The latter, like Tanguma, played the accordion sometimes accompanied by bajo sexto, and both resided in Monterey from 1938 (Ayala Duarte 2000, 38–42).

Despite being relatively inexpensive, these instruments were tremendously valued, to such a degree that some lovers of the squeezebox had to learn to play secretly, as was the case with Pedro Ayala. The accordionist, who was born in General Terán, Nuevo León, in 1911, and grew up in the town of Donna, in the Rio Grande Valley (Burr 1999, 55), was one of the pioneers of norteño music. He began playing secretly with his older brother's instrument, but on one occasion when his family had gone out, the man who became known as the "monarch of the accordion" ate salmon while practicing, and his smelly secret was soon discovered. But, upon discovering the little boy's ability, rather than admonishing him, his brother brought the child with him to a ranch to play that same night (Martínez 2011, 48–49).

Pedro Ayala was not the only one to extend the influence of norteño music in Texas. One might also mention such players of the accordion as Lolo Cavazos, who was born in 1906 in Matamoros and settled in Alice (Strachwitz 1995, 9). Another musician from Tamaulipas, Agapito Zúñiga de la Garza (b. Burgos, Tamaulipas, 1924; d. Corpus Christi, Texas, 2015), recorded in Mexico City for Peerless, although much of his artistic career was spent in Corpus Christi, his music distributed through Ideal, Falcon, Hacienda, and BEGO Records. From Nuevo León, Camilo Cantú, born in 1907 in the town of Sabinas Hidalgo, became known as *El Azote de Austin* ("The Scourge of Austin"), and was identified as the best musician in central Texas for more than thirty years from the 1930s to the 1960s. Cantú learned to play thanks to Leopoldo Guajardo, who arrived in Texas from Monterrey early in 1920 (Shorkey 2012, 98–99).

Andrés Berlanga, who was born in northeastern Mexico in 1907 and grew up near San Antonio, began by playing guitar and later shifted to bajo sexto. The musician, who made his first recording in the spring of 1934 (Strachwitz 1994b), used to sing during his old age in the streets of downtown San Antonio, accompanied only by a bajo sexto.

The migration of many norteño musicians to Texas brought about very complex phenomena related to the hybridization of music and identity. In Austin, in the Texas Music Museum, there is a photograph of Camilo Cantú and his group of musicians in 1946, an early date in the development of conjunto. In spite of being a Mexican accordion player, he soon integrated into American culture, as we can see not only by his use of the electric guitar—not often seen in conjunto norteño at the time—but also by the appearance of the man beside him, dressed in suit and tie: his manager or representative. Years later, this figure would become indispensable to many musicians south of the border. We should note, as well, the improvised stage, complete with a concrete block holding down the weak roof, and, above all, the symbol of the bicultural condition of both musicians and audience: the Stars and Stripes in the foreground, in front of the Mexican tricolor with its nineteenth-century image of an eagle perched on a prickly pear, devouring a snake.

No Mexican made a more lasting contribution to *Tejano* music than Narciso Martínez. The accordionist, who would soon be dubbed "the Hurricane of the Valley," was born in Reynosa, Tamaulipas, on October 29, 1911 (Peña 1985, 54). He was one of the first conjunto musicians to travel outside of Texas, and he was sporadically able to make a living from music, combining it with periods in which he drove a tractor or picked tomatoes in Florida (Burr 1999, 147–148). This musician is recognized as the father of Texan-Mexican conjunto. After "playing solo for years with just the accordion" (Tejeda 2001a, 318), he abandoned the use of the left hand and concentrated solely on melody. He was the first to record accompanied by the Mexican-American Santiago Almeida on bajo sexto, forging the foundations of what would be conjunto. Previously, people had played the accordion solo, or accompanied by the guitar or *tambora de rancho*, as heard in Bruno Villarreal's recording of the polka "La bella Italia" from January 1935.

Narciso Martínez can also be considered one of the initiators of conjunto norteño, because his records, which first appeared in 1936, were pioneering on both sides of the border. These recordings were promoted under his own name in Chicano territories but under the pseudonym of Louisiana Pete in Cajun areas and Polski Kwartet in Polish communities (Burr 1999, 19). The recordings of Narciso Martínez are an extraordinary legacy, because his music does not hide his deep knowledge of its European heritage—German in particular—which the accordionist learned through his attendance at dances and concerts given by Germanic bands in South Texas (Strachwitz 1995, 8). We can see this European influence, combined with traditional Mexican music, in the mazurka "Luzita." If the second part, in a major key, has some air of *norteño* about it, the first part is surprising for its theme in a minor key, because of its languid and evocative nature, something that would come to be very rare in the repertoire of conjunto. Here, he displays his virtuosity in passages with rapid successions of scales and arpeggios. At the same time, we also perceive that his style of interpreting announces something new, without actually breaking with tradition.

The recordings of this stupendous Mexican-American musician enjoyed international distribution, being welcomed in many countries of the Americas, but not in Mexico City, where the music of the north was still frowned upon (Hickinbotham 2012, 497–507). In Monterrey, records made by the Hurricane of the Valley were often promoted in local newspapers. During the 1940s, for example, albums from the label Ideal could be found at Beattie's, located on Villagrán Street, and for only six pesos people could acquire *valses bajitos,* polkas or corridos, played or accompanied by Martínez. During his old age, the musician alternated his work as an animal caretaker at the Brownsville zoo with sporadic recordings and concerts. Before Martínez's death, Texas recognized the legacy of the father of Texas-Mexican conjunto and established in his honor the Narciso Martínez Cultural Arts Center in the city of San Benito, Cameron County, very close to the place where he had spent much of his life.

Considering the transcendence of musicians from northeastern Mexico in the development of *Tejano* conjunto, discussions among fans about the superiority of this genre over norteño music, or vice versa—as if they were antagonistic families—would seem hilarious. But this discussion around the authenticity of interpretations must be related to a desire to break the "legitimacy of the system of classification of [musical] genres" (Lena 2012, 152–153), in order to promote the concerts and albums of the respective genres. It should be pointed out that such battles between rival musical types are often useful, because they mold musical opponents, giving chroniclers an opportunity to describe a genre in comparison to another. In this regard, there are rumors of alleged struggles and criticism between norteño and *Tejano* musicians, although in the course of my own fieldwork, respondents had only respect and admiration for their counterparts living on the other side of the border, as typified by Ramiro Cavazos: "There is little difference ... we [norteños] care a little more about the Spanish language, but they [*Tejanos*] work perfectly fine. When I started, there were few tex-mex conjuntos, and they played a lot like norteños, but we have always been very good friends with them" (personal communication, July 24, 2013).

In the beginning, the norteño and *Tejano* conjunto shared an ideology of class, but at present, can we consider their differences on the basis of ethnic and socioeconomic diversity? Without taking into account the parallel development of both ensembles, some scholars, such as Manuel Peña or José Limón, have published research on *Tejano* musical culture, but they completely ignore the role that norteño music has played north of the Rio Bravo/ Grande. Applying Marxist theory in Texas, Peña (1985, 150–151) states that the music of *Tejano* conjunto has served as a defensive space of protest and resistance, with an anti-ideological power, with which it is possible to resolve the conflict of Anglo-American racism. For her part, Cathy Ragland (2009, 201) speaks of an immigrant norteño music, essentially adopted by the Mexican diaspora in the United States. But in that case, how can we explain the analogous development of conjunto in northern Mexico, when in the northeast of the country there was no inter-ethnic conflict? Can we consider conjunto norteño a testament to a lack of identification of northeastern Mexican citizens with their federal government and with people in the rest of the country?

Returning to our theme, along with the musicians from Tamaulipas and Nuevo León who enriched the Texan soundscape, we also find other players, born in Texas of Mexican parents or grandparents, who promoted the new music of conjunto. This may give us a clue to the great importance of music as a unifier within the social networks that Mexicans and Texans expanded north of the Rio Bravo/Grande. These networks carried information about migrant destinations, provided assistance in finding jobs, and mobilized collective action in hostile environments (Ogilvie 2000, 13). One of the few accordionists who had the luxury of competing against the great popularity of the "Hurricane of the Valley" was Santiago Jiménez. The so-called *Flaco* (skinny one) of San Antonio was born in the popular neighborhood of La Piedrera and recorded his own compositions in 1936, including the polkas "El aguacero" ("The Downpour") and "Dispensa el arrempujón" ("Pardon the Shoving"). Ethnomusicologist Manuel Peña (1985, 59–64) rightly points out that, while Jiménez shows a great deal of the influence of Narciso Martínez, he departs from the *marcato* style that characterized him, preferring a technique more identified with *legatto*. Peña also claims that the *Flaco* was the first to be accompanied by contrabass, or, as it is known in the region, upright bass or *tololoche*. Accordionist Pedro Ayala's family, however, claims that the Monarch of the Accordion was using tololoche before Jiménez (Martínez 2011, 54).

If in the image of Camilo Cantú in the Texas Music Museum we perceive that the accordionist from Nuevo León had assimilated a certain degree of American culture, then, in a picture of Santiago Jiménez (with guitarist Lorenzo Caballero) held by The Institute of Texan Cultures in San Antonio we note that Jiménez, born in the United States, wears a Mexican regional costume and large *sombrero* (hat). In both cases, identity was thus being negotiated and constructed daily, borrowing from both cultures with which these instrumentalists coexisted every day. Clothing is one of the most obvious indicators of identity construction in any musical tradition. Throughout the history of conjunto, the most common attire has been jeans, shirt, boots, and cowboy hats, both north and south of the Rio Bravo/Grande, and in northeastern Mexico often the traditional jacket called *cuera tamaulipeca*. However, there are many pictures from the early years of conjunto in which performers appear in suits and ties, as in one promotional image of Narciso Martínez from Ideal Records. This practice has not died, and currently Ramon Ayala, Paulino Bernal, and Los Tigres del Norte appear in photo sessions or at press conferences similarly attired, trying to set aside the stereotype that identifies conjunto artists with a dissipated life and the music of conjunto with the poor and uneducated. But this trend is not unique to this genre; practitioners of other musical traditions often want to get closer to the intellectual elite, probably through a desire to give their music status above their own social or ethnic stratum (Lena 2012, 58).

THE RECORDING INDUSTRY OR THE COMMODIFICATION OF TRADITIONS AND ART

The second half of the nineteenth century was an era of amazing inventions and discoveries, many of them in the area of science and communication. As early as 1856, Antonio Meucci was operating a device he called the "electromagnetic telephone" (Kloosser 2009, 210–211). The German physicist Heinrich Hertz demonstrated the nature of radio waves in 1886, which today we call Hertz in his honor (Hewitt 2004, 365).

In July 1877, Thomas Alva Edison developed a microphone, although his discovery was accompanied by a legal battle to be recognized as its inventor (Beyer 1999, 120–121). But it would be another patent that would turn Edison into a national hero by the end of that same year—one of the most important years in the history of music—when he discovered how sounds could be stored (Gronow and Saurio 1998, 1). The phonograph, called the "talking machine," not only helped shape musical traditions all over the world but was also an event with multiple social and economic implications. Initially, however, Edison himself did not envision the scope of his invention, and its promotion was primarily a device designed to replace secretaries: "The main utility of the phonograph is for the purpose of letter writing and other forms of dictation" (cited in Katz 2012, 13).

The phonograph was a fairly rudimentary item, and storing sound on a wax cylinder was complicated. Thus, a few years later, a competitor emerged: the telegraphone, a machine capable of recording magnetically (Morton 2000, 3). Then, ten years after the introduction of the phonograph, Emile Berliner, a fervent rival of Edison, would patent yet another apparatus, which he called the "gramophone," a contraption with many similarities to the phonograph, since it was necessary to turn a handle to begin the recording procedure in a mechanical manner. A needle transmitted sound vibrations and then carved them, not on a cylinder, but onto a flat disc. Berliner also had a very clear idea of the purpose of *his* machine: to reproduce musical pieces on an industrial scale (Gronow and Saunio 1998, 8).

It is not my intention to trace the history of the industry that generated these inventions. Rather, one must emphasize their importance to economy and culture, because some scholars claim that modernism resulted from the impact of American popular music and its dissemination by mechanical means (Pople 2002, 601–619). In this way, once acetate discs and playing equipment were popularized, their sales grew exponentially. This meant that musicians could spread their art to many distant places; at the same time, however, the music went from being part of a social activity that people embraced to delight themselves and their neighbors to being a commodity "produced and consumed on a previously unknown scale" (Taylor 2012, 2–3). That is why the title of this section mentions commodification, in the sociological sense, which occurs when innovative ideas and things are appropriated by the dominant culture, incorporating them into capitalist and bureaucratic systems.

Let me look in more detail at the pros and cons. In the early decades of the twentieth century, the dissemination of phonographs and jukeboxes generated a genuine revolution, citizens praised them for inaugurating a cultural democracy, and suppliers quickly jumped to the vanguard of marketing (Suisman 2009, 90). By popularizing the phonograph, crafty suppliers introduced a brand-new niche into the global economy, offering to the public both discs and phonograph players simultaneously. Album manufacturing created not just a national market in the United States; its expansion was global, making it one of the few American industries of its time that had a greater volume of sales abroad than at home (Miller 2010, 157–158), forging an incipient process of globalization at the dawn of the twentieth century. At that time, for just a few cents you could listen to the best symphony orchestras of the world in the tranquility of your own home or gain access to new music collections from any number of ethnic minorities. In this sense, record companies tried to create a halo of distinction, since classical music recordings occupied a privileged space in their catalogues before 1945, despite the fact that this repertoire was the most expensive to produce and that the higher sales came not from this genre but from popular music (Miller 2010, 161; Morton 2000, 23–24).

Another contribution of the recording industry relates to the musical interpretations of some accordion players. It would be almost impossible to write into a score the fine details of some performances, like the way in which they contain and expand the tempo, which we only know because we can hear this in recordings. But ethnomusicology was not the only beneficiary: there were also music magazines, one of the many parallel businesses generated by the recording industry. Through the journal *Talking Machine World*, we see that "the anthropologists and philologists also are finding it [the phonograph] a great aid to their investigations" (Miller 2010, 179). The advent of these recording technologies brought with them a way to "freeze" performances artificially, "annihilating time and making the music experience repeatable" (Morton 2000, 7); they also attenuated, rearranged, and obscured the social relations of the practice of music (Suisman 2009, 90). In addition, each of the early cylinders and 78 rpm discs could contain only two or three minutes of music (Morton 2000, 22), meaning musicians were forced to simplify their traditional executions to ensure they conformed to the new commercial format. For this reason, several writers strongly criticized this new cultural industry, claiming that it commercialized and standardized art. Music, they said, "has participated in the growth and the creation of capital and spectacle; fetishized as merchandise, music has become an example of the evolution of our whole society: deritualizing a social form, repressing an activity of the body, confining an exercise, then selling it as a spectacle, generalizing its consumption and then organizing its storage until it loses its meaning" (Attali 1995, 13).

The recording industry thus generated profound changes, both positive and negative, although Attalli's opinion is pessimistic and excessive, since it is impossible to drain music of all meaning. It was during the 1920s when some of the subsidiaries of the major recording labels, such as Decca, Columbia, and RCA, began to make recordings of *Tejano* and Mexican music under the rubric of "race records" (Peña 1985, 39). In the early years, approximately two-thirds of the music sold by these corporations consisted of vocal duets (Peña 1999a, 51), and, usually, the singers accompanied themselves with one or two guitars. The inaugural recording sessions in Texas were a watershed event in the dissemination of regional music. As we have seen, the first accordionist who had this privilege was Bruno Villarreal, of San Benito, in 1928. However, Narciso Martínez was the first to record polkas played on the accordion, accompanied by Santiago Almeida on bajo sexto.

The aspiration to promote their music, and earn some money at the same time, attracted a good number of singers to Texas—especially to San Antonio—where a group of engineers sent by the Edison Company had recorded, in 1893, a representation of a traditional *pastorela* (Hickinbotham 2012, 497). During the 1930s, the city of the Alamo became a mecca for Mexican and Mexican-American artists. For instance, the vocalist and guitarist Lydia Mendoza recorded more than 200 songs for the Bluebird label between 1934 and 1940, which were distributed globally (Hickinbotham 2012, 500). The advent of radio broadcasting, the stock market crisis, and the beginning of World War II caused the record industry to collapse in the United States (although not in the rest of the world) (Miller 2010, 157–159). During the war, the rationing of oil meant that there was a lack of materials with which to make records (Hartman 2008, 40; Hickinbotham 2012, 501).

Although Mexico did not produce phonographs in the early decades of the industry, its proximity to the United States led to the prompt circulation of records and phonographs throughout the country. In the case of Mexican migrants to the United States, anthropologist Manuel Gamio calculated that, in 1927, every Mexican who was returning to his or her homeland brought back 1.18 records (i.e., 118 recordings per 100 persons), and almost 22 of every 100 brought a phonograph acquired in the United States (Peña 1999a, 92). Unfortunately, there is no sales data on these recordings, but there is a reference to the payment made to artists for each piece of music, which was between $15 and $20 dollars (Peña 1985, 42). If we take into account that each record was sold for 35 cents, and in the absence of the payment of royalties, it seems that the music business for this regional genre was not a bad deal for investors, nor for some musicians, who sometimes recorded up to twenty songs in a single session (Peña 1985, 57). The career of Armando Marroquín, owner since 1946 of the first local recording business in the state of Texas, Ideal Records, is very illustrative. Marroquín owned a number of jukeboxes at sites along the border, with which he was making money and, at the same time, promoting his own albums, recorded by musicians who had not signed any contract and who sometimes did not receive remuneration for their work (Peña 1985, 72–76).

South of the border, in Monterrey, the record company Orfeo flourished somewhat later, at the end of the 1940s, although its distribution was poor. Since 1922, however, people had easily been able to get any number of records of the most varied musical genres, as well as phonographs, in the city (Ayala Duarte 2000, 42). By the 1960s, a good number of companies had been founded, reaching farther afield from the border, in Monterrey (Disa, Del Valle Records, DLV); in Corpus Christi, Texas (Hacienda Records and

Freddy Records); and even in places as far away as San Jose, California (Fama, currently Fonovisa). All of them are still active today.

If I have argued that records flattened and generalized a musical culture, it is also a fact that they resulted in musicians experiencing a decline in their professional activity in the territory under discussion. In 1932, the Unión Filarmónica de Monterrey (Philharmonic Union of Monterrey) asked Monterrey City Council to limit the operation of "autophonic" devices that dominated the aural spaces of the municipality, in order to stem unemployment of the union's members (Ayala Duarte 2000, 46). This request was not granted, but this did not discourage the musicians, who continued with their demands and managed to win some battles. Among other things, by the end of the decade, they had succeeded in winning regulation that dictated that cantinas in Monterrey could use any "electro-mechanical musical apparatus" no later than 9 p.m.

The historical archives of Monterrey include some documents related to the clashes between musicians and modern machines. For example, the Sindicato Único de Filarmónicos de Monterrey (Sole Philharmonic Union of Monterrey) ensured that City Hall issued a regulation limiting the operation of *sinfonolas* (jukeboxes), and demanded that all new businesses established in the red-light district be forced to hire orchestras, and that permission for mechanical musical apparatuses be rejected. Even as late as 1960, the Sindicato Nacional de Trabajadores de la Música de la República Mexicana (National Union of Music Workers of the Mexican Republic), appearing before the municipality's Entertainment and Revenue Commission, expected that mechanical musical devices would be regulated. But these had come to stay, as seen in a 1930 item in the newspaper *El Porvenir* by Lucio M. Dávila, who proposed to compete against all those "aberrations" of modernity:

> The radio—said a musician, a professional, friend of mine—is for us an obstacle, as are the orthophone, the vitaphone, the Victrola, and all the appliances that have already appeared; we almost no longer exercise the profession; nobody hires us.
>
> No—I said to him—Why? You, the musicians (the professionals), must strive to be better musicians than they are until you dominate them. The Victrola, vitaphone, orthophone, the radio, and a thousand other things that will come after can never exceed the gift of art with which those already born are blessed.

As a final point, another wonderful invention, cinema, made a particular demand on musicians, who had to adjust their repertoires to the diversity of films. In Monterrey, the local cinema already had had live music since 1890, first a pianist and later an orchestra (Ayala Duarte 2000, 66), although a few years later, these would be replaced by recorded music.

EARLY RADIO, THE PHONOGRAPH'S COMPETITOR

It is likely that the first transmission of a human voice over distance, without any type of cable, was made in December 1900 by the Canadian Reginald Aubrey Fessenden, who, six years later, from the New England coast, achieved what is regarded as the world's first radio transmission (Greb and Adams 2003, 30–31). In Texas, in 1911, J. B. Dickinson built the necessary apparatus to allow engineering students to become familiar with radio transmissions, both at the University of Texas at Austin and Texas A&M, College Station.

There has been a debate over the origin of radio in Mexico, which may be the result of a struggle between the center and the periphery of the nation. Some centralist authors claim that Mexican radio began with a transmission by brothers Adolfo and Pedro Gómez Fernández, who, from Teatro Ideal in the center of Mexico City, organized a program to showcase the new invention on September 27, 1921. The same writers mention that Constantino de Tarnava Garza was the second Mexican to use radio, since his first "official" broadcast was on October 9, 1921 (Robles 2012, 23–26). However, that was made from a private radio station in Monterrey; de Tarnava, an engineer, had in fact been sending out Hertz waves since the summer of 1919, for which he is recognized as the father of Mexican broadcasting by the Cámara Nacional de la Industria de Radio y Televisión Mexicana (National Chamber of the Mexican Radio and Television Industry).

Constantino de Tarnava was born in Monterrey on February 26, 1898, and died in the same city in 1974. He studied at the University of Notre Dame, in Indiana, from which he graduated as an engineer. The first acronym for his station was TND (Tarnava Notre Dame) in honor of his Alma Mater; afterward the call sign was changed to CYO, then to CYH, and from 1929 it was XEH. He sold the station in 1962. For all that, radio seems to have been simply entertainment for de Tarnava, who came from a wealthy family. He was, among other things, RCA Victor's authorized dealer in Mexico, manager and authorized representative of the firm Patricio Milmo and Sons, and treasurer for the Matehuala Railway Company, from the state of San Luis Potosí.

At the dawn of radio, there was an intense competition between record companies and the owners of radio stations. This era was characterized by broadcasting of live music, at the same time as entrepreneurs were trying to convince the public that recordings were second-class entertainment (Morton 2000, 8). Radio spread quickly in both big cities and the most isolated places, promoting consumerism, and not only offered classical and popular music but also launched news and gossip, dramas and comedies, and civic and patriotic celebrations. In the United States alone, between 1921 and 1922, 556 new stations began operations (Fowler Jr. and Crawford 2002, 3). In

Mexico, as in the United States, the required equipment was inexpensive, as, shortly after the earliest radio broadcasts, various stores began to sell the material needed to build radios. Among those stores was the famous La Casa del Radio (the Home of Radio), established by Raúl Azcárraga in Mexico City (Robles 2012, 37).

For all these reasons, radio began to replace the phonograph. In the United States, record sales, which had grown exponentially (Shuker 2005, 189), plummeted toward the mid-1920s; several companies went bankrupt or changed owners. There would be no recovery until the end of the 1930s (Morton 2000, 26–28). In the United States, from the dawn of the industry, stations that broadcast in English had sold ad space to Hispanics to schedule music and news of community interest (Miranda and Medina 2008, 482–496), but Mexican-Americans would have to wait until 1946 for an all-Spanish station: KCOR of San Antonio. This was because copyright laws had been used to exclude Latinos and African Americans from the radio station system (Lena 2012, 117–118).

Meanwhile, south of the Rio Bravo/Grande, radio could not ignore the Mexican government's attempts to construct a modern nationalist identity in the wake of the Revolution. The first president to benefit from the new mass communication medium was Plutarco Elias Calles. His broadcast of April 1924 was directed not only at Mexicans in the country but also at those in the United States, and at United States authorities, as the message was also broadcast in an English translation (Robles 2012, 35). The federal government was not happy with simply owning some frequencies; they also sought social control by regulating private stations. It was very important for the State that music, as a symbolic activity that could move or contain masses, be supervised. In the 1930s, for example, stations were forced to offer a minimum of 25 percent "traditional Mexican music" in their schedules (Robles 2012, 47). The so-called "traditional Mexican music" did not initially include the sounds of conjunto norteño, even in the state of Nuevo León. It would be 1937 before Constantino de Tarnava's XEH broadcast accordionist Antonio Tanguma, for example.

In this post-revolutionary society that was redefining and consolidating its identity, radio and cinema also facilitated the creation of regional Mexican stereotypes (Madrid 2010, 231). Recall that Eulalio González, "Piporro," debuted as an announcer for a radio station in Monterrey in December of 1942 (González Ramírez 1999, 37). In the decades between 1930 and 1980, the northern border of Mexico became a popular site for powerful broadcasters seeking to evade conditions imposed by U.S. regulations. These frequencies, known as *border blasters*, which could reach as far as New Zealand, Sweden, or Japan with admirable clarity, reached power levels of up to one million watts (Fowler Jr. and Crawford 2002, 1–9). Both radio and records were of enormous importance in the creation and development of musical tastes, even shaping preferences. Current directors of record labels interviewed denied their involvement in the creative process of the groups they promoted, but they help set the style from the moment they favor one group over another. Similarly, anyone responsible for radio programming listens to a large number of recordings every day, and, based on his or her own tastes and preferences, chooses the songs that will play "six or seven times a day," because usually, after a week, "if we play a song a lot, people begin to like it" (mentioned in Simonett 2001, 42–43).

The music of conjunto is usually transmitted orally among members of the same family, but radio and records have also been exceptional channels for keeping up to date with new trends in the genre. As an example, Jorge Hernández, singer and accordionist with Los Tigres del Norte, absorbed in his rural village the style of groups, such as Los Donneños and Los Dos Gilbertos, thanks to a Philco radio that only received a signal from a norteño music station from Harlingen, Texas (mentioned in Gurza et al. 2012, 129).

THE SPACES OF DISSEMINATION FOR CONJUNTO: FROM CANTINAS TO BALLROOMS

The recording industry produced fabulous economic benefits for the people involved in the business, but also generated transformations in the history of music. Based on my experience as a guitarist, one can say that, among other things, while a recording will always resonate in exactly the same way, no live musical performance is equal to any other: the audience at a concert participates in an interaction with artists (see Katz 2010, 1st chapter) that can result in outstanding, unrepeatable, and unique moments. In addition, when music is recorded and later reproduced in another place, it loses its context, "its unique spatial and temporal identity," and, above all, it generates "new experiences, traditions, and indeed rituals" (Katz 2012, 17). As sound is intangible, at the dawn of the phonograph, the strangest thing to listeners was the lack of the formerly ubiquitous "visual experience" that affected all musical genres. Musicologist Richard Leppert emphasizes that this visual ingredient is crucial "for locating and communicating the place of music and musical sound within a society and culture" (mentioned in Katz 2012, 23). It is true that recordings helped promote the emerging tradition of conjunto, but the music then departed from its "natural" spaces, which until then had been rural celebrations or city streets and cantinas.

Jennifer Lena (2012, 11) reminds us that "It is extremely important to analyze the spaces in which music is experienced because spatial arrangements impact the form and nature of community engagement." So, in the early years of the twentieth century, the rustic dances of northeastern Mexico and the southwestern United States were often

> enlivened by a couple of musicians. [They] lit the stage with oil lamps, while the suitor requested permission from a girl's parents for a dance. Then he led her to sit down, because otherwise it could be interpreted that the couple were engaged and would soon formalize their matrimonial union. From this rural practice came terms such as: *taconazo* (heel), *punta y talón* (tip and heel), *zapateyenle* (move your shoes), *pedida y dada* (requested and given), and other argot from the *ejidal* (common) feasts, where they also served a luxuriant feast including *barbacoa de pozo* (pit barbecue), *picadillo* (meat with potatoes), rice, noodle soup, grilled pork, and *hojarascas* (cookies) for dessert. (Mentioned in Ramos Aguirre 2006, 38)

In addition to the ranches and *ejidos* (commons), cantinas and cabarets were other sites of exposure for early conjunto in northern cities and towns. Musicians like Antonio Tanguma or Abelardo García migrated to Monterrey, and others went to Texas, but many more were seduced by the development of the northeastern frontier, especially in the city of Reynosa. In the mid-1930s, the Algodonera Mexicana (Mexican Cotton Company) was founded here (González 2012), part of the region's cotton boom, but economic growth was also stimulated by Prohibition (Ramos Aguirre 2006, 39–40), which attracted drunks from South Texas. Norteño musicians who installed themselves in this Tamaulipas border city included Mario Montes and Ramiro Cavazos, who later formed the group Los Donneños, as well as Tomás Ortiz and Eugenio Ábrego, of Los Alegres de Terán, and, subsequently, Ramón Ayala and Cornelio Reyna, who began their careers by joining forces to create Los Relámpagos del Norte (The Lightning of the North). All of them later settled in the Lower Valley of the Rio Grande, in South Texas.

For its part, the spaces of dissemination of conjunto in South Texas were not very different from those of Mexico; country weddings were the community's really important events, at times lasting 24 hours or more, and at which the unfortunate musicians had to play without a break (Peña 1985, 36–37). Since the end of the nineteenth century, the so-called *bailes de regalo* (gift dances), at which a smitten lad was expected to offer candy or a similar present to the lady with whom he wanted to dance, had also been common, and finally there were also *bailes de negocio* (business dances), at which a man paid a young woman—or a madam—approximately 15 cents per dance (Peña 1985, 48–49). Similar social events also existed in Mexico: in the 1940s, in the red-light district of General Terán, Nuevo León, known as *El Zumbido* (The humming), "some fifteen unhappy women, squalid [and] malnourished . . . were seated . . . waiting for someone to invite them to dance, for a charge of 20 cents piece" (Ramos Aguirre 2006, 89). The following chapter discusses how conjunto took some venues by storm and how this music managed to cram large halls and sports stadiums through the use of technology.

In this chapter, we explored the early history of conjunto norteño, as well as the great importance of Mexican musicians in the dissemination of this newfangled style throughout South Texas. We noted the manner in which conjunto assimilated and modified the various musical forms transported to the region by Germans, Czechs, and Poles, as well as the hybridization of the musical instruments that would become representative of the tradition. In particular, we discussed the lives of accordionists who, facing a lack of recognition for their work, managed to promote their art throughout the region. In addition, we saw the impact of the introduction of technology for storing sounds and the monumental growth of the recording industry, which contributed to blurring the divisions among social classes and engendered a globalization process, and the equally significant history of radio, which transformed ideas of private and public space.

Chapter 4

Conjunto

From Subaltern Mexican Culture to American Cultural Treasure

At the end of World War II, the panorama of popular culture and "official" culture was shaped by the importance of the Chicano movement in the United States, in the case of Texan-Mexican conjunto. In Mexico, the growth of the music industry and wider dissemination through theater, radio, film, and television, as well as popular celebration of the displaced groups in the industrialized areas of northeastern Mexico, spread a taste for the music of conjunto norteño. In the post-war period, until the end of the 1970s, although conjunto remained marginal, it also made significant progress. The technological development that facilitated large dances and concerts came to be the ideal way to boost the genre in a meaningful way, including beyond the region, without any official support. Here, we face mass culture. In terms of popular music, we must judge whether it is essentially conservative in nature, favoring groups that wield political and economic power in a capitalist society, or expresses an alternative identity, as in the case of the music of conjunto norteño and Tex-Mex conjunto, spreading despite the dominant culture, due to the fact that both personify the authenticity and identity of the working class. Also, we must note the importance of migrants, because if initially conjunto and *banda* (traditional brass band) were quite localized in northeast and northwest Mexico, respectively, citizens from the states of Michoacán, Guerrero, Oaxaca, and Veracruz played a very prominent role in the dissemination of such traditions throughout the nation, adopting them almost as symbols of the economic success of their families, which were rooted in the United States (Madrid 2013b, 73–74).

INNOVATIONS OF THE POST-WAR PERIOD: INSTRUMENTS, CROSSOVER, AND *BAILES*

The musical ensemble known as conjunto would undergo changes in the 1940s and later. Tomás Ortiz, a member of Los Alegres de Terán, was still playing guitar by the middle of the decade, when he switched definitively to bajo sexto. In fact, journalistic notes and photographic archives reveal that, from the early to mid-twentieth century, groups in this region used the guitar and bajo sexto interchangeably. This was the case with the Orquesta Típica Fronteriza ("Typical Orchestra of the Border"), which during the 1930s delighted the community of El Paso, Texas, with performances featuring violins and mandolins, but also two guitars and two bajo sextos (Peña 1999a, 125). The often-cited Ramiro Cavazos alternated the guitar and bajo sexto until approximately 1954, when his companion, accordionist Mario Montes, told him that he did not like the guitar (personal communication, July 11, 2011).

There are pictures of enthusiastic players of stringed instruments who are normally identified as players of bajo sexto. In spite of the fact that some old images are blurry, it is possible to distinguish several hybrid instruments, combinations of seven-string guitars, six-string guitars with double courses, and bajo sextos, suggesting the possible genealogy of the artifact that would later become the favorite accompaniment to the accordion. As an example, in a 1925 photo of musician Juan Flores that appears in a book by Juan Alanís Tamez (1998, 51), one may distinguish an instrument with thirteen or even fourteen wooden pegs, demonstrably not a bajo sexto, which can have no more than twelve pegs; this is, instead, a seven-string guitar with double courses, although with a much larger body than normal.

In a promotional image of Los Donneños, from the Falcon Records label, we recognize the young Ramiro Cavazos with suit and tie, and an instrument that definitely can be called bajo sexto: this is confirmed by the position of the player's left hand, the number of strings, and even the moustaches—the ornaments usually placed on either side of the bridge—but it is striking that, as late as the mid-1950s, this bajo sexto has a quite thin body, similar to the guitar rather than one as wide as those currently made. The bajo sexto features a cutaway, a curve in the body to facilitate access to the frets that sit high on the neck, and thus to the highest notes, and it is important to distinguish in these photographs the instruments without the traditional cutaway. As well, instruments used by pioneers of norteño and *Tejano* music have no tailpiece behind the bridge, as did the first instruments built in Mexico. As mentioned earlier, we do not know where the bajo sexto emerged, but there is little doubt that its development was consolidated at the U.S.-Mexico border. Therefore, one could suggest that, at some point around the dawn of the twentieth century, an ingenious musician probably employed a different tuning on his six- or seven-string guitar of double courses, finding that, when altering this bigger-bodied instrument down to a lower register, it could be used in the range between the guitar and the *bajo de armonía* of typical orchestras, and would also be better suited to accompanying the accordion. Carlos Cadena, guitarist in a trio of romantic *boleros* (a genre of slow-tempo Latin music and its associated dance) and a native of Reynosa, supported this theory, as indicated by his grandson:

> He traveled a lot, from here to there and back, but on his way he encountered fellow musicians of norteña music, and he told me at that time that more than 60 years before, more or less in the late 1930s or early 1940s, the northern groups used guitar and usually were three (accordion, guitar, and tololoche), but out of necessity the bajo sexto was invented, because when the trios became duos, the sound of the guitar was very soft compared to the accordion, and was insufficient to bear the bass notes, which [are] very important for our norteño music, hence the idea of building an instrument [that was] half guitar and half tololoche.

Such a practice would not be new: throughout history, musicians have changed their instruments to suit their needs or simply the fashion of the time. As early as 1555, Juan Bermudo wrote: "For my part (convinced that I am not mistaken), I believe that these players, being musicians, invent more types of instruments, and among those already invented, innovate every day" (cited in Cruz 1993, 76–77). According to Peruvian ethnomusicologist Julio Mendívil (2016, 100), musical instruments are modified and adapted to the most varied social practices: "musical instruments are transformed as they spread to different territories, coming into contact with heterogeneous musical traditions and different material environments." Many norteño and *Tejano* conjuntos continue to use the bajo sexto today, although since the early twenty-first century it has not been considered a referent of identity, and proof of this is that we can see today many groups that interchangeably use the twelve-string folk guitar or *bajo quinto* (which is just like the bajo sexto, but without the lower course).

On the other hand, it was in these years when conjuntos began to use the *tarola* (snare drum) and tololoche, the last of which was soon replaced by the electric bass in the United States, in the late 1950s (Peña 1985, 60). But if there are experiments with musical instruments, the same goes for the voice: in the various recordings made in the 1940s and early 1950s, we cannot speak of an established *Tejano* or norteño conjunto, especially in terms of the *style* of singing. The records that appeared in the late 1940s, recorded by founders of conjunto norteño like Maya y Cantú and Los Donneños, reveal a style very similar to the vocal duets mentioned in the second chapter, so common in Mexico and the southern United States in the late nineteenth century. The timbre of the voices, as well as the use of melodies in thirds and frequent *glissandos*, make it seem that some duets are no more than old northern vocal duos that have simply swapped guitars for accordion and bajo sexto. In this way, *norteño* duets consisting of *grave* (lower) and *contra alta* (medium) voices began to be identified with a region. The change in instrumentation was made not only for the sake of greater resonance, which allowed players to be heard by a greater number of people in cantinas, squares, parks, and markets, but also because the bajo sexto and accordion became representative of the geographic area.

The introduction of voices into traditionally instrumental music produced a change of direction in conjunto; there was no longer any doubt that the music was the region's heritage. The first recording with this new concept was made by the duo of Jesús Maya and Timoteo Cantú in 1946, although it took a couple of years for it to be released by Ideal Records (Strachwitz 1999). But it would be two young boys from General Terán, Nuevo León, who lifted the low profile of conjunto until it became a phenomenon. They were originally known as Ortiz and Abrego, and shortly after, Los Alegres de Terán. Passing on old rural traditions, Tomás Ortiz (bajo sexto) and Eugenio Abrego (accordion) arrived in Monterrey and recorded their first albums for the small record company Orfeo in May 1949. Subsequently considered "the fathers of norteño music," they recorded on both vinyl and acetate more than 2,500 songs. Initially, their enormous regional fame was thanks to the Texan company Falcon Records, and their international profile to the giant Columbia Records. Columbia's director in Mexico, composer Felipe Valdez Leal, proclaimed that Los Alegres de Terán represented "a blank check," since each one of their albums "was assured high sales" (Ramos Aguirre 2006, 49–105).

To understand the significance of Los Alegres de Terán in the history of norteña music, one need only glance at the largest collection of recordings of Mexican and Mexican-American music in the world, the Strachwitz Frontera Collection, located at the University of California Los Angeles, which has more than 16,000 78s and roughly 25,000 45s, in addition to 4,000 LPs and 650 cassettes (Gurza et al. 2012, 9). There, among the 12,000 musicians represented, Tomás Ortiz and Eugenio Abrego are ranked ninth among the listed composers, with 205 songs, as well as first among performers, with a total of 811 recordings (Gurza et al. 2012, 162–167).

At Los Alegres de Terán's concerts, people thronged the front of the stage to listen, forgetting about dancing while the duo was singing, which was rare (according to composer Reynaldo Martínez, personal communication, July 24, 2013). The duo also influenced artists of later generations: the members of Los Tigres del Norte became familiar with norteño music through Los Alegres' recordings (Gurza et al. 2012, 129), while Los Relámpagos del Norte began to interpret Los Alegres' lyrics when Paulino Bernal wanted to hear them with a view to promoting the duo through his record company. One of the secrets of Los Alegres' fame, their "complex vocal style" (Madrid 2013b, 82), could not conceal its debt to the famous romantic bolero trios, among them Los Panchos and Los Tres Reyes, refined groups of singers, accompanied by two guitars and *requinto* (a type of small guitar), who primarily interpreted boleros, which delighted Latin American audiences throughout the 1930s and 1940s (Madrid 2013b, 52–53). Los Alegres remained faithful to their genre's tradition, however, always including polkas and other instrumental pieces on their records.

If conjunto norteño admits the influence of musical forms from the south of Mexico, *Tejano* conjunto takes into account musical genres and technology from the northern United States. A good example is the accordionist Tony de la Rosa, who, according to Manuel Peña (1985, 86–87), introduced the use of microphones, drums, and electric bass, as well as the amplification of bajo sexto and accordion, and in the 1950s made his conjunto into the most popular in Texas. From this moment on, one can already speak of an established conjunto. Part of the second generation of regional musicians, de la Rosa incorporated elements of Mexican musical tradition, recording the songs of José Alfredo Jiménez and Cuco Sánchez, but spiced with other music that he loved: Western swing and honky-tonk (Cano Jr. 2012, 160–161).

In addition to reforms in the field of musical styles and instruments—and nuancing Manuel Peña's assertion (1999a, 94–95) that between 1947 and 1970 *Tejano* conjunto achieved complete emancipation from *norteño* conjunto—we have a postwar period characterized by unequal socioeconomic circumstances and musical influences to the north and south of the border, although there is a rapprochement between the two traditions. Between 1942 and 1964, the American and Mexican governments defended the Bracero Program, through which about five million Mexicans were invited to work legally in the United States. In the field of norteña and *Tejano* music, that meant greater sources of employment for musicians, as well as confluence and exchange between these two traditions.

Escorting the Mexican diaspora on its way north, norteño groups such as Los Rancheritos del Topo Chico staged tours in the United States that could go on for more than six months, visiting places increasingly far away from the border, such as Illinois, Kansas, Georgia, or Nebraska (Garza Torres 2013, 47). This group from Nuevo León, and others of the time assimilated Texan musical trends and spread their own, as they frequently alternated in concert with prominent American groups, such as when El Palomo y el Gorrión played with the Texan Conjunto Bernal (Berrones 2013, 141). This last group was one of the most ambitious ensembles of the entire history of conjunto, because they featured three voices and were accompanied by two chromatic button accordions played with virtuosity. The accordionist and leader of Conjunto Bernal, Paulino Bernal, made several recordings with norteño musicians, including one in 1954 with Ramiro Cavazos on bajo sexto, accompanying singer Chris Sandoval; Bernal also worked with drummer Leonel Sánchez in one of the first appearances of this percussion instrument in the genre (Ramos Aguirre 2006, 100). It is worth remembering that Bernal, in his role as producer with BEGO Records, was the person who discovered norteña legends Ramón Ayala and Cornelio Reyna in a Reynosa cantina and made them famous.

Both norteño and *Tejano* conjunto absorbed influences from the music of their respective countries but rather than a "complete emancipation" of one from the other, they in fact had a tendency toward crossover. Contrary to the claims of various authors, we can confirm that *Tejano* and norteño conjunto have dedicated to build more bridges than walls between them. For instance, from the mid-1950s onward, Conjunto Bernal, from Texas, recorded a large number of Mexican songs, rancheras, and boleros while in the next decade Ayala and Reyna, then known as Los Relámpagos del Norte, recorded norteño music with American mainstream influences. A fine case in point is "Qué tal si te compro" ("What if I Buy You"), by Cornelio Reyna. In the first eight bars of the instrumental introduction, the composer presents a traditional Mexican melody that, if played on piano, could be confused with a nineteenth-century waltz, but from the ninth bar has an air of *swing*. While the ascendancy of rock 'n' roll is quite subtle in this example, in subsequent years, Ramón Ayala would mix elements of that genre with the cumbia, as in the case of his version of the song "Despeinada" (Disheveled). This illustrates the elasticity of conjunto in terms of the assimilation of concepts from other musical traditions, quite the contrary to what had happened with the mariachi, which, when converted into a living image of the Mexican nation, was frozen on a pedestal for decades, playing the same old tunes, in a very similar way, as we can hear on a compilation album featuring several versions of "El son de la negra" (Jáuregui 2012). In addition, these examples serve as evidence that norteño and *Tejano* conjunto are very close, sharing ideas and symbols mutually as well as with other genres of music, contrary to what some scholars believe.

For example, in order to emphasize the stylistic differences underlying the norteño and *Tejano* conjuntos, Cathy Ragland (2009, 125–133) transcribed the famous "Corrido de Gerardo González," played first by the Nuevo León accordionist and singer Ramón Ayala, and later by the south Texas group Los dos Gilbertos. She accepts the influence of Tex-Mex conjunto on Ayala—who has lived in Texas for many years—but points out that his version is in compound meter, that the accordion is simply for accompaniment and that his scales are "simple and repetitive," while she argues that Los Dos Gilbertos' interpretation uses binary meter and has "much more elaborate improvisation" by the accordionist. Certainly the duo Luis y Julián or the group Pesado adhere to Ayala's conservative interpretation of the mentioned corrido, but there are also Mexican groups that relate more to Los Dos Gilbertos, such as the group Honorable from the state of Sonora, or Abraham Beltrán y Los Rayitos, who, despite both featuring compound meter, alter it with aggressive syncopation, in addition to having a much more participatory accordion. At the end of the day, if we were to listen to all the recordings of the "Corrido de Gerardo González," we would find differences in each of them, regardless whether it involved *Tejano* or norteño artists. After all, in some cases, these artists are playing songs that have been circulating for almost a century, seeking to offer the hottest version—or the more traditional, if the audience wants that—that will ensure high visibility and good record sales.

During this period, many norteño musicians experienced a rise in their social status thanks to their work in the United States, because in the mid-1950s, there still was no such thing as a concert circuit in Mexico. The closest things were "caravans," such as those organized by a particular beer company, and in which Eulalio González "Piporro" participated (1999, 233). These caravans were "traveling all over the country, inch by inch, with comedians, singers, musicians, and mariachis forming the Corona Caravan, performing in cities both large and small." Such tours were little more than updated *carpa* (tent) shows, in which a great variety of radio and movie stars appeared on stage. These were not exclusive to norteño musicians, who normally played in rural areas over the course of strenuous journeys, gathering in red-light districts, *ejidos*, or cantinas, "lighted by oil lamps and singing at the tops of their lungs," without any amplification, or at best using speakers manufactured by "Radson, [made with a] cone of very low quality" (Berrones 2013, 86–104). In fact, in many northeastern Mexican towns, it was not possible to use electrified musical instruments speakers, or microphones, because even in the late 1950s such places had no electricity (Ramos Aguirre 2006, 70–71). Times were hard south of the border: accordionist Catarino Leos, founder of Los Rancheritos del Topo Chico, was part of Los Gorriones del Topo Chico but abandoned the group when he found a more secure job as an employee at a Coca-Cola depot (Garza Torres 2013, 38). In addition, interpreters of corridos in rural areas of Mexico claimed their songs were causing conflicts within their audiences, which often ended in fistfights or even with gunfire, as verified by El Palomo y el Gorrión in Zacatecas and Michoacán, where "things get red hot," or by Los Alegres de Terán in Pablillo, Nuevo León, where there were several murders at a dance (Berrones 2013, 137–138).

The earliest radio stations programmed chamber music and opera concerts, but no conjunto norteño until they had been in operation for decades. Radio station XEBU, known as La Norteñita, had played regional music in the state of Chihuahua since 1937, while in Mexico City, local broadcasters such as XECM, and those with national coverage like RCN (called La Norteña), seem to have included accordion and bajo sexto music assiduously during the 1950s (Berrones 2013, 66–67), shortly before broadcasters in Nuevo León, because La Doña de la Música Norteña and La Norteña del Cuadrante were founded in Monterrey at almost the same time (Zapata Vázquez 1990, 45–46).

Once again, fortuitous historical references confirm that the music of conjunto enjoyed approval first to the north of the Rio Bravo/Grande: at the end of the 1930s, Don Santiago Jiménez was already playing regularly on a program called "La hora Anáhuac," broadcasting from San Antonio (Peña 1985, 63). In Texas, Spanish-language radio has always disseminated Mexican and *Tejano* music in equal parts, by mixing conjunto norteño with the varied local sounds. This trend changed at the start of the 1990s, when *Tejano* conjunto was relegated in favor of norteña music, which recent migrants preferred.

WOMEN IN CONJUNTO

There is no doubt that dedication to music is rewarding. Regardless of the society of which we speak, the person who transmits a vocation for the art of music gains social prestige and becomes part of the intellectual elite. But charm is not everything; a musician must have absolute discipline, singing or playing an instrument many hours each day, and rehearsing for years before it pays off. In many instances, the work requires one to be away during the most important family moments. Perhaps the lack of women in the world of conjunto is the result of a regional culture that favors close blood ties.

The public began to listen to women in conjunto groups until the 1950s, quite late if we take into account that the first female singers to leave evidence of Mexican music were sisters Rosa and Luisa Villa, recorded on a wax cylinder by Charles Loomis in Los Angeles in 1904 (Herrera-Sobek 2006, 49). In our region of research, Lydia Mendoza sang and played guitar in front of a microphone in San Antonio at the end of the 1920s; another singer, Rosita Fernández, recorded for Bluebird in 1931 (Burr 2001, 88); and the duo of Carmen and Laura Hernández was accompanied by Narciso Martínez in the mid-1940s (Peña 1985, 72). But here we are speaking of traditional Mexican music in the United States, and not yet the cheerful sounds of conjunto.

One of the first female accordion players in Texas to lead her own conjunto was Eva Ybarra, who began playing in her father's group at the age of 6, in 1951 (Tejeda 2001b, 295–297). This outstanding musician, who was born in

San Antonio, continues to perform today, but she has had a difficult career in a musical world dominated by men and has been accused of being a lesbian, which she denies (Ragland, 2012, 94).

Linda Escobar, a singer born in Alice, Texas, and daughter of composer Eligio Escobar, also began to shine at an early age, recording for Ideal Records in the early 1960s, when she was 7 years old. She says that she has struggled to develop her musical career, because men have great solidarity with each other, but not with women (personal communication, May 18, 2013). She believes that, at present, things are "a little easier" for women in the music business, but what is certain is that at the thirty-second *Tejano* Conjunto Festival in San Antonio in 2013, both Escobar and Ybarra were booked to play in the afternoon, not during the evening prime time, which was reserved for male soloists and groups like Los Hermanos Farias, Mingo Saldívar, or Leonardo "Flaco" Jiménez.

Escobar and Ybarra started their careers during a period of expansion for conjunto, at a time when the genre was becoming known beyond Nuevo León, Tamaulipas, and Texas, as since 1964 Las Incomparables Hermanas Ortiz had already been propagating the new sounds in California. Isabel Ortiz was a particular standout, an accordionist and singer who would later be known as the Lady of the Accordion, and as leader of Chavela y su Grupo Express. Ortiz claimed that she never encountered difficulties in the music business until she led her own group (Burr 2001, 91–92). After enjoying great popularity, however, the native of Fresno, who was married to Los Tigres del Norte leader Jorge Hernández, died tragically in an accident (Burr 1999, 73–74).

In Mexico, some female duos perceived that the norteña niche was being neglected by music producers, so Las Norteñitas, Las Hermanas Degollado, and Las Jilguerillas began to combine mariachi accompaniment with northern conjunto around the end of the 1950s, although their favorite genre continued to be ranchera music. The discography of Las Jilguerillas reveals that approximately 60 percent of their recordings were accompanied by mariachi—which eventually included accordion—while another 20 percent were backed by brass bands with a rustic sound, and the remaining 20 percent was conjunto norteño, sometimes backed by Los Alegres de Terán. Everything seems to indicate that the taste for the sounds of norteño conjuntos and brass bands was primarily a response to a regional marketing strategy.

In their time, a famous duo that inclined more toward norteño music was Dueto Río Bravo, formed by Eva Gurrola Castellanos and María de la Luz Pulgarín Gurrola, both from the community of Rio Bravo, in the municipality of Allende, Coahuila. For their part, the career of Las Norteñitas exemplifies the regional-transnational character that the music industry acquired along the border: they recorded in the United States for Falcon Records, but their music was distributed in Mexico by Discos Tambora from Mazatlán, Sinaloa. Las Potranquitas del Norte was one of the first Mexican norteño groups comprised exclusively of women from various Mexican states, including Zacatecas, Chihuahua, and Michoacán. This group performed in many places in Mexico and the United States and entered Billboard's Hot Latin LP's chart in the early 1970s with the song "Abre el corazón" ("Open Your Heart"). Unfortunately, the greater part of this interesting repertoire has fallen into oblivion, and it is now very difficult to get these recordings.

If a feature of conjunto accordionists has been their image as sexually aggressive "tiger" dandies, women for whom the accordion is a *modus vivendi*, as ethnomusicologist Sydney Hutchinson (2008, 37–56) observed, develop a female counterpart to the masculine role: They become assertive and sensual. The author analyzes the role of the ladies of the accordion in the merengue genre, but there is a striking parallel with what happens in conjunto. As an example, we have contemporary *Tejano* and norteño groups, which play mainly cumbias and are sexually integrated, exploiting this eroticism, such as in the case of Chicas de Canela and Las Fénix in the United States; while in Mexico, we find male groups that are headed by women, including Priscila y sus Balas de Plata and Saraly y la Promesa.

THE CHICANO MOVEMENT AND REGIONAL MUSICAL PRIDE

Bajo sexto player Frank Alonzo is one of the best examples of the transformations suffered by the Mexican-American community in the period around World War II. In 1938, this musician debuted the group Alonzo y sus Rancheros (Alonzo and his Ranchers), featuring violin, accordion, tololoche, and bajo sexto, and playing a repertoire very similar to that of Los Montañeses del Álamo. The ensemble played in the Houston area, but by the end of World War II, Alonzo decided to emphasize his bicultural condition—and reach a larger audience—by renewing and expanding his group: he dressed them in tuxedos, introduced saxophones and trumpets into his lineup, played big-band numbers, and changed the group's name to Alonzo y su Orquesta ("Alonzo and his Orchestra"). If that were not enough, another symbol of these new times was that Frank's wife, Ventura Alonzo, played the accordion in the group, and even took on a leadership role in her husband's band. Chicanos, however, do not forget their Mexican heritage, and in the first row of Alonzo y su Orquesta, right beside the brass instruments, were the accordion and bajo sexto, which of course would be unthinkable in the bands of Glenn Miller or Benny Goodman (Peña 1999a, 130–132).

*Tejano*s were living a different reality from that experienced by their families and friends residing south of the Rio Bravo/Grande, including having to deal with armed conflict; thousands of Mexican-Americans were sent into battle during World War II (McKenzie 2004, 93). But this was also a time of opportunity, because the war against Germany and its allies meant that the state of Texas industrialized and urbanized rapidly: between 1940 and 1950, the urban population of Texas grew by almost 70 percent. Due to the emergency situation, in many cities the laws and segregationist policies against *Tejano*s were relaxed (Mon*Tejano* 2010, 262–268). At this time, *Tejano*s temporarily left their traditional romantic themes behind in favor of describing their impressions in harsh terms, as in the corrido "El Veterano," (Table 4.1) by Eligio Escobar:

During the Cold War, and in relation to the Korean War, they also sang *Ya volví de Corea* (Table 4.2).

Finally, "El corrido de Johnny López" (Table 4.3) praised a Mexican-American who died in Vietnam. These verses were recycled in the 1990s, and the singers substituted the word "Iraq" for "Vietnam":

It is not the intention of this book to analyze the poetry of songs and corridos, which is already a complex issue due to the polysemy between music and text. These are cited simply because while in the corrido *El veterano* ("The Veteran") there is a marked melancholy not only about the brutality of war but also about the lost homeland, which we see in symbols, such as the Guadalupana or the mention of the Aztec race, in the later ranchera songs *Ya volví de Corea* ("I've Returned from Korea") and *El corrido de Johnny López* there are no such references, which may suggest a growing rapport between

Table 4.1 Cited in Dorsey and Díez-Barriga 2011

El Veterano	*El Veterano*
. . . mi virgen guadalupana me protegió de la muerte . . .	. . . my Virgin of Guadalupe protected me from death . .
En los campos de batalla,	In the fields of battle,
se mostró su valentía, ser mexicano	He showed his courage, to be Mexican
para que el mundo lo sepa,	so that the world may know,
que no se afrenta de nada el que tiene sangre azteca.	That he who has Aztec blood is afraid of nothing.

Table 4.2 Ranchera song "Ya volví de Corea," recorded in 1951, 45 rpm, Conjunto de Henry Arizméndez

Ya volví de Corea	*I returned from Korea*
Ya volví desde Corea amigos míos,	I returned from Korea my friends,
con la voluntad de Dios vengo a decirles,	with the will of God I come to tell you,
que no vengo dichoso ni contento,	that I don't come blissful or happy.
traigo una pena que mucho me hace sufrir.	I bring a grief that makes me suffer.

Table 4.3 "Corrido de Johnny López," sung by Oscar Chávez, available at: https://www.youtube.com/watch?v=gx1Jrgspu-g

El Corrido de Johnny Lopez	El Corrido de Johnny Lopez
Les cantare este corrido,	I will sing this corrido,
con sentimiento y dolor,	with feeling and pain,
que trata de un mexicano,	which is about a Mexican,
con diferente sabor.	of a different stripe.
Sus padres y sus abuelos	Hi parents and grandparents
vinieron de Monterrey,	came from Monterrey,
Johnny nacio en Sausalito,	Johnny was born in Sausalito,
americano por ley.	American by law.

Chicanos and American traditions. However, the fact that these melodies are sung in Spanish, accompanied by accordion and bajo sexto, may pose a contradiction, by which anthropologists Margaret Dorsey and Miguel Díaz-Barriga (2011, 208) interpret this as an expression of belonging to the United States that is articulated through Mexican-American cultural forms, hence the concept of "cultural citizenship." In this case, the music is an unequivocal reference to Mexican-American identity in multicultural American society and adapts itself to the definition of the term "cultural citizenship," understood as the "right to be different with respect to the norms of the dominant national community, without compromising one's right to belong" (Chavez 2013, 15).

We have seen the idea of cultural citizenship put into practice since the mid-nineteenth century in the form of popular *fandangos*, and like these, conjunto in Texas was also an open-air activity. Regardless, Mexican migrants and *Tejano*s soon considered their music to be of more exclusive value. In Rio Grande Valley communities like Pharr, La Villa, Weslaco, and Santa Rosa in the 1950s, people attempted to reform the unrefined image of conjunto, preferring indoor dances at which beer was not sold and that the whole family could attend. Residents along the border tried to ward off the stigma that had weighed on the imaginary of conjunto and make their regional music a vehicle for values, such as the importance of family, work culture, loyalty, and solidarity. At the same time, they sought to distance themselves from the degraded Mexican tradition through particular ways of dancing, such as *El tacuachito*, a very popular dance throughout Texas, whose movements resembled those of another amusing inhabitant of the region: the opossum.

By the end of the 1960s, the Chicano movement had transformed the perception of *Tejano* conjunto from that of "cantina trash to cultural treasure" (Peña 1999a, 115). In subsequent years, there was a reassessment of the genre in Texas thanks to the boom in *Tejano* music, which enjoyed a period of celebrity beyond the region, when artists like Selena and La Mafia replaced the bajo sexto and accordion with electric guitar and synthesizer, capturing international attention. At the same time, a group of fans of traditional conjunto began to promote meetings and festivals, highlighting the *Tejano* conjunto Festival in San Antonio.

Eventually, government recognition also came. Once the National Endowment for the Arts established the National Heritage Awards in 1982, the first beneficiary of the program in Texas was the singer Lydia Mendoza. The following year, Narciso Martínez was recognized as one of the founders of Texan-Mexican conjunto. Since then, others have been granted the distinction of National Heritage Fellowships: Valerio Longoria (1986), Santiago Almeida (1993), Santiago Jiménez Jr. (2000), and Mingo Saldívar (2002). The most recent awards were presented in 2012 to Leonardo "Flaco" Jiménez, and in 2017 to Eva Ybarra, in a ceremony in which they not only received $ 25,000 but were also declared living national treasures of the United States.

But if the United States came to cherish *Tejano* conjunto as a cultural treasure, south of the border, in Nuevo León, there would be quite limited and belated recognition of the value of norteña music. It is true that Bonifacio Salinas, governor of the state between 1939 and 1943, was an enthusiast of accordion music, and often hired Antonio Tanguma to raise spirits at private and public events (Ayala Duarte 2004, 150). But this was an isolated case, because Tanguma himself spread this music for many years, playing mainly on the streets, and only obtained government support in his old age, in the early 1970s, when the Secretary of Public Education of Nuevo León commissioned him to accompany the activities of promoters of local folklore (Ayala Duarte 2000, 109). Nonetheless—and acknowledging there is huge acceptance of norteña music in the mass media—even now, at the start of the third decade of the twenty-first century, conjunto norteño is invisible to the cultural institutions of the Mexican government at the national level.

As an example, the Fondo Nacional para la Cultura y las Artes ("National Fund for Culture and the Arts") established in 2001 the program "Musicos Tradicionales Mexicanos" ("Traditional Mexican Musicians") with the objective of "fostering the creation and performance of musical works, both instrumental and vocal, that take up the forms of various traditional Mexican genres." In the calls for applications, there is an invitation to composers of *chilenas,* danzones, or *jarabes* to submit their projects but genres, such as the polka, redova, or chotis, are not mentioned. While it is true that they accept applications from "other representative music types of the country's regions," the reality is that the overwhelming majority of successful applicants to this program are composers of *sones jarochos* (traditional music and dance from the state of Veracruz), and in the years of the program's existence no norteño musician has received a grant from it. Here the allusion is to norteño groups unknown to the mass media, such as Los Líricos de Terán or Los Rancheros de Terán, performers who continue to create songs based on the traditional musical forms discussed here. It is clear that although groups as popular as Pesado and Ramón Ayala play polkas occasionally, the sales of hundreds of thousands of recordings come mainly from the interpretation of romantic songs, corridos, and ballads.

Here, one must make a fundamental distinction between Texan-Mexican conjunto and norteño conjunto. Both began their days as marginal genres, but today norteño music has become a visible, multimillion-dollar industry—contemptuously called norteño light or norteño pop (which does not mean, however, that we find no traditional norteño musicians here)—while *Tejano* conjunto has become a traditionalist genre. We will return later to this discussion. First, however, it must be acknowledged that some defenders of traditional conjunto strongly criticize narcocorridos and the marketing of norteña music, arguing that, in the first case, corridos about drug trafficking have "kidnapped" the corrido genre, and that, in the second, marketing has resulted in a "homogenization" and "simplification" of the genre. In this regard, the use of long-standing Marxist premises—especially of the Frankfurt School—to criticize mass culture, using concepts such as "standardization" and "repetition," is paradoxical, because both "commercial" norteño music and narcocorridos are indisputable heirs of traditional conjunto.

REPRESENTATION OF NORTEÑO AND TEJANO IN THE COLLECTIVE IMAGINARY

After World War II it was possible for interpreters of conjunto to make a living exclusively through music, thanks to the phenomenon of ballrooms on the "taco circuit"—as the concert circuit of regional Mexican music in the southwestern United States was called—and *caravanas* (troupes). Manuel Peña (1999a, 94–95) asserts that the years between 1947 and 1970 were a golden or classical era for *Tejano* conjunto, adding that, during these years, it broke completely free of conjunto norteño. No doubt there have been improvements, such as those in the field of electronics, as well as the emergence of remarkable groups, such as the Conjunto Bernal. However, the available information indicates that conjunto continues to be a markedly unpopular popular music form, as blues was at its beginning, and one may continue to identify more affinities than differences between *Tejano*s and norteños.

In this sense, the autobiography of Eulalio González Ramírez, "Piporro," is invaluable for understanding the ups and downs of the period, as the famous actor, singer, composer, and dancer experienced in person the birth and transformations of norteño and his music in the collective imaginary. Truly, he became a symbol of the regional culture. The friendly González wanted to be a famous radio announcer but became a comedian by pure chance, answering a call at station XEQ to join a group of performers who would take part in the series *Ahi viene Martín Corona* ("Martin Corona is Coming"). González (1999, 95–110), bragging about his natural *norteño* accent, won the role of the "old northern man, jolly and talkative," who appeared in the script with the name of Piporro, and who would form a duo with the famous charro singer Pedro Infante. Shortly after, in 1951, the story of Martín Corona was successfully translated to the big screen, after which González never quit the character of Piporro.

However, in spite of the acceptance of his friendly character, the actor stated that it was no easy task to have his songs received as "something so very Mexican," because even in the 1950s, when Piporro was working in theater, audiences in Mexico City expected to hear tangos when he appeared on stage accompanied by accordion and guitar. Before González, musical groups, such as Los Montañeses del Álamo and Los Alegres de Terán, were virtually unknown in the capital, and the typical image of northerners was a caricature, one of repugnant men, "horrible types" with ten-gallon hats, moustaches, and enormous pistols (González Ramírez 1999, 123–126), popularized in tent shows since the end of the 1930s by Luciano Esquivel, a comedian from Zacatecas, when he was characterized as Don Matías, and then as a member of the duo Los Codos (The Elbows) (Ayala Duarte 2000, 89–90).

Unlike Esquivel, Piporro represents a norteño ideal that was different from the cliche, and that even enjoyed a degree of economic prosperity, because of which he cannot be considered an archetype of the 'rascuache-norteño" ("penniless wretch") nor a "different kind of pelado," as Cathy Ragland (2011, 349) has it. She attempts to locate Piporro in the artistic tradition of the *peladito*, as a continuation of the actors in the old tent shows, like Cantinflas, but as César Garizurieta (1979, 171) has mentioned, in Cantinflas there are no aspirations: "He does not want a better world . . . he wants to live as is." It is true that Piporro was influenced by Cantinflas, and in some of his movies, he integrates the working class, but he was not vulgar: although he is harvesting tomatoes in the field, he never appears dressed in rags, and his language and clothes are not associated with those of a beggar. From the beginning of his career, González (1999, 406) was aware of the tremendous influence of attire on the formation of symbols within the framework of Mexican cultural diversity, and, without giving any regard to these garments' association with fields and cantinas, he dressed in traditional jackets, or *cueras tamaulipecas*, ordering from a tailor in Ciudad Victoria, Tamaulipas, through which he managed to be "identified more symbolically with people from the north, in the same way as the *charro* became the hallmark of Jalisco."

In addition, Piporro converted music into another *norteño* and transnational symbol, making it quite odd that in his autobiography he provides very little data on his songs, the musicians who accompanied him, or his recordings. This apparent omission may be due to the fact that he was a contemporary of some of the most influential composers and singers in Mexican popular music, among them José Alfredo Jiménez, Mario Ruiz Armengol, and Manuel Esperón, and among singers like Pedro Infante or Jorge Negrete. In his role as composer, González enjoyed a certain status, as the aforementioned Frontera Collection indicates. When one searches the most outstanding songwriters in this database, Piporro appears in twenty-seventh place, with 78 recordings of his songs, higher than musicians as brilliant as Lorenzo Barcelata, Rubén Méndez, Gonzalo Curiel, or Ignacio Fernández Esperón, known as "Tata Nacho" (Gurza et al. 2012, 162). For Eulalio González, the distinctive feature of the norteño persona was his biculturality, manifested by, among other things, use of the English language (even if it was *pizquero* English, spoken by laborers), in addition to a love of the border, which resulted in films such as *El terror de la frontera* (*The Terror of the Border*) (1963) and *El rey del tomate* (*The Tomato King*) (1963), as well as *El bracero del año* (*Laborer of the Year*) (1964), or songs like "Chulas fronteras," (Table 4.4) where he employs his characteristic scream, "¡Ajúa!".

The objective of Piporro's lyrics, and films, such as *El Pocho* (The Mexican-American) (1970), was to draw attention to that wound known as the border, as well as to make visible and uphold the Mexican-American people: his interest resided "in the lack of interest that has always been shown in these characters, the Mexicans born 'over there' . . . who, being of our color and having the same blood that runs through our veins, have never awakened anything but the contempt with which we call them *pochos*, as though they were renegades" (González Ramírez 1999, 245). The solidarity with the Mexican-American people proclaimed by González was counter to the usual distrust of the Mexican government, which did not consider that the diaspora had "the same blood" as Mexicans. For instance, after González had written, directed, and produced, out of his own pocket, *El Pocho*—with its subject then considered a "hot potato"—the administrator of the Banco Cinematografico (the Mexican national film commission) did not consider

Table 4.4 Chulas fronteras, by Eulalio González, "Piporro." Available at: https://www.youtube.com/watch?v=2tgmCzIuaCM

(*Ajúa*, ajúa . . .)	
Antes iba al otro lado	I used to go to the other side [the US]
escondido de la gente	hidden from people
pues pasaba de mojado.	Well, I was illegal.
Ahora tengo mis papeles	Now I have my papers
ya estoy dentro de la ley	I am already within the law
tomo whiskey o la tequila	I drink whiskey or tequila
hasta en medio del *highway*.	even in the middle of the highway.

it of "national interest," and Piporro had to overcome many bureaucratic obstacles to get the film screened (González Ramírez 1999, 239–248).

The film *El bracero del año,* mentioned in the first chapter, manifested an ideological line that did not sympathize with migration, carrying a message that encouraged working the land in Mexico and not in the United States. In general, Mexican and American cinema were quite harsh in their representation of Mexican-American people and recent migrants, seeing no clear difference between the two groups and accusing them equally of being passive, loose, and devoid of family values, even going so far as to call them immoral, dishonest, and criminal (Martínez 1998, 31–50; Nuñez Arellano 2010, 41; and De la Garza 2005, 111). It is not necessary to mention the hatred that President Donald Trump promoted toward Mexicans in recent years, which has also affected the Chicano community.

The descendants of migrants in the United States have been rejected twice: not only by official discourse and Mexican society but also by public opinion in the country where they were born. As an example, the Movimiento Estudiantil Chicano de Aztlán (Chicano Student Movement of Aztlán, known by its acronym, MEChA), whose members seek to promote education among Mexican-American people, non-discrimination, and pride in the culture and history of their ancestors, has been compared to the "fascism of Mussolini," and described as separatist and "unabashedly racist" by U.S. politician Patrick J. Buchanan (2007, 107–110). In his paroxysm, he went so far as to assert that *MEChA* wants to reintegrate the American southwest into Mexico. The claims of this native of the District of Columbia conveniently underscore one of the ideas discussed here; in his books, Buchanan provides historical information on the U.S.-Mexico border region, but he observes from a distance and does not *live* the reality of the border.

Historically, and also from a distance, the Mexican federal government, as well as academics from central Mexico, have had unfortunate ideas regarding the border and compatriots who decide to live in the United States. In a recent book by José Ángel Hernández (2012, 8), the author provides a historical overview of the relationship between the Mexican government and Mexican expatriates, who were considered responsible for the loss of the country's northern territories. Hernández analyzes these contentious links through documents in the Archivo Histórico Militar Mexicano (Mexican Military Historical Archive) entitled "Circulars for the Training of Police in each *Comandancia General* [territory] for the Purpose of Pursuing the *Bad Mexicans* who Rouse the People to Be Annexed to the United States. 1853" (emphasis added); through the description of Guillermo Prieto, who considered the United States was "polluting" the *californios*; the "extremes" noted by Octavio Paz in those "sinister clowns" known as *pachucos*; and, finally, the chauvinism shown by Elena Poniatowska, who was sure that "The nation of the poor, the lousy, and the *cockroaches* is advancing in the United States" and that "Mexico will recover the territories ceded to the United States with migratory tactics." Hernández observes that all of these critics share the idea that Mexicans living outside Mexico lack the culture of those who reside in the center, namely, in Mexico City (Hernández 2012, 8–10).

Certainly, some Mexican-American people call themselves Mexicans, and even today think of how to "win the Alamo peacefully." Discussions with musicians, friends, and family members who reside in the United States—both migrants and permanent residents—reveal the dream that the American southwest will be returned to Mexico, which frightens the American government and thrills the Mexican State, is a fantasy. Mexicans have gone north for many reasons, among them recurrent economic crises, lack of employment, violence, and corruption of the Mexican government, so they are not "working" in favor of a supposed "Reconquista," as Pat Buchanan and historian Josefina Zoraida Vázquez have called it.

But if, to an outsider, the Chicano and Mexican communities in the United States appear to be equal, there are indeed differences between these groups, as we can see in the statements of Dan Arellano, a *Tejano* activist cited by the American intellectual José E. Limón (2011, 121–122), who believes that "aside from being American of Mexican descent, we have little in common [with Mexicans]. We speak, read, and think in English while they do not. . . . *Tejano*s are senators, congressmen, doctors, lawyers, professors." However, if Chicanos hold important positions in government and the academy, in the last few years, and probably thanks to uninterrupted migration, conjunto norteño has become the favorite music of radio stations in Austin, San Antonio, and the Lower Rio Grande Valley, leaving very little space for *Tejano* conjunto. Recent migrants, with their growing economic power, bear no resemblance to "the poor Mexicans [who] couldn't afford anything," whom record producer Chris Strachwitz met in the late 1950s, when he thought that the music of conjunto could not be marketed (Gurza et al. 2012, 15–16).

Chapter 5

Transformation and Recent Trends in Conjunto

This chapter discusses the development of *Tejano* and norteño conjunto from the 1970s, during which time the music began to flourish as a mass phenomenon, measured on the basis of growing record sales and massive concerts. Ramón Ayala earned his first gold record in 1974, and Los Tigres del Norte extended the taste for their regional music with corridos about drug trafficking such as *Contrabando y traición* ("Smuggling and Treason") and *La banda del carro rojo* ("The Band of the Red Car") (Ramírez-Pimienta 2011, 88–92). But in Texas, "nobody was paying attention" to conjunto, and to illustrate this, we can point to the fact that two remarkable accordionists, Santiago Jiménez and his son Santiago Jr., were during those years working as concierges in Dallas (Strachwitz 2012, 21–22). As Monterrey received a large number of migrants throughout the period discussed here, it is likely that some of these people brought recordings of norteña music with them when they returned to their home villages located in the southern Mexican states of Veracruz, Chiapas, and Michoacán. However, the taste for the genre remained predominantly in the north of Mexico at least until the 1990s, when, with the momentum of the so-called *onda grupera* (a rock-inspired genre of regional Mexican music), it became ubiquitous in the mass media (Madrid 2013b, 73).

CONJUNTO IN CINEMA

If during the formative years of conjunto, musicians visited small cantinas and town squares, in the late 1960s and early 1970s, their audiences grew due to migration from the countryside to the cities, in what Elias Canetti (1981, 62) called "festive crowds":

Nothing and no one threatens, and there is nothing to flee from; life and pleasure are assured while the party lasts. Many prohibitions and separations have been suspended, and they favor less usual personal approaches. The atmosphere for the individual is distension and not discharges. There is no identical goal that people have to attain together. The party is the goal and it has been achieved.

These feast crowds not only filled the halls and later the big stadiums, they also began to buy thousands of records and magazines and attended movies to be thrilled by their new idols. On several occasions here, there have been allusions to films, both Mexican and American, from which it is possible to learn about the idea of the border that the movie industry tried to impose on the collective imaginary. It is now crucial to point out the contribution of the music of conjunto to this field.

One of the first appearances of norteña music on the big screen was thanks to Eulalio González "Piporro". In the 1954 film *Cuidado con el amor (Watch Out for Love)*, actor Óscar Pulido and Piporro crooned the duet *Agustín Jaime (Augustine James)*, accompanying themselves with two guitars. Subsequently, in 1957's *Los chiflados del rock and roll (The Stooges of Rock and Roll)*, Lalo González was actor, singer, and composer of the *norteña* song "El cascarazo" *(The Rind)*, singing a cappella. Two years later, Piporro was seen with accordion in hand, humming "El ojo de vidrio" *(The Glass Eye)*, in the film *Dos corazones y un cielo (Two Hearts and One Heaven)*. It was not until 1960, however, with his involvement in *Calibre 44 (.44 Caliber)*, that González was flanked by a norteño group on screen, Los Broncos de Reynosa having that honor. The introduction of norteña music into the tastes of national Mexican audiences was thus very slow.

Los Alegres de Terán were also part of this first approach of norteña music to celluloid. Their first appearance was in the 1962 production *Pueblito (Small Town)*, directed by Emilio "El Indio" Fernández, in which Los Alegres—who were frequent guests in the home of the famed director—sang *Ingrato amor (Ungrateful Love)*, *La fonda chiquita (The Little Tavern)*, *Las Mañanitas (The Early Mornings)* and *Las golondrinas (The Swallows)*. They also contributed the music of hits such as *El contrabando del Paso (The Smuggling in El Paso)* (1980), and *El güero Estrada (Blond Estrada)* (1997) (Ramos Aguirre 2006, 141–143).

In the 1970s, a growing number of norteño musicians appeared on screen, not only as singers but also as actors in leading roles, many of whom would continue to appear in cinemas during the 1980s and 1990s. Examples include Cornelio Reyna, the main character in *Lágrimas de mi barrio (My Neighborhood's Tears)* (1973), and Ramón Ayala in *Dinastía de la muerte (Dynasty of Death)* (1977). Cinemas all over the country also presented famous groups like Los Cadetes de Linares, who appeared in *Los dos amigos* (*The Two Friends*) (1980), and Los Broncos de Reynosa in *Rosa de la Frontera* (*Rose of the Border*) (1985). In films like *Lágrimas de mi barrio* (*Tears from My Neighborhood*), and also *Guadalajara es México* (*Guadalajara is Mexico*) (1975) and *El norteño enamorado* (*The Northerner in Love*) (1979), Cornelio Reyna was the lead, and usually sang, although he did it with guitar or mariachi accompaniment, showing that even in the 1970s, conjunto norteño did not have an important place in the Mexican national popular culture.

In referring to norteña music on the big screen, one cannot ignore the work of Los Tigres del Norte. During the same decade that was internationally dominated by disco music, the popularity of their song "Contrabando y traición" was so great that the history of this corrido was brought to cinemas in 1977; this would be the beginning of a long list of audiovisual productions on which they would collaborate. The song was played by the Sinaloan group in the Miguel Galindo film *La banda del carro rojo* (*The Gang of the Red Car*) the following year. With these films and others, such as *La camioneta gris* (*The Gray Pickup*) (1990), the members of Los Tigres del Norte became synonymous with low-budget productions about drug trafficking. But they also excelled with films about migration issues, such as *La jaula de oro* (*The Golden Cage*) (1987) and *Tres veces mojado* (*Three Times Illegal*) (1989), on which they also served as producers.

Los Tigres serve as a good barometer by which to measure the rise and fall of the drug trafficker film genre. They had been involved in film since 1978, with success over the following decade; their last production was in 1993 with *Amor a la medida* (*Love Made to Measure*). From Nuevo León, another composer of corridos, producer, and prominent actor in this film genre was Julián Garza Arredondo, known later as *El Viejo Paulino* (Old Paulino), whose *Pistoleros famosos* (*Famous Gunmen*) (1981) became a cult film. While the movie was certainly not award-worthy, it drew crowds throughout its fifty-seven weeks in Monterrey cinemas. This can be explained by the fact that audiences now recognized themselves, and also their city, in the film; it was no longer a production imported from the capital. In the same way as Los Tigres del Norte, however, Julián Garza's career on the big screen declined in the early 1990s. There was a resurgence of violence in Mexico during the six-year presidency of Felipe Calderón, who declared open war against the drug trade. Film directors and producers were among the few who benefited from this "war," making films like *El infierno* (Hell) (2010), *Salvando al soldado Pérez* (Saving Private Perez) (2011), and *Heli* (2013).

Tejano conjunto, for its part, has never had the sort of approchement with the film industry enjoyed by its norteño counterpart. The previous chapter mentions the placement of the Tex-Mex conjunto in the traditionalist category, in which committed players, fans, and genre-supporting businesspeople decry what they identify as the adulterating consequences of the "commercial exploitation" of their music (Lena 2012, 47). Perhaps because of this pursuit of authenticity, the few audiovisual productions involving Texan musicians are of a documentary character, as is the case with *Chulas fronteras (Beautiful Borderlands)* (1976) and *Del mero corazón (From the Heart)* (1979), both directed by the late Les Blank and produced by Chris Strachwitz. These movies are bilingual, and feature appearances by accordionists Santiago Jiménez and Narciso Martínez. *Chulas fronteras* begins with images of the Rio Bravo/Grande at the border between Texas and Tamaulipas; in the background "Cancion mixteca," interpreted by Ramiro Cavazos and Conjunto Tamaulipas, can be heard. Later, Cavazos appears again, accompanying Narciso Martínez with bajo sexto. In general, these films not only illustrated regional musicians' low standard of living, but were also a pretext to make visible the important contribution that Mexicans and *Tejano*s made to the construction of the United States, both culturally and economically. At the same time, it seeks to make clear the influence of norteño musicians in Texas, with performances by Los Alegres de Terán and Ramiro Cavazos, who by then were already living in the Rio Grande Valley.

INFLUENCE OF THE AMERICAN MAINSTREAM IN TEJANO CONJUNTO

The musician Martín Zapata recalls that while he was performing at a dance during the 1950s, a couple approached him to say that he played very well, but they were ready to faint because the music was too fast. Zapata thus asked the bass player to calm down and sing more slowly, as people would like: "We learn from [these] people . . . the people tell us what to do." This example is in no way unusual, because historically conjunto artists have put their talents at the service of dancing. In this section we will see that some conjuntos in Texas moved away from that basic premise.

The previous chapter also noted that since the 1950s Tony de la Rosa had taken up some elements of the Mexican musical tradition and recorded songs by José Alfredo Jiménez and Cuco Sánchez, but always flavored with music from the American mainstream, including Western swing and honky-tonk. In addition to musical forms, other key elements that make clear the influence of American popular music on conjunto are the introduction of technological advances and new musical instruments. In a recording from 1948 made by accordionist Valerio Longoria's group, drums are included for the first time, and by the mid-1950s Tony de la Rosa was performing in ballrooms with electric bass, amplified bajo sexto, and microphones for the singer and the accordion (Peña 1985, 84–87). There is also the matter that even by the late

1950s the use of electrical instruments and microphones was not possible in Mexico, because there were simply no outlets available in most venues to connect the equipment. El Palomo y el Gorrión was perhaps the first norteño conjunto to employ professional amplification, in the late 1960s, thanks to a trip to Los Angeles, where they acquired several 300-watt Cerwin Vega loudspeakers (Berrones 2013, 87–88).

In recent decades, *Tejano* conjunto has boasted of artists who perform daring fusions of sound, with jazz and rock harmonies. Of note is accordionist Albert Zamora, who identifies his music as a mix of *Tejano* and norteño conjunto, and adds on his Facebook page: "spice that tradition with the funk/punk/rock gyrations of the Red Hot Chili Peppers, and the metallic rage of Guns N' Roses, Papa Roach, and you've got a sound that speaks directly about one individual: Albert Zamora."

But it seems to me that the best representative of the turn in *Tejano* conjunto toward assimilating the influence of American popular music in Texas, without ignoring any southern heritage, is the late Esteban "Steve" Jordan, called *El Parche* (The Patch), born in February 1939 in the Rio Grande Valley and known as the Jimi Hendrix of the accordion (Burr 1999, 124). We can appreciate his talents from the ranchera song *La Bicicleta* (*The Bicycle*), which begins with two male voices in a high register singing, *Voy a cantar un corrido* (I'm Going to Sing a Corrido), which recalls interpretations of the Mexican music from the early recording industry. Meanwhile, *Si te portas mal* (*If You Misbehave*) includes brass instruments that owe a debt to the big bands. El Parche was not afraid to play versions of songs that defied any generic classification, blatantly personal and mixing lyrics in English and Spanish, like classic rock and jazz numbers like "Louie Louie," "You've Lost that Loving Feeling," or his inspired interpretation of "Summertime." Of course, some of his songs invite us to dance, such as "Cumbia con salsa" ("Cumbia with salsa') or "My Toot Toot," but in general his music is composed simply to be listened to, without the dance floor in mind; he two times once said to a reporter, "I am working for me." Surely no music critic could define the music of Steve Jordan better than he did himself:

> I like to play everything, that's what I like to do, but, sometimes, you mix it up too much. If you're in the Valley, you can't be playing jazz, rock, and then turn around and play them some real tasty salsa, and then a good, solid bolero, like a *danzón*, and then a polka because they'll kill you! There's no such thing as that. But in California, yes. Paulino Bernal . . . Valerio Longoria . . . Tito Puente, Machito, Tito Rodríguez, Count Basie . . . Buddy Rich. . . . That influenced me, bro. I mix it into the polka, I mix it into the redova, wherever I f'ing feel like it. (Tejeda 2001e)

By his way of speaking we can discern that Jordan accepted his chicanismo, his bicultural—and musically, multicultural—condition because he was influenced by some prominent Texan accordionists, but his music is a hybrid that owes a debt to genres such as conjunto, rock, bolero, swing, salsa, and jazz. He is a good example of the *transetnicidad* (trans-ethnicity) mentioned earlier. Jordan devoted many years to recording music in his own home, although most of this material has not been released. Unfortunately, there are virtually no record sales for Jordan registered with Del Valle Records, and the producer Chris Strachwitz indicated that there would be no "real demand" for the unreleased material. After battling cancer for several years, Esteban "Steve" Jordan died in the summer of 2010, but his sons continue to spread their father's outstanding legacy through his group Rio Jordan, which includes the blind accordionist Juanito Castillo, Steve's disciple and protégé.

CUMBIA! A PAN-AMERICAN MUSICAL GENRE

Like Mexico, the Republic of Colombia is a Latin American nation with enormous cultural diversity. The category of *musica costeña colombiana* (Colombian coastal music) alone includes styles ranging from "*paseo, porro, gaita, merengu* (unrelated to the Dominican genre), *fandango, bullerengue* and *mapalé*," to the best-known at the international level, *cumbia,* and its close relative, the *vallenato* (Pacini Hernandez 2010, 110–111). At the beginning of the twentieth century, cumbia was played by small instrumental ensembles along the Caribbean coast of Colombia, an area characterized by a population consisting largely of people of African and indigenous descent. With the passage of time, the mixture of these cultures with European traditions gave rise to new sounds, spread by varied ensembles, which fused instruments such as the maracas and the vertical flute called *gaita*, both of indigenous origin; the *tambor alegre* (merry or mid-drum) and the *marímbula*, of African derivation; and the accordion, from Europe (D'Amico 2013, 29–48). In spite of their instrumental and rhythmic richness, cumbia and vallenato were considered unculturedd by the upper classes, unrefined and even grotesque (Contreras, 2003). And where have we heard that before?

By the 1940s the musical groups that had been emulating the big bands introduced cumbia into their repertoires, and thanks to LPs, this music became known first in the interior of the country and later outside of Colombia (Pacini Hernandez 2010, 117). Regardless of its marginalized origin, cumbia has shown great capacity for adaptation: it is considered a pan-American genre, and a cultural representative of Colombia internationally. Arriving in Argentina at the end of the 1930s, it was influenced by musical forms like the *cuarteto* and the *chamamé*. Years later, the cumbia arrived in

Perú, where it was called *chicha* after merging with the *huayno* and other Caribbean rhythms (Blanco Arboleda 2008, 73–78). At the beginning of the 1960s, this genre was consolidated in Mexico by the Colombian group *Los Corraleros de Majagual*, which did extended tours in the north of the country and would set the pattern for Mexican tropical groups. However, Los Corraleros were not the first Colombian international performers; since 1945, Luis Carlos Meyer, a musician from Barranquilla known as *El Rey del Porro* (The King of Porro), had been performing in Panama, Venezuela, Cuba, and Mexico (Blanco Arboleda 2008, 45–54).

Texan singer and songwriter Linda Escobar composed and recorded the porro "Frijolitos pintos" ("Little Pinto Beans") in 1965, which on some records is identified as cumbia. The 45 rpm disc sold over a million units (personal communication, May 18, 2013), a good example of the acceptance—and the whirlwind—caused by the new Colombian rhythms in south Texas. However, it is likely that cumbia was appropriated and brought to the American southwest by Mexicans, not by Colombians. One of the researchers who supports this theory is the Colombian Darío Blanco Arboleda (2008, 35), who also underlines the importance of cumbia in the construction of identities:

> In the northeast, particularly in Monterrey, there is a phenomenon without parallel within the youth culture of the country, the use of cumbia for the construction of the most important and influential youth and popular class identities in the city and nearby areas. The phenomenon [is] known as *La Colombia de Monterrey* (the Colombia of Monterrey). Both the sonority of regio-Colombian cumbia (cumbia made in Monterrey) and *sonidera* and tropical cumbia have crossed over to the USA and Canada, becoming a bulwark and tool of Mexican and Latin American identity from the "other side" of the border.

Blanco also believes that the enormous popularity of cumbia in various Latin American countries is due to the fact that it was assimilated by migrants from rural areas, by 'peasants living in the cities," explaining that "it is a crossroads, where the challengers of sound and their products, across the continent, allow themselves to be impressed by, affected by, and sensitized to each other" (Blanco Arboleda 2008, 40). We should not be surprised, then, that those "peasants living in the cities" of northeastern Mexico and the American southwest, who had absorbed the music of conjunto, also endorsed cumbia, which reminded them of the polka and its well-known binary rhythm.

For his part, sociologist José Juan Olvera Gudiño (2013, 87–104) mentions that, thanks to cinema, the contagious rhythm appeared in Monterrey from the 1950s, giving rise to cumbia styles such as the cumbia norteña, cumbia grupera, cumbia colombiana, and cumbia villera. Olvera states that at the end of the following decade, Beto Villa y Los Populares de Nueva Rosita, a conjunto from the state of Coahuila, became the first group to include cumbias norteñas in their repertoire. The band's leader, who was born in 1947 and agrees that he has been strongly influenced by Los Corraleros de Majagual, alleges that when he wished to include cumbias in his group's catalogue, his bandmates mocked him, as they felt the idea was absurd. Beto Villa y Los Populares de Nueva Rosita, which still performs, is quite unorthodox in its instrumentation, since the lineup usually includes a keyboard accordion, bajo sexto or electric guitar, saxophone, synthesizer, drums, and percussion.

By the 1970s it was even clearer that this music could justifiably be called transnational. Monterrey began to dominate the regional recording industry, as indicated by the fact that Villa and his band recorded for Mex-Melody Records in Mexico, whose discs were distributed in the United States by Escobedo Enterprises of Dallas, Texas. The cumbia played in Mexico and the southern United States is usually simpler and slower than its Colombian sibling. Cumbia may no longer cause the commotion it did years ago, but it remains among norteño and *Tejano* conjunto's favorite genres.

ONDA GRUPERA, OR THE POWER OF MUSICAL MARKETING

During the 1970s and 1980s, a musical movement called *onda grupera* (group wave) (Madrid 2013a, 105–118), or the *grupero* movement, arrived. This label does not refer strictly to a musical genre. It was, rather, an invention of the music industry designed to popularize recordings by a wide variety of groups across different instrument lineups and genres, in which there was generally no identifiable frontman (Olvera Gudiño 2013, 93). These groups leaned toward cumbia and ballads, and featured music with rural roots, but with a greater influence from technology and urban culture, and with cosmopolitan ambitions.

Just as Mexico City had attracted musicians for decades, during the grupero boom Monterrey consolidated its reputation as the center of a cultural industry based on popular music and supported by radio, film, television, and record labels, and became the *grupero* capital (Olvera Gudiño 2013, 92–93). With centralist vision, the music critic Antonio "Toño" Carrizosa (1997, 199–200) expressed his astonishment in this way:

It was 1986 when we began to hear that the north of the country had such a large number of groups that were soon to come to the capital. . . . How could the province beat what was playing on the radio in the DF [Federal District]? The capital was considered the basis of what would be heard on radio all over the country, and there was nothing else. Surely didn't all the groups and musicians from the southeast had to establish themselves in the DF to make it big? While solo artists kept doing their own thing on the radio and Miguel Ríos was the great hope for the rebirth of rock in Mexico, little by little, the ground was being prepared for the groups from the north to dominate us.

In fact, Monterrey was now a big city: as of 1966 its metropolitan area was home to a population of one million, and by 1970 it could justifiably be called the "industrial capital of Mexico," because it generated 10.5 percent of the country's gross domestic product (GDP) (Cavazos Garza and Ortega Ridaura 2010, 227–232). The city reclaimed its prestige as an artistic center, not only for the cultural industries mentioned above, but also as the gateway to the American entertainment market. After establishing its regional-transnational power, the next step was to assure its cultural preeminence internationally.

Just as the taste for the novelty of acoustic grupero was spreading, the boundaries between musical genres were blurring, so it was possible to find norteño or tropical arrangements with rock influences. To get an idea of the unprecedented success of grupero: Rigo Tovar played to a verified crowd of some 400,000 people in Monterrey in 1982 (Madrid 2013a, 108); the band Los Temerarios sold more than 35 million albums over the course of their career; and the group Bronco founded its own brands of boots and clothing, as well as participated in movies, cartoons, comic books, calendars, advertising, and even a reality show. In addition, in October 1994, *Billboard* magazine created a category called Regional Mexican Song, independent of the old Latin genre. Another magazine, *Furia Musical*, a noted grupero publication from 1993 to 2006, contained gossip, stories, horoscopes, interviews, and photographs of musicians, and had a circulation of 750,000 in the United States alone (Simonett 2001, 45).

This success within the grupero movement, initiated by artists such as Rigo Tovar in the 1970s, later served to position conjunto as a mass phenomenon. This transformation has no antecedent in the history of Mexican popular music, as here, the working class—a marginal culture and its economically powerful market—its worldview, and its aspirations were eventually accepted and celebrated by the middle and upper classes (Madrid 2013a, 115–116). What is more, such an event was transnational, with Monterrey and Houston as the axis of the development of an identity and economy based on the music industry, specifically on tropical and norteña cumbia (Olvera Gudiño 2005, 40). At the beginning of the 1990s, cumbia was the musical genre that supported one of the fastest-growing segments of the Latin music market in the United States: *Tejano*. After EMI Latin signed a contract with the *Tejano* singer-songwriter Selena in 1989, the label's profits increased 800 percent within three years (Paredez 2009, xi). The murder of the charismatic "Queen of Tex-Mex" in 1995, however, may have been a harbinger of the end of the *Tejano* music movement, which shortly after began slipping in the charts in the face of the arrival of new norteño groups that also embraced cumbia and ballads, like Límite and Los Tucanes de Tijuana (Burr 1999, 38).

FROM CHRISTIAN MUSICIANS IN THE US TO THE RISE OF THE NARCOCORRIDO IN MEXICO

In the early 1970s, after having remained among the most important groups on the scene for years, members of Conjunto Bernal and Los Alegres de Terán became evangelical Christians, and shifted from traditional corridos and love songs to praising God. This coincided with the initial boom in *Tejano* and norteño conjunto in the mass media. In 1973, Paulino Bernal became a "born-again preacher," and shortly thereafter was followed by all the members of his conjunto (Peña 1985, 105). According to Bernal, the reason for this was that, early in his musical career, "vices began to accompany celebrity, starting with beer . . . then liquor, until we started with marijuana . . . LSD, cocaine, and heroin." Coupled with this, the members of Conjunto Bernal saw the brutality of war close-up when they spent twenty-one days as musical ambassadors in Vietnam. Additionally, Bernal admitted that "a young man opened the Bible and explained things that transformed my life" (2014 interview on www.soylibreencristo.wordpress.com, later deleted). At that time, radio stations did not want to air Christian music, so Bernal founded his own station; he now owns sixty. Tomás Ortiz and Eugenio Abrego, from Los Alegres de Terán, who by then already lived in the Rio Grande Valley, also began to follow the path of evangelical Christianity.

But while some conjunto musicians in the United States repented, others began to sing more violent verses in Mexico. Here we can see one of the most important changes in the history of conjunto. As the genre that began as the music of marginalized rural groups began to evolve and modernize in the 1970s, so it eventually confronted in its lyrics the problems faced by disenfranchised urban communities. As discussed in the previous chapter, this process started in the United States because of that country's technological development and the armed conflicts in which it had been involved from the 1950s onward.

When one speaks of the narcocorrido, the first name that comes to mind is, without doubt, Los Tigres del Norte. However, it would be simplistic to attribute their visibility solely to this famed subgenre of corrido, because the group is also a model for migrants, its members having become millionaires although born in poverty, thus personifying the "American dream." Despite that, these so-called *ídolos del pueblo* (idols of the people), also called *la voz del pueblo* (the voice of the people) (Aguilar Cruz 2012, 5), maintain a formidable closeness to their followers, typically performing a mere eight or ten songs at the beginning of a concert before turning themselves over to requests scribbled by the audience on small pieces of paper that make their way to the stage. In the same way, at the end of a concert they hold a "photo session," in which hundreds or even thousands of people from the audience can approach the musicians to talk and take a photograph with them, regardless of whether this activity goes on till dawn. It is contradictory that Los Tigres del Norte achieved international fame playing corridos on the subject of drug trafficking, considering that they turned away from narcocorridos for years, and their vocalist confesses he feels embarrassed singing about drugs (Ramírez-Pimienta 2011, 104). As we shall see later, this group from Sinaloa invented nothing new; they just revitalized a genre that had been forgotten for several decades. Due to the complexity of the topic, this discussion of corridos on drug trafficking is divided into three sections: a) the historical background of the corrido; b) the importance of the U.S.-Mexico border in its development; and c) the meaning of narcocorridos in popular culture.

Having made reference several times to the musical genre called corrido, it is necessary to be aware of the ancient roots of this tradition. Despite the age of the following definition of corrido, devised by Mexican folklorist Vicente T. Mendoza (1996, IX), it continues to be one of the most complete:

> The corrido is an epic-lyric-narrative genre, in variable rhyming quatrains, assonant or consonant in the even verses, a literary form on which rests a musical phrase generally composed of four parts, which recounts events that powerfully touch the sensitivity of the masses; the epic element derives from Castilian romance, and normally maintains its general form, preserving its narrative character of warlike exploits and battles, then creating a history by and for the people. Its lyrical element derives from the *copla* and *cantar* [types of folk songs], as well as the *jácara*, and it also includes sentimental stories.

In the second chapter, there was mention of satirical verses written during the colonial and independent period to criticize the government, an essential role that the Mexican corrido takes up in becoming the voice of the marginalized classes, and it is therefore "a history by and for the people." Those old rhymes have had a great influence on the development of the genre but, as pointed out by Mendoza (1996, xiv), they cannot be considered corridos, because they do not boast a "narrative or epic character." The same author considers the first corridos to be those that appeared in the late 1870s, "when they [sang about] the exploits of certain rebels against the government of President Porfirio Díaz" (1996, xv). This means that a basic characteristic of the genre, in addition to events that powerfully touch human sensibilities and the narrative and epic aspect, lies in the conflict introduced to a powerful regime by a tough guy, dubbed Leandro Rivera, Macario Romero, Juan Alvarado, Valentín Mancera or Heraclio Bernal.

Cuauhtémoc Esparza (1976, 11–12) stated that "Las mañanas de Hidalgo" (The Mornings of Hidalgo), from 1811, was the first known corrido; it is necessary, however, to qualify this assertion, for even if such verses were specifically composed to be sung, surely the music would differ much from the corrido as we recognize it now. If we take into account the era proposed by Mendoza for the birth of corrido, that is, the last quarter of the nineteenth century, we can see—with Américo Paredes (2008, 134)—that the "intensification of nationalism" experienced by residents of the U.S.-Mexico border caused this genre to bloom from the mid-nineteenth century, about twenty years before it did in central Mexico. In this sense, the oldest corrido of which we know, with the characteristics described by Mendoza, is the corrido of Juan Nepomuceno Cortina, a citizen of Tamaulipas and owner of most of the land on which the city of Brownsville is located today, who took up arms to defend his rights in 1859 in the face of aggression from Anglo-Americans.

Brave men were by no means the only characters featured in border corridos. From the beginning, the experience of migration was also a privileged theme. An example of this is the first corrido that has come down to us intact: "El Corrido de Kiansis" chronicles the adventures of cowboys in the first cattle drive from Texas to the state of Kansas in the late 1860s (Paredes 2008, 141). As well, in the so-called Corrido de los quinientos novillos (Corrido of the Five Hundred Steers), the competence of Mexican cowboys is weighed against the incompetence of Anglo buckaroos.

Speaking specifically of corridos about traffickers, these also emerged in the border area, which highlights the importance of the U.S.-Mexico border in the development of norteña music. There had been smuggling in the area since the colonial period, and by 1822 it was "scandalous in its volume" in the towns of northern Mexico (Vizcaya Canales 2006, 7). Prohibition in the United States, which began in 1920, encouraged smuggling from Mexico and Canada, as well as corridos about traffickers of spirits (Ramírez-Pimienta 2011, 35). In 1933, as Prohibition ended, criminals like Enrique Fernández Puerta, known as the Al Capone of Ciudad Juárez, exchanged the business of liquor for that of drugs. A little earlier, in 1931, the Vocalion company recorded the first corrido that I know of on the subject of drug trafficking: "El Pablote" (Big Paulie), performed by Norverto [sic] González and Jose Rosales in the traditional format of vocal duet with guitar accompaniment.

The verses were dedicated to the morphine trafficker Pablo González, alias El Pablote (Big Paulie), who dominated the trade in this drug after eliminating a group of Chinese immigrants who had previously controlled it (Ramírez-Pimienta 2011, 52–53). In the following years, other corridos appeared on the subject of drug trafficking, such as *Por morfina y cocaína* ("For Morphine and Cocaine") and *Carga blanca* ("White Cargo"). Shortly after this, however, the subgenre was abandoned, perhaps due to the economic boom of the mid-twentieth century known as the Mexican miracle (Ramírez-Pimienta 2011, 17). During this time, corridos about narcotics and their distributors were probably composed, but the fact that we do not know them speaks of their negligible social impact, certainly nothing compared to what happened in the 1970s, when severe economic crises caused a huge resurgence of illegal activity, and the drug trade began to occupy spaces of power that both State and Church had left vacant.

Since that time, members of the Mexican government have tried to obstruct the spread of the narcocorrido, alleging it "incites violence" and can be considered an "apology for crime." One of the more recent examples of this occurred in the capital of Chihuahua, where the municipal council banned Los Tigres del Norte because they performed the song "La reina del sur" ("Queen of the South") at the local fair, explaining that public performance of such corridos had been prohibited since 2011. In the same line, the Technical Secretary of the National Security Council in turn supported, through his blog on the official website of the presidency (now deleted), Sinaloa's prohibition of the subgenre. In 1991 the state of Sinaloa had prohibited the broadcast of narcocorridos, and in 2011 banned them from "bars, nightclubs, and ballrooms." Celebrating the event, the official said in a column entitled "A Position Against 'Narco-Corridos'":

> The fight against organized crime is taking place not only with the deployment of the security force; there is also a *cultural struggle* that we must recognize. The violence is generated not only by bullets; the incorporation of this type of song in places that have been ravaged by criminals represents an attempt to imbue the social fabric with patterns of unacceptable values for our country.

Trying to justify the incursion of the State into individual security, the bureaucrat indicated that we must recognize the above-mentioned "cultural struggle," with the purpose of "preventing killers, kidnappers, extortionists, and drug traffickers from hijacking norteña music." To be fair to this official, it is possible to assert that, indeed, in recent years norteño music has become synonymous with drug trafficking, and several of its interpreters have been killed in a violent manner, as was the case of Zayda Peña, Sergio Gómez, Valentín "El Gallo" (the Rooster) Elizalde, Fabián "El Halcón de la Sierra" (the Hawk of the Mountains) Ortega, Sergio "El Shaka" (Zulu warrior) Vega, and, of course, Rosalino "Chalino" Sánchez, singer and composer of corridos, who was born in Sinaloa—surely the first musician to appear with a pistol or rifle on the covers of his albums—and who alternated conjunto norteño with *banda sinaloense*.

But we must ask ourselves, why is the music of Sinaloan bands, and specifically the corrido norteño, associated with drug trafficking? Why are there no musical genres such as *narcobolero* or groups of *narcojaraneros*? Possible answers include the fact that, in the first place, corrido identifies with the lower classes: it does not sing about politicians, but rather the rebels who oppose them. The corrido speaks of individuals, as narcocorridos continue to do. This musical subgenre offers "three minutes of a 'super powerful Mexican' to a person who feels devoid of power," especially the undocumented (Perasso, 2013). That is to say, expressive culture can be a way to sublimate and forget, at least for a few minutes, a life of deprivation. One of the arguments of the Mexican State against the narcocorrido, however, is precisely the idea that someone may feel attracted by the life of power and easy money captured in the songs, although we must also remember that many narcocorridos end in tragedies, commenting on the premature and violent death of the "super powerful Mexican."

The State has not had the ability to appropriate institutionally the popular symbols of the dispossessed majority, and if narcocorridos appear in the north of Mexico it is because this area is a smuggling model par excellence; in addition, the inhabitants of this region have maintained their autonomy from centralized power. Also, it is no great feat to grow marijuana in the center and south of the country, or produce cocaine in South America: the real challenge is to cross the United States border with narcotics. It is of this that they sing, and that is why regional border music has arisen as a means of expression for the narco. The campaign against narcocorridos implemented by the Mexican federal government and various states and municipalities across the country has been indulged, assimilated, and then defended by a part of the citizenry, which makes it clear that "what is known or believed to be known about them [narcos] and their world is mostly the result of a process of construction and imposition of meaning whose monopoly has been wielded by the state" (Astorga 1997). The truth of this can be seen on various blogs and online newspaper comments, where many people who clearly do not listen to narcocorridos claim that they are an "arm of organized crime," repeating doctrines promulgated by authorities. The following is typical:

> For the *nacos* (lowbrows), in order to cultivate the further disintegration of the family, to feed the chaste ears of *narcos*, they pay famous musicians and ask for a new corrido to praise their destructive work; this is what we've come to

call popular culture, driven by a multitude of frivolous people, consumers who sooner or later will end up in psychiatric hospitals, in prison or in the cemetery; it is the culture of death that ennobles these drunkard musicians who are expanding alcohol's huge market day by day (Ordaz 2009).

This example also shows how people with aspirations toward upward mobility use music to feel superior to and discriminate against others, because they believe their own tastes and education are better than others'. Unfortunately, this trend has grown in recent times in Mexico due to the so-called "outraged generation," members of which label lowbrow or ignorant anyone who does not share their opinions. This is another point of view, which was approved by several readers of this newspaper: "There are many topics, why corridos about narcos, exactly (?) . . . and ones in which they're always triumphant. Gentlemen, it's praise, they're hymns to drug trafficking, yes, they are guilty, and they damage the minds of young Mexicans who follow their mediocre music. Prison for these [the article refers to the imprisonment of Ramón Ayala] and for others as well, the Tigres [del Norte], etc." (Ordaz 2009).

It is also possible that the opposition to narcocorridos simply camouflages the center-periphery conflict, as was illustrated by the opinions of those who celebrated on social networks when the *El Komander* concert in Cuernavaca, Morelos, was cancelled: "Well, I hope they send him to . . . and also his followers, who already believe they're all from the north or Sinaloa." It is also worth noting that composers of traditional corridos do not agree with the production of narcocorridos, as is the case with Ramiro Cavazos who, although he respects them, says:

> We never try to do very aggressive things, talking about narco and those things, we respect the people, and everybody does what they want. We sang simpler corridos: that they killed a guy, and we did a corrido, but good, not that he was a narco. Right now they are doing very different things, very strong, I do not agree that they should sing about very heavy things or try to cause harm to the people who work: if they want to work in drug trafficking, it's their problem (Personal communication, July 11 2011).

But if on the one hand governments want to suppress corridos, on the other hand, over roughly the last ten years government at various levels has also sponsored large-scale concerts, such as the Fiestas de Octubre in Guadalajara (featuring Los Tigres del Norte), the Festival Internacional Cervantino in Guanajuato, and performances in the Zócalo (main square) of Mexico City. Everything indicates that the Mexican government is in a process of transformation associated with its cultural policies, since the introduction of norteño bands and rock groups to festivals such as the Cervantino of Guanajuato and the Festival Cultural Zacatecas, which were previously oriented toward chamber groups and symphonic orchestras, speaks to an attempt by the State to try to identify with marginalized or young people. However, after the crusade to discredit those musical groups identified with the narcocorrido, such attempts look desperate, and frankly pathetic.

Despite all of the above, narcocorridos helped revitalize the corrido genre. Folklorist Vicente T. Mendoza (1996, xvi) had proclaimed the decadence and death of corrido as a genre of the people, due to the fact that from 1930 onward it became "cultist, artificial, often false, with no genuinely popular character." The corrido did not die, but ethnomusicologist Helena Simonett (2001, 229) suggests that recent corridos can no longer be regarded as popular ballads in which "the common folk express their sentiments and points of view regarding their social reality." Confronted with these positions and accepting that the narcocorrido can qualify in effect as commodified music, many norteño artists frequently record songs and corridos offered to them by humble and unknown authors, and even Los Tigres del Norte have on their web page a mailing address for anyone who wants to submit their musical compositions. The narcocorrido thus does not arise spontaneously; it is anchored in the long tradition of the Mexican corrido, in the sense of being an echo of the social base.

This subgenre of the corrido is very similar to the typifications of the theater: if we see a murder on stage we know it is a fantasy; no one goes out into the street frightened, or wanting to kill a patron, because "when the curtain falls [or, in our case, when the narcocorrido ends], the viewer is back to reality . . . to the supreme reality of everyday life in comparison with which the reality presented on stage now seems tenuous and ephemeral" (Berger and Luckman 1995, 41). Following the time-honored function of the corrido as a means of disseminating news, if a narcocorrido asserts that a drug trafficker built a school or helped people in some way, it is because this actually happened; a composer of corridos makes no apology for something that does not exist, except in the cases of "corridos por encargo" (commissioned corridos), which is discussed below. Curiously, the Mexican State tries to impede the spread of narcocorridos, a form of imagined reality, while on the other hand it promotes and subsidizes bullfights, an immediate reality in which there is no need to imagine anything, and where the culture of death is presented in all its pain and horror as a lesson in torture.

An outstanding example of a criminal who favors his community and is protected by it is Joaquín Guzmán Loera, alias "El Chapo," leader of the Sinaloa Cartel. According to *Forbes*, this man is one of the most powerful in the world, and has a fortune of over a billion dollars. Guzmán can be considered a type of the "social bandit" described by British historian Eric

Hobsbawm (2003, 19), because he "challenges the economic, social and political order by challenging those who hold or lay claim to power, law and the control of resources . . . [he] simultaneously challenges the economic, social and political order." He escaped from a federal prison in 2001 and was subsequently included on the most-wanted list by Interpol and the FBI until he was recaptured in 2014. Even when they are caricatured in a corrido, social bandits retain a universal appeal, and with the help of his neighbors El Chapo evaded justice for thirteen years. The same neighbors organized mass protests in the towns of Culiacán and Guamuchil to demand the release of Guzmán Loera, because, they said, "to us he is a good person," and "he's the one who helps the people . . . the government needs to round up kidnappers, not people who help us." The drug lord escaped again in the summer of 2015, to be recaptured in January 2016. He was later extradited to the United States and is currently serving a life sentence at the Florence "Supermax" prison in Colorado.

In the field research carried out in the north of Mexico by sociologist Mark Edberg (2004, 81–82), the greater part of his interviewees did consider the protagonists of old corridos—like Pancho Villa—to be heroes, but did not feel the same way about modern drug traffickers. Even numerous marginalized young people Edberg spoke to classified narcocorridos' lyrics as the same kind of fun as that found in cartoons or professional wrestling (Edberg 2011, 67–82). Commissioned corridos, composed specifically to exalt traffickers, idealize them to hyperbolic levels, so they can be easily recognized. In addition, the judicious Mexican writer José Emilio Pacheco claims "the narcocorrido is a perfect romance, which came to those who relay them orally"; he adds that it is equivalent to the epigram: the only way to criticize power today.

This suggests that the policy of the Mexican State toward this music has several functions: on the one hand, it registers disapproval of a popular form of protest that makes clear the government's inability to fulfill its role of safeguarding the rule of law and ensuring the integrity of all citizens. In this way, the narcocorrido may be considered an "uncomfortable" musical genre, the kind of music that stole from government the "monopoly . . . on symbolic production about traffickers" (Astorga 1997, 5). In this case, the State seeks to inculcate the idea that certain writers and performers of corridos are something like "exclusive artists" for a specific drug dealer, but the composers interviewed during this research stated that no customer asks for exclusivity: they create corridos for any person on request and always with complete freedom. Drug traffickers also employ architects, engineers, designers, lawyers, accountants, and many other professionals, so the hatred propagated by members of the Mexican government (and some mayors and governors) against musicians is unjustifiable. This may be the result of the fact that, unlike the mariachi—a tradition invented with the approval of authority—the narcocorrido is a form of expressive representation over which government has never had control.

On the other hand, the State still adheres to an outdated paternalism, verging on authoritarianism, and makes a mistake when it considers the population to be no more than young children who must be protected: "people with an immense ability to be persuaded, who lack the capacity to discern what they hear or see" (Lara, 2003). Mario Quintero, singer, bajo sexto player, and leader of Los Tucanes de Tijuana, has expressed sincerely that "we aren't doing anything harmful. We are an effect of the drug traffic, not a cause. If we were to stop singing corridos, there would still be people doing what they do [smuggling drugs]" (Wald 2001, 117–118).

The prohibition of narcocorridos in several Mexican states only makes the genre more desirable to the public, as stated by Mario Quintero: "sometimes, inadvertently, [what happens is that] what is prohibited is what people seek with the greatest interest; morbid curiosity sometimes intensifies this, and people try by various means to obtain information that the news or media do not give them and that they find in this type of music" (Durand 2011). The morbidness Quintero mentions must be the reason why many norteño groups, hoping for quick and easy success, now begin their careers singing narcocorridos; the more "hard" or explicit they are, the greater the interest they attract. In fact, since the 1990s, there has been an increase in descriptions of violence in corrido lyrics, which has led to them being called *perrones* or *pesados* (heavy), and subsequently *empecherados*, *enfermos* (sick), *blindados* (armoured), and *progresivos* (progressive), leading in the early years of the twenty-first century to *corridos alterados* (altered) (see Ramírez-Pimienta 2013). The so-called Movimiento Alterado, located mainly in Sinaloa and California, recounts in detail violent events that have taken place in Mexico; this subgenre of corrido was propagated by Omar and Adolfo Valenzuela, better known as Los Cuates Valenzuela (The Valenzuela twins), music producers from Sinaloa, but based in Los Angeles, California, for over twenty years (Ramírez-Pimienta 2013, 306). Some of the representative musicians of the Movimiento Alterado are Alfredo Ríos, known as El Komander, as well as Los Buknas de Culiacán and Los Nuevos Elegantes. Their world includes such symbols as skulls, luxury cars, AK-47 machine guns also known as *cuernos de chivo* (goat horns), bulletproof vests, and, of course, marijuana leaves and white powder. Their instrumentation is varied, with a basic lineup of accordion, bajo sexto, and drums, opting for the tuba instead of the electric bass, highlighting the hybridity between norteño conjunto and Sinaloan brass bands. They use traditional musical forms such as corrido and huapango, but some groups, among them Los Buchones de Culiacán, also show the influence of rap and hip hop.

El Komander, composer of custom-made corridos, who has more than double the number of followers of Los Tigres del Norte on his Facebook page, is an example of the social context in which the Movimiento Alterado is located. In his concerts in Mexico and the US, where fights among audience members are common, Alfredo Rios takes to the stage carrying bandoliers and *empecherado* (wearing a bulletproof vest), and then begins to sing a corrido like "Carteles Unidos" ("United Cartels"), (Table 5.1).

During his show, El Komander shares a bottle of wine with the audience and at a given moment he invites a young girl up on stage to dance while she takes off her skirt or blouse. Like many other musicians from the north, his life is not easy; they are often caught in the crossfire between rival criminal organizations. The risks are explored in an episode of the Mexican television show *Los héroes del norte* (Heroes of the North), which deals with the adventures of a group of norteño musicians. In this episode, the protagonists are abducted by a narco boss and taken to play for several days at a mansion in the mountains, any resemblance to the real world being entirely coincidental. Record producer Omar Valenzuela describes the danger thus: "They [the musicians] go back and forth, playing, and they know what they'll get and the risks they take" (González, 2014).

In spite of the enormously popular acceptance of narcocorridos in Mexico, the same is not true in Texas, where *Tejano* conjuntos usually do not perform them. As I was able to attest during a phase of fieldwork, en route through diverse music stores in the Rio Grande Valley, San Antonio, and Corpus Christi, there seems to be no market in Texas for this musical subgenre, although it is possible to acquire a few recordings related to the topic, performed by twitchy conjuntos norteños, in shops in Los Angeles and Chicago. This can be construed as a part of *Tejano* being rooted in a certain brand of conservatism particular to the Lone Star State, which does not prevail in larger cities with more mobile populations and more migration.

In a similar manner, the phenomenon of the narcocorrido has extended into Central and South America, as evident in Colombia, which since the 1980s has broadcast norteño music on radio stations in Barranquilla, Medellín, and Bogotá. The subsequent interest in narcocorridos allowed Los Tigres

Table 5.1 Cárteles unidos, available https://www.youtube.com/watch?v=aPhDF-6a9Zo

... que siga y que siga, a guerra sta (sic) abierta, todos a sus puestos ponganse pecheras, suban las granadas pa trozar con fuerza, armen sus equipos la matanza empieza ...	... it goes on and on, the war is open, everybody to your posts, put on your bulletproof vests, lob those grenades hard, put your teams together, the massacre begins ...

del Norte and Los Tucanes de Tijuana to make several tours throughout Colombia. Known there as *corridos prohibidos* (forbidden corridos), songs about the traffic of narcotics are sung mainly by those who engage in that activity and by the working class, and popularized by groups like Los Tigres del Sur (Tigers of the South), who use the same instruments and clothing worn by norteño artists.

In summary, norteña music has been promoted by and assisted in the inititation of the current process of norteñization of Mexico, and has created a cultural region, not only in the place where it arose, but wherever in the United States the Mexican diaspora and even other Latin Americans live. In recent years, some states in the United States have legalized marijuana for medicinal and recreational purposes, and in November 2020 the same happened in Mexico, so it is likely that the narcocorrido will cease to be significant and may disappear, because there will be few adventures to narrate. However, this will not kill the northern corrido, which will still have migratory experiences and social conflicts to narrate, plus a long list of other topics: love and heartbreak, joys and sorrows, feasts and drunkenness, the struggles of children and the elderly. It may be pertinent to ask whether there is any real difference between the *corridistas* who witnessed the Mexican Revolution and those who describe the recent war on drugs. It seems that, except for the access to technology and financial resources, the answer is probably no.

Conclusions

We have had the opportunity to trace the cultural traditions of the border, specifically, its perception from colonial times until the end of the twentieth century. We observed the way in which the various social actors used their music in local situations to set limits: "to erect boundaries, to maintain distinctions between us and them" (Stokes 1997, 6). As discussed in the second chapter, which examines the invention of the mariachi tradition, people in this region built new and different signs and networks of meaning that drifted away from national myths. We also note that the region and its inhabitants' feelings about it were defined through this musical expression, at the same time as they rejected the homogenizing national imaginary that the governments of Mexico and the United States tried to impose.

This book documents the marginalization—and even outright contempt—to which the cultural manifestations of our region of research have been subjected. After having been isolated for centuries, the states of Nuevo León and Texas can at present in no way be considered marginalized and both are important engines of the economies of their respective countries. Unfortunately, however, even today there still is much prejudice and ignorance about their representative art forms. On YouTube one can find numerous performances by the talented Dutch accordionist Dwayne Verheyden, among them a performance of the song "Camino Real de Colima" ("The Royal Road of Colima") from the 2010 *Tejano* Conjunto Festival in San Antonio. Among the comments right below the video is this most unfortunate one:

> The huapango is MEXICAN [*sic*]. The one interpreted on this occasion by the Dutch boys is called: Camino Real de Colima. Perhaps the stupid Texans know where Colima is? The evil Texans are so stupid and ignorant that they must

think Colima is in Texas or in some other part of their repulsive kingdom called United States. No my Texans donkeys, you are children of Mexico, although this hurts you, and types of music like NORTEÑA music is [sic] a tradition inherited from Mexico, [signed] your dad.

But here, we have discovered that, since colonial times, Texas has shared the culture of the northeastern states of Mexico, so the above statement only shows a lack of knowledge about regional interactions. It also seems that the loss of the original northern territories is still an open wound for many Mexicans when, in fact, before their separation only a handful of stoics wanted to live in Texas, and the most dangerous criminals were sent to California. Furthermore, in the mass media, and at middle- and upper-class gatherings and family reunions both in Mexico and in the United States, conjunto music is still rejected, still seen as simplistic, sentimental, and corny, unimaginative, and even vulgar. It is probable that marketing has brought about a certain homogenization in the music, but, as Richard Hoggart (1958, 131) points out, we cannot deny that "some of the melodies are lovely, and . . . can move a listener in much the same way as the arias from the lusher Italian operas. Like these operas, the songs have limited and bold emotional equipment."

For her part, Cathy Ragland (2009, 203) declares that the emergence of Texas-Mexican conjunto presents a "fascinating opportunity to study the construction of a separate regional society" whose identity is based on "selective local acculturation and assimilation." I, however, have argued that Tex-Mex conjunto was not a product of acculturation, which refers to the acquisition of a culture different from one's own (Ortiz 1987, 96). The inhabitants of South Texas who embraced the music of bajo sexto and accordion were descendants of or came, for the most part, from the northeastern states of Mexico, and therefore their musical expressions exteriorized the "intensification of nationalism" of which Américo Paredes spoke. Thus, although this migration of symbolic capital generated neo-cultural processes, it in no way "altered the musical culture of Mexican Texas," as suggested by Manuel Peña (1985, 107); rather, one could argue it enriched it. In any case, we can speak of an intertextuality between the norteño and *Tejano* conjunto, due to their fluid and constant interaction throughout history.

The recent regionalist pride that has emerged in the northeast of Mexico in defense of the origin of norteño conjunto bears no relation to the feelings generated in the early days. Then, a large number of soloists and groups from Nuevo León and Tamaulipas, like Pedro Ayala, Lolo Cavazos, Camilo Cantú, Narciso Martínez, Agapito Zúñiga, Los Donneños, Los Alegres de Terán, and subsequently, Los Relámpagos del Norte, Los Tigres del Norte, the duo Carlos y José, or Juan Villarreal, had to settle in the Rio Grande Valley, San Antonio, Austin, and even in the state of California, bound by the indifference, and even rejection, of their fellow countrymen. Others, such as Piporro, discussed earlier, or the group El Palomo y el Gorrión, tried their luck during the 1950s in Mexico City, where they were soon embraced by the public (Berrones 2013, 66–69).

It is likely that bajo sexto was probably an adaptation that players of stringed instruments made to accompany the resounding accordion in the American southwest and the northeast of Mexico, and not in Durango, Guanajuato, and Michoacán, where their acoustic traditions did not need such a powerful musical instrument. If we now see a bajo sexto in those latter states, it is simply because they play norteña music. It is important to note that this research has turned up similar findings to those obtained by American ethnomusicologist Thomas Turino (1984), who studied the social function of the *charango* in Peru. There, as in northeastern Mexico, important migrations took place from rural to growing urban areas in the early twentieth century due to, among other factors, the transition from an agrarian society to a capitalist economy. In Mexico, as in Peru, the adoption of a musical instrument from a marginalized culture, used both by peasants and then by urban workers, could be the result of the lack of identification of the people with the "official" or "national" culture that powerful groups sought to impose from the developed areas of the country. The bajo sexto, like the charango, is seen by some as a crude instrument of low social status, removed from European refinement. It is true that it is the heir of the Spanish guitar, but it is also true that its intense and bright sound separates it from the artistic model of the dominant culture. However, unlike the charango, and thanks to the current economic power of the inhabitants of northeastern Mexico and Mexican-Americans, the bajo sexto transmuted from peasant to urban instrument, from marginal to public, becoming ubiquitous in the mass media and crossing social classes. Affordable instruments are still built on production lines and by humble luthiers, but we can also find handmade bajo sextos, made with fine woods, that can cost thousands of dollars, played by artists who are part of a powerful transnational industry. The bajo sexto is essential to building social spaces symbolizing regional identity, which empower participants and oppose national myths.

From Monterrey to San Antonio, and from Reynosa to Corpus Christi, the music of traditional conjunto serves to do more than simply enliven a festive evening with dancing and humming. The performers are transformed into representatives of a collectivity, non-conformist and critical of the dominant culture. In a humble cantina or a huge stadium, the performance is a true rite, where there is social cohesion and where bonds of solidarity are forged; where a message of identity is sent to the interior and the exterior, although this does not necessarily imply an isolation from the rest of society, because at any given time, there are communicative vessels approaching other melodic traditions. The ritual of the performance of conjunto suppresses the label that unfolds in the concerts of classical music, where the audience is required to be silent, and they are seated below the musicians. On the contrary, and despite being at the center of the historical construction of their identity, at a conjunto fiesta the beer steins clink, people are hissing and screaming, singing and tapping along with the performers, developing a collective self. This way, they create a private social space, where the music helps to empower working people for a few hours. The crowds gather to listen to music and dance in each space endorsed by the conjunto not only to delight their ears; they are celebrating the cultural diversity of the region, especially in the state of Nuevo León, where norteña music is the only Mexican folkloric genre that has the accordion as a central instrument of its tradition.

Even today many people associate the conjunto solely with the working class, but as we have seen, its influence has spread to all social strata and even delved into other worldviews. If conjunto norteño began its days as the sound of the marginalized, eventually the values it represents were assimilated in unexpected places: the *waila*, the music of community dances of the Akimel and Tohono O'odham people (known as Papagos in Mexico), who live in southern Arizona and northern Sonora, decades ago exchanged the violin for the button accordion and bajo sexto (Titus, 2011), and also appropriated norteño cumbias and traditional songs of the Guadalupan cult. Similarly, in the streets and squares of the states of Jalisco and Zacatecas, one can hear groups of Wixáritari people (also known as Huicholes) who, with violin, guitar, and tololoche, interpret polkas composed by Antonio Tanguma. In addition, in rural communities of northern Mexico, the traditional accompaniment to the ancient dances called *matachines*—and also *matlachines*—has replaced the violin with the accordion.

Contemporary music could not be understood without the inspiration of the transnational *conjunto* and its musical instruments: the Avanzada Regia, an aesthetic movement that includes pop and rock groups like Plastilina Mosh or Kinky, lives somewhere between tradition and modernity. The young people approaching this movement do so often driven by a desire to be cosmopolitan and move away from the music style of their grandparents, but even the group Control Machete, when they rap, pick up narrative forms of corrido norteño (Corona, 2011). At the same time, the phenomenon of electronic music from Tijuana known as Nor-tec is based on conjunto and banda from Sinaloa, altering recordings made by street musicians or fragments of studio sessions, which contain chords strummed on a bajo sexto and improvisations with accordion (Madrid 2008, 66). Finally, the Mexican composer Gabriela Ortiz created her first opera by taking up the story of the corrido "Contrabando y traición" by Los Tigres del Norte, calling it "Camelia la Texana: Only the Truth."

Some people in Texas may deny the southern heritage of their conjunto, claiming that the American mainstream has a greater influence. In fact, a

Figure C.1 Conjunto performance in San Antonio, photo of the author.

small group of *Tejanos* considers it an insult to compare their conjunto to norteño conjunto. However, during the 2013 *Tejano* Conjunto Festival en San Antonio (Figure C.1), surrounded by the lovely aroma of traditional Tex-Mex food and enjoying some beer, it was impossible to overlook that couples sat when the conjunto on stage began to play a song influenced by country or rock, while the melodies composed by Mexicans José Alfredo Jiménez or Juan Gabriel thrilled the audience and filled the dance floor. Events of this nature seem to suggest that if Chicanos honor this music, it is precisely because of its connection with Mexico, thanks to the "romantic attachment to *lo mexicano,* especially *lo ranchero*" (Peña 1999b, 3). And yet, conjunto is authentic American roots music, such as blues, country, or folk.

South of the border, some municipal or state governments in Mexico have sponsored performances of famous norteño groups, but we are very far from the momentum and prestige enjoyed by *Tejano* conjunto, with its television programs (*The Johnny Canales Show* and *Acordeones de Tejas*, for example), museums (like the conjunto museum of San Benito in the Narciso Martínez Cultural Arts Center, the *Tejano* R.O.O.T.S. Hall of Fame and Museum in Alice, or the conjunto section of the Texas Music Museum of Austin), festivals (El Veterano Conjunto Festival, in Corpus Christi, or the *Tejano* Conjunto Festival in San Antonio), organizations (the South Texas Conjunto Association), and fellowships and awards (the National Heritage Awards). If Mexican mariachi has been selected as an Intangible Cultural Heritage of

Humanity by the Organization of the United Nations Educational, Scientific, and Cultural Organization (UNESCO), it is time for Mexico to recognize regional diversity and to ask the UN for a similar declaration for traditional conjunto norteño. After all, the music of accordion and bajo sexto will soon be 100 years old and is an unofficial reference for Mexican and Chicano identity anywhere in the world.

Today, forty million Mexicans and Mexican-Americans live in the United States. Mexican writer Carlos Monsiváis (2001, 201) said that each migrant brings with him or her a panoramic definition of Mexico and elaborates the idea of nation and the national while they are in the United States and each time they return. One may add that, within the migrant imaginary that invents and reinvents the nation each time such people come and go, both migrants and Mexican-Americans owe a debt to the music of conjunto, which occupies a vital place in the construction of meaning, reality, consciousness, and identity in two nations. It is undeniable that the socioeconomic realities of the Mexican-American and of Mexicans are very different, but the music of norteño and *Tejano* conjunto, as a living heritage and a cultural tradition shared by Mexico and the United States, are two sides of the same coin: a transnational group that builds bridges, not walls.

Glossary of Musical Terms

Chord: Two or more notes played simultaneously.
Blues: Musical genre originating in African American communities, born at the end of the nineteenth century in the southern United States. The main instruments are the guitar and the piano.
Cajun: Music representative of the state of Louisiana, having its roots in the ballads brought by the first French arriving in the American continent, settling in Canada and known as Acadians. In this musical genre, we find the accordion and violin as the main instruments.
Capo: An apparatus of wood, metal, or plastic that is placed on the fingerboard of the guitar and other similar instruments and that serves to change the tonality.
Corrido: A musical form from Mexican popular culture, probably derived from the Spanish romance, characterized by its storytelling nature.
Couple dances (or partner dances): Basically, a dance with some choreography in which a couple, rather than a group, participates. An example of a couple dance is the polka.
Group Dance: Dance that has choreography, involving several people dancing in a circular fashion or forming a square, such as the *quadrille*.
Glissando: Musical ornamentation that moves quickly from a high to a low note, or vice versa, while including the intermediate notes. Some traditional musicians in the region researched for this text call this "columpiar" (swing) or "cucharear" (with the voice).
Legato: Connected notes played smoothly, without interruption.
Marcato: A note or chord to be played with greater force than the surrounding passages.
Mazurka: Polish folk dance, very popular throughout the world during the nineteenth century; usually rapid and in three-quarter time.

Minuet: Social dance of French origin, in three-quarter time.
Organology: Study of musical instruments and their classification.
Score: Sheets of paper on which to write music.
Plectrum (also called pick): A small device, usually made of plastic, which is held in the strumming hand to play the strings of the guitar and other stringed instruments.
Ranchera (music or song): Traditional musical genre of Mexico, which had its first manifestations at the end of the nineteenth century. The ranchera takes advantage of polka or waltz, and even the bolero.
Syncopation: In music, stressing the weak beat in a measure to temporarily change the meter.
Social dances: A category of various dance forms that includes both group and couple dances, and in which socialization is the main objective of the dance.
Tambora de rancho: Medium to large drum with a very powerful sound, made of wood and goatskin, popular since colonial times in the rural areas of Nuevo León, Tamaulipas, and Texas.
Tarola: Drum, also called "caja" (box) or "redoblante" (snare drum).
Tejano (or *Tejano* music, also Tex-Mex music, musical genre): This is the name of a wide variety of folk and popular music created by Mexican-American communities in Texas, usually sung in Spanish. In many instances, *Tejano* music is nothing other than *Tejano* conjunto played with electric instruments.
Tempo: The time signature in which one plays a particular piece of music.
Timbre: Also called tonal color or tonal quality, this refers to the characteristics of a sound that make it different from another, as, for example, the inequality that exists between a saxophone and a piano when each plays the same note with the same force; in such a case, the timbre of each instrument is different.
Tololoche: a four-stringed musical instrument from northern Mexico and the southern United States, a bit smaller than the double bass, played without a bow.
Vals Bajito: Also known as redowa in the southern United States and northern México.
Virtuoso: One who has an outstanding gift or ability; here, used to refer to musicians.
Zydeco: A very popular musical form from the state of Louisiana and southeast Texas, emerged from Creole music. It is usually played with piano, accordion, violin, and guitar.

A Selection of Recorded Music

Alegres de Terán, Los. *Los Alegres de Terán, 1947–2006, Éxitos inmortales*. Sigala Records: Hesperia, 2006.
———. *Los Alegres de Terán: Puros éxitos*. Discos Continental: Mexico, n.d.
Almaguer, Chuco. *Chuko Almaguer y su Carta Brava (norteñas), Éxitos, Grupo Brindis (chicanas)*. Fonodíaz Records: Santa Paula/San Juan de los Lagos, 1992.
Ayala. Ramón. *La colección Ramón Ayala Vol. 2*. GC Musical: Mexico, 2005.
———. *Ramón Ayala y sus Bravos del Norte: Puras buenas con el rey del acordeón*. Freddie Records, Corpus Christi, 2012.
———. *Grandes éxitos de Ramón Ayala*, Vol. 1. Emi Music: Mexico, n.d.
-Aztlán, Conjunto. *Conjunto Aztlán*. Blue Cat Studio: San Antonio, 1998.
Bernal, Conjunto. *16 Early Tejano Classics*. Arhoolie Records: El Cerrito, 1997.
———. *25 coritos con la familia Bernal*. Bernal Christian Recordings: McAllen, n.d.
Bernal, Paulino. *Paulino Bernal, El maestro del acordeón y sus polkas*. Urbana Records: Houston, 2008.
Broncos de Reynosa, Los. *Los Broncos de Reynosa, 75 años Peerless*. Warner Music: Mexico, 2008.
De la Rosa, Tony. *Tony De la Rosa, 35 golden hits*. Hacienda Records: Corpus Christi, 2005.
Donneños, Los. *Los Donneños, Mario y Ramiro. 30 éxitos: Sus inicios*. Discos Rodej: Monterrey, 2004.
———. *Los Donneños, Mario Montes y Ramiro Cavazos, Grabaciones originales, Historic First Recordings, 1950–1954*. Arhoolie Records: El Cerrito, 2006.
———. *Los Donneños de Ramiro Cavazos y Beto Espinosa, Tu perro guardián*. Discos RyN: McAllen/Monterrey, 2011.
Dueto Carta Blanca. *Polkas y redovas que dan vibra*. Discos Amor: Mexico, 2008.
Dueto Río Bravo. *Dueto Río Bravo. Mexicanísimo*. Sony Music Latin: Coconut Grove, 2013.
Escobar, Linda. *Linda Escobar, Featuring Special Guests: Eligio Escobar, Los Dos Gilbertos and Cielo Band*. Hacienda Records: Corpus Christi, 2005.

Flores de Durango, Los. *Los Flores de Durango: Puros corridos bravos*. AJR Discos: Oak Hills, 2000.
González, Eulalio. *Colección de oro "El Piporro."* Discos Musart: Mexico, 2002.
Gorriones del Topo Chico, Los. *Los Gorriones del Topo Chico: Mis primeros 20 éxitos*. Libertad Musical: Mexico, 2008.
Jiménez, Leonardo. *Flaco Jiménez, Ay te dejo en San Antonio y más!* Arhoolie Records: El Cerrito, 1990.
Jordan, Steve. *Steve Jordan, 25 Golden Hits*. Hacienda Records: Corpus Christi, 2005.
Luis y Félix. *Los dos amigos: Luis y Félix, 15 corridos con tololoche, bajo y acordeón*. Discos RyN/Rodej: Monterrey, 2011.
Luis y Julián. *Luis y Julián, 21 golden disc, Vol. 2*. De oro: Mexico, 2008.
———. *Homenaje a Luis Garza*. Universal Music Group: Mexico, 2010.
Luera, Lorenzo, y su Conjunto. *Soy texano*, de Oscar Argumedo. 45 rpm, Gabe Records Inc.: Fort Worth, n.d.
Martínez, Narciso. *Narciso Martínez: Father of the Texas–Mexican conjunto*. Arhoolie Records: El Cerrito, 1993.
Maya y Cantú. *Maya y Cantú, El primer conjunto norteño famoso, 1946–1949*. Arhoolie Records: El Cerrito, 1999.
Miguel y Miguel. *Corridos ca%?@&... es de Sinaloa*. Platino Records: Northridge, 2010.
Montañeses del Álamo, Los. *Primeras grabaciones, 1940–1950, Los Montañeses del Álamo*. Arhoolie Records: El Cerrito, 2002.
———. *Los Montañeses del Álamo, Puras polkas*. Discos Amor: Mexico, 2008.
Mora. Lalo. *Lalo Mora: También de los ranchos bajan*. DISA: Mexico, 2004.
La Norteña y la Texana, La. *La Norteña y la Texana, A puro pico*. Discos RyN: McAllen, n.d.
Norteños de China, Los. *Los Norteños de China de José Ángel Reyes*. Discos RyN: McAllen, n.d.
El Palomo y el Gorrión, El. *15 grandes éxitos: El Palomo y el Gorrión*. Discos Amor: Mexico, 2008.
Pedraza, Andrés. *Andrés Pedraza, El azote de Hualahuises*. Discos RyN: Monterrey, 2003.
Rancheros del Norte, Los. *Los Rancheros del Norte, de Eugenio Abrego*. Discos RyN: Monterrey, n.d.
Relámpagos del Norte, Los. *Los Relámpagos del Norte, Nuestros primeros 20 éxitos*. Discos Amor: Mexico, 2008.
Reyes. José. A. *José Ángel Reyes: Tampico Hermoso, polkas, huapangos y chotis*. Discos RyN/Rodej: Monterrey, 2011.
Saldívar, Mingo. *Mingo Saldívar, Rueda de Fuego, 20 super hits*. Hacienda Records: Corpus Christi, 1995.
Salvajes de la Frontera, Los. *Los Salvajes de la Frontera: 20 éxitos, Vol. 1*. Golden Disc: Mexico, 2011.
Sánchez, Chalino. *Chalino Sánchez, mis mejores corridos*. Musart: Mexico, 2004.
Tanguma Jr., Antonio. *Raíces de Nuevo León*. CONARTE: Mexico, 2011.

Tigres del Norte, Los. *Jefe de jefes*. Fonovisa: Mexico, 1997.
Troqueros, Los. *Los Troqueros, Venganza y tragedias*. Discos Centenario Musical: Mexico, 2004.
Tucanes de Tijuana Los. *Corridos, La más completa colección*. Fonovisa: Mexico, 2010.
Various. *Texas–Czech, Bohemian & Moravian Bands, Historic recordings 1929–1959*. Arhoolie Records: El Cerrito, 1993.
Various. *Mexican-American Border Music, Pioneer Recording Artists, 1928–1958*. Arhoolie Records: El Cerrito, 1994.
Various. *Norteño & Tejano Accordion Pioneers, 1929–1939*. Arhoolie Records: El Cerrito, 1995.
Various. *The Soulful Women Duets of South Texas*. Arhoolie Records: El Cerrito, 2000.
Various. *San Antonio's Conjuntos in the 1950's*. Arhoolie Records: El Cerrito, 2009.
Vela, Rubén. *Rubén Vela, El coco rayado power mix y mucho más*. Hacienda Records: Corpus Christi, 1996.
Villarreal, Frutty. *Polkas tejanas con Frutty Villarreal y Los Mavericks*. Discos Rodej: Monterrey, 2003.
Villarreal, Nick. *Nick Villarreal: La Pass It Around*. Discos Joey: San Antonio, 2010.

A Selection of Norteño/Tejano Performers

Alegres de Terán, Los: Norteño duet formed in the late 1940s by Tomás Ortiz and Eugenio Abrego.

Ayala, Ramón (born Ramón Covarrubias): Started his career in the early 1960s as accordion player and singer with *Los Relámpagos del Norte*, and later with his own group: *Los Bravos del Norte*.

Bernal, Paulino: *Tejano* accordion player and leader of Conjunto Bernal.

Broncos de Reynosa, Los: Norteño conjunto from the state of Durango, started in the late 1950s by composer Paulino Vargas.

De la Rosa, Tony: Master accordion player from Sarita, Texas.

Cadetes de Linares, Los: Norteño group from Linares, Nuevo León, formed in 1974.

Donneños, Los: Established in 1948 in the town of Donna, Texas, by accordionist Mario Montes and bajo sexto player Ramiro Cavazos, both natives of Nuevo León.

Dos Gilbertos, Los (known as *Los Dos Gs*): Founded in 1965, in Edinburg, Texas, by accordion player Gilberto García and Gilberto López.

Dueto Río Bravo: Formed by Eva Gurrola Castellanos and María de la Luz Pulgarín Gurrola, from Allende, Coahuila.

González, Eulalio, "Piporro": Norteño singer and composer born in 1921.

Grupo Pesado: Norteño group formed in Monterrey in 1993.

Humildes, Los: Formed in 1972 in California, with members from Sinaloa and Michoacán.

Jiménez, Santiago: Accordionist born in San Antonio, Texas, in 1913. His sons became eminent accordion players too: Leonardo "el Flaco" (born in 1939) and Santiago Jr. (1944).

Jordan, Steve, "El Parche": *Tejano* accordion player born in 1939, in Elsa, Texas.

Luis y Julián: Brothers Luis y Julián Garza, from Nuevo León, began to sing corridos in the early 1970s.

Martínez, Narciso: Father of *Tejano* conjunto, born in Reynosa, México.

Maya y Cantú: Norteño duet, they made their first recording in 1946.

Montañeses del Álamo, Los: Traditional group from Nuevo León.

El Palomo y el Gorrión, El: Founded by brothers Miguel and Cirilo Luna, from Nuevo León.

Saldívar, Mingo: *Tejano* accordion player and composer, from Marion, Texas, born in 1936.

Tam y Tex, Los: Formed in 1979 with musicians from Tamaulipas and Texas.

Tigres del Norte, Los: Norteño group from Sinaloa, created in 1968.

Tremendos Gavilanes, Los: Norteño conjunto from Monterrey, established in 1962.

Tucanes de Tijuana, Los: Norteño band with members from Baja California, Sinaloa, Guanajuato, and Zacatecas.

Interviews

Anonymous. Music producer, Corpus Christi, Texas, July 12, 2011.
Anonymous. *Tejano* composer and accordion player, Selma, Texas, July 14, 2011.
Cavazos Gutiérrez, Ramiro. Composer and bajo sexto player, founder of Los Donneños, owner of Ryn records, McAllen, Texas, July 11 and December 21, 2011, and July 24, 2013.
Chamorro Escalante, Arturo. Ethnomusicologist affiliated with the University of Guadalajara, April 2, 2014.
Cruz, Eloy. Player of historical instruments and instructor at the National School of Music of the National Autonomous University of Mexico (UNAM), Mexico City, May 9, 2012, and April 10, 2014.
Escobar, Linda. Singer born in Alice, San Antonio, Texas, May 18, 2013.
García, Abel. Manufacturer of musical instruments from Paracho, Michoacán, Zacatecas, April 20, 2014.
Hernández Cándido, Frumencio. Manufacturer of traditional musical instruments, Texquitote, Municipality of Matlapa, San Luis Potosí, July 25, 2007.
Juárez Frías, Ernesto. Composer and performer of corridos, Zacatecas, May 23, 2012.
Martínez, Reynaldo, "El Gallero." Composer of corridos, McAllen, Texas, July 24, 2013.
Tejeda, Juan. *Tejano* accordionist, San Antonio, Texas, July 15, 2011.
Verheyden, Dwayne. Dutch accordionist, San Antonio, Texas, May 17, 2013.

Newspapers

El Aldeano, 1908.
El Bejareño, 1855–1856.
El Correo, 1858.
El Cronista, 1888.
El Demócrata, 1915.
El Economista, 2009–2013.
El Imparcial de Texas, 1918.
El Lampacense, 1891–1892.
El Mañana, 2012.
El Porvenir, 1922–1950
El Progresista, 1903.
El Ranchero, 1856.
El Regidor, 1904–1915.
El Siglo Diez y Nueve, 1844–1889
El Universal, 2010–2013.
Época, 1923.
La Gaceta de Monterrey, 1864–1866.
La Jornada, 2007–2013.
La Libertad, 1902.
La Prensa, 1919–1925.
La Revista del Norte, 1887–1888.
Milenio, 2008–2013.
Periódico Oficial del Estado de Nuevo León, 1925–1929.
Revista científica y literaria, 1845.
The Monterey News, 1903–1907.

Archives

City Archive of Monterrey.
Dolph Briscoe Center for American History, the University of Texas at Austin.
General Archive of the state of Nuevo León.
Harry Ransom Center, the University of Texas at Austin.
Historical Archive of the State of Zacatecas.
Institute of Texan Cultures, San Antonio.
Mauricio Magdaleno Library, Zacatecas.
National Newspapers Archive of México, México City.
San Antonio Central Library.
Texas Music Museum, Austin.

Bibliography

Aboites Aguilar, Luis. "Poblamiento y estado en el norte de México, 1830-1835." In *Indio, nación y comunidad en el México del siglo XIX*, edited by Antonio Escobar Ohmstede, 303–313. México: Centro de Estudios Mexicanos y Centroamericanos/CIESAS, 1993.

Adams, John A. *Conflict and Commerce on the Rio Grande: Laredo, 1755-1955*. College Station: Texas A&M University Press, 2008.

Aguilar Cruz, Jorge Luis. "¡Vámonos al baile! Corridos, regionalism & cultural symbolism: An expressive narrative approach to Los Tigres del Norte." Master's thesis, The University of Texas at El Paso, 2012.

Alanís Tamez, Juan. *Los Montañeses del Álamo, 1938-1994*. Monterrey: UANL, 1994.

———. *Un barrio lleno de música, Historia musical de Santiago, Nuevo León*. Monterrey: Consejo para la Cultura de Nuevo León, 1998.

Alarcón, Rafael. "El proceso de norteñización: impacto de la migración internacional en Chavinda, Michoacán." *Movimientos de población en el Occidente de México*, edited by Thomas Calvo and Gustavo López, 337–357. México: CEMCA/El Colegio de Michoacán, 1988.

Alcocer, fray José Antonio. *Bosquejo de la historia del Colegio de Nuestra Señora de Guadalupe de Zacatecas y sus misiones, año de 1788*. Mexico: Editorial Porrúa, 1958.

Alessio Robles, Vito. *Coahuila y Texas en la época colonial*. México: Editorial Porrúa, 1978.

Amastae, Jon. "Lenguaje e identidad en comunidades inmigrantes de los Estados Unidos." In *Población, frontera, cultura y desarrollo: una aproximación desde la historia*, edited by José F. Román Gutiérrez and Leticia I. del Río Hernández, 293–301. México: UAZ-IZC, 2010.

Amescua, Cristina. "Análisis regional de las proclamaciones de Obras Maestras del Patrimonio Oral e Inmaterial de la Humanidad." In *Compartir el patrimonio cultural inmaterial: Narrativas y representaciones*, edited by Lourdes Arizpe, 103–127. México: CONACULTA-UNAM, 2011.

Anderson, Benedict. *Imagined Communities, Reflections on the Origin and Spread of Nationalism.* London: Verso, 2006.
Anteo, Mario. *Texas y Nuevo León, 1821-1911.* Monterrey: UANL, 2010.
Arias Jirazek, Rita. *Mexican Chicago.* Chicago: Arcadia Publishing, 2001.
Astorga, Luis. "Los corridos de traficantes de drogas en México y Colombia." Lecture presented at the 1997 Meeting of the Latin American Studies Association in Guadalajara, México. Accessed February 24, 2014. http://136.142.158.105/LASA97/astorga.pdf.
Attali, Jacques. *Ruidos: ensayo sobre la economía política de la música.* México: Siglo XXI Editores, 1995.
Ayala Duarte, Alfonso. *Breve historia gráfica de la música en Monterrey.* Monterrey: CONARTE/CONACULTA, 2004.
———. *Desde el Cerro de la Silla, origen y consolidación del conjunto norteño en Monterrey.* Monterrey: Herca, 2000.
Bartók, Béla. *Escritos sobre música popular.* México: Siglo XIX Editores, 1997.
Berger, Peter, and Thomas Luckman. *La construcción social de la realidad.* España: Amorrortu Editores, 1995.
Berrones, Guillermo. *Ingratos ojos míos, Miguel Luna y la historia de El Palomo y El Gorrión.* Monterrey: UANL, 2013.
———. "Los montañeses del Álamo." In *Primeras grabaciones, 1940-1950, Los Montañeses del Álamo,* Arhoolie Records, 2002.
Betts, Raymond, F. *A History of Popular Culture: More of Everything, Faster and Brighter.* New York: Routledge, 2004.
Beyer, Robert T. *Sounds of our Times: Two hundred Years of Acoustics.* New York: Springer-Verlag, 1999.
Blanco Arboleda, Darío. "La cumbia como matriz sonora de Latinoamérica: Los colombias de Monterrey-México (1960-2008), Interculturalidad, identidad, espacio y cuerpo." PhD diss., El Colegio de México, 2008.
Bourdieu, Pierre. *La distinción, criterio y bases sociales del gusto.* México: Taurus, 2002.
Broyles-González, Yolanda. *Lydia Mendoza's Life in Music/La historia de Lydia Mendoza.* New York: Oxford University Press, 2001.
Buchanan, Patrick J. *State of Emergency: The Third World Invasion and Conquest of America.* New York: St. Martin's Press, 2007.
Burke, Peter. "El 'pueblo' y su 'cultura.'" In *La nueva historia cultural: La influencia del postestructuralismo y el auge de la interdisciplinariedad,* edited by Ignacio Olábarri and Francisco Javier Caspistegui, 191–216. Madrid: Ed. Complutense, 1996.
———. *Popular Culture in Early Modern Europe.* Farnham: Ashgate Publishing, 2009.
Burr, Ramiro. *The Billboard Guide to Tejano and Regional Mexican Music.* New York: Billboard Books, 1999.
———. "Women in Conjunto Music." In *Puro Conjunto, an Album in Words & Pictures,* edited by Juan Tejeda and Avelardo Valdez, 85–95. Austin: University of Texas Press, 2001.

Calderwood, Michael, and Gabriel Breña. *México: Una Visión de Altura, Un Recorrido Aéreo del Pasado al Presente.* La Jolla: Alti Publishing, 1992.

Campos, Rubén M. *El folklore musical de las ciudades, Investigación acerca de la música mexicana para bailar y cantar.* México: SEP, 1930.

———. *El folklore y la música mexicana, Investigación acerca de la cultura musical de México (1525-1925).* México: SEP, 1928.

Cano Jr., Ray. "De la Rosa, Tony." In *The Handbook of Texas Music second edition,* edited by Laurie E. Jasinski, 160–161. Denton: Texas State Historical Association, 2012.

Canetti, Elías. *Masa y poder,* Barcelona: Muchnik, 1981.

Cárdenas, Lázaro. *Ideario político.* México: Ediciones ERA, 2000.

Carrizosa, Antonio. *La onda grupera: Historia del movimiento grupero.* México: Edamex, 1997.

Castellanos, Pablo. *El nacionalismo musical en México.* México: Seminario de Cultura Mexicana, 1959.

Cavazos Garza, Israel, and Cesar Morado Macías. *Fábrica de la frontera. Monterrey, capital de Nuevo León (1596-2005).* Monterrey: Ayuntamiento de Monterrey, 2006.

———, and Isabel Ortega Ridaura. *Nuevo León, historia breve.* México: FCE, 2010.

Cernusak, Gracian, Andrew Lamb and John Tyrrell. "Polka." In *New Grove Dictionary of Music and Musicians,* vol. 20, edited by Stanley Sadie, 34–36. London: Macmillan, 1980.

Cerutti, Mario. *Burguesía y capitalismo en Monterrey, 1850-1910.* Monterrey: Fondo Editorial de Nuevo León-UANL, 2006.

———. *Propietarios, empresarios y empresa en el norte de México: Monterrey: de 1848 a la globalización.* México: Siglo XXI Editores, 2000.

Chartier, Roger. *El presente del pasado: escritura de la historia, historia de lo escrito.* México: Universidad Iberoamericana, 2005.

Chavez, Leo R. *The Latino Threat: Constructing Immigrants, Citizens, and the Nation.* Stanford: Stanford University Press, 2013.

Chew Sánchez, Martha. *Corridos in Migrant Memory.* Albuquerque: The University of New Mexico Press, 2006.

Contreras, Juan Guillermo. "Bajos de espiga." In *Diccionario de la música española e hispanoamericana,* vol. 2, edited by Emilio Casares Rodicio, 67–69. Madrid: Sociedad General de Autores y Editores, 1999.

Contreras, Juan Vicente. "Carlos Vives and Colombian Vallenato Music." In *Musical Cultures of Latin America: Global Effects, Past and Present,* edited by Steven Loza, 337–345. Los Angeles: UCLA, 2003.

Corona, Ignacio. "*La Avanzada Regia*: Monterrey's Alternative Music Scene and the aesthetics of transnationalism." In *Transnational encounters, Music and Performance at the U.S.-Mexico Border,* edited by Alejandro L. Madrid, 252–284. New York: Oxford University Press, 2011.

Cruz, Eloy. *La casa de los once muertos, historia y repertorio de la guitarra.* México: UNAM, 1993.

Cuéllar, José. B. "El Saxofón in Texano and Norteño Music." In *Puro Conjunto, an Album in Words & Pictures*, edited by Juan Tejeda and Avelardo Valdez, 135–154. Austin: University of Texas Press, 2001.

D'Amico, Leonardo. "Cumbia Music in Colombia: Origins, Transformations, and Evolution of a Coastal Music Genre." In *Cumbia! Scenes of a Migrant Latin American Music Genre*, edited by Héctor Fernández L'Hoeste and Pablo Vila, 29–48. Durham: Duke University Press, 2013.

De la Garza, María Luisa. *Ni aquí ni allá, el emigrante en los corridos y en otras canciones populares*. Cádiz: Ayuntamiento de Cádiz, 2005.

De la Teja, Jesús F. *San Antonio de Béxar: A Community on New Spain's Northern Frontier*. Albuquerque: The University of New Mexico Press, 1995.

De León, Arnoldo. *They Called them Greasers, Anglo Attitudes Toward Mexicans in Texas, 1821-1900*. Austin: University of Texas Press, 1983.

Del Hoyo, Eugenio. *Historia del Nuevo Reino de León (1577-1723)*. Monterrey: Fondo editorial, Tecnológico de Monterrey, 2005.

Díaz-Santana Garza, Luis. *Tradición musical en Zacatecas (1850-1930), Una historia sociocultural*. Zacatecas: IZC-FECAZ, 2009.

Dickson, Jean. "Carlos Curti: ¿compositor, director, rey del xilófono, camaleón? ¿Quién fue Carlos Curti?" *Heterofonía, Revista De Investigación Musical* XLI, no. 140 (Enero-junio 2009): 61–75.

Dorsey, Margaret E., and Miguel Díaz-Barriga. "Patriotic Citizenship, the Border Wall, and the "El Veterano" Conjunto Festival." In *Transnational Encounters, Music and Performance at the U.S.-Mexico Border*, edited by Alejandro L. Madrid, 207–227. New York: Oxford University Press, 2011.

Duggan, Anne Schley, Jeanette Schlottmann and Abbie Rutledge. *Folk Dances of the United States and Mexico*. New York: A. S. Barnes & Company, 1948.

Durand, Jorge. "Origen y destino de una migración centenaria." In *El país transnacional: migración y cambio social a través de la frontera*, edited by Marina Ariza and Alejandro Portes, 55–81. México: UNAM, 2007.

Durand, Nayeli. "Narcocorridos, 40 años de espectáculo y controversia." *El universal*, May 30, 2011.

Edberg, Mark C. *El Narcotraficante: Narcocorridos & the Construction of a Cultural Persona on the U.S.-Mexico Border*. Austin: The University of Texas Press, 2004.

———. "Narcocorridos: Narratives of a Cultural Persona and Power on the Border." In *Transnational encounters, Music and Performance at the U.S.-Mexico Border*, edited by Alejandro L. Madrid, 67–82. New York: Oxford University Press, 2011.

Eisenhower, John S. D. *So Far from God: The U.S. War with Mexico, 1846-1848*. Norman: University of Oklahoma Press, 2000.

Elbein, Saul. "Get your Norteño out of my Conjunto." *Texas observer*, May 20, 2011. http://www.texasobserver.org/dateline/get-your-norteño-out-of-my-conjunto.

Esquer, Ismael. "La música de clarinete y tambora de San Carlos, Tamaulipas." In *A tambora batiente*, edited by Carlos Jesús Gómez Flores, 19–22. Monterrey: Dirección General de Culturas Populares, 1997.

Esparza Sánchez, Cuauhtémoc. *El corrido zacatecano*. México: INAH, 1976.

Fehrenbach, T. R. *Lone star, a History of Texas and the Texans.* Boston: Da Capo Press, 2000.

Felis de Espinosa, fray Isidro. *El peregrino septentrional atlante: Delineado en la exemplarissima vida del venerable padre F. Antonio Margil de Jesús.* México: Joseph Bernardo de Hogal, 1737.

Felix, David. *America Rising: Power and Political Economy in the First Nation.* Piscataway: Transaction Publishers, 2009.

Florescano, Enrique, and Margarita Menegus. "La época de las reformas borbónicas y el crecimiento económico (1750-1808)." In *Historia General de México versión 2000*, 363–430. México: Colmex, 2002.

Fowler Jr., Gene, and Bill Crawford. *Border Radio: Quacks, Yodelers, Pitchmen, Psychics, and other Amazing Broadcasters of the American Airwaves.* Austin: University of Texas Press, 2002.

Frith, Simon. *Performing Rites, on the Value of Popular Music.* Cambridge: Harvard University Press, 1996.

———. "Towards an Aesthetic of Popular Music." In *Music and Society: The Politics of Composition, Performance, and Reception*, edited by Richard Leppert and Susan McClary, 133–149. Cambridge: Cambridge University Press, 1987.

Galindo, Miguel. *Historia de la música mexicana, desde sus orígenes hasta la creación del Himno Nacional.* Colima: Tip. de "El Dragón," 1933.

García Flores, Raúl. "De tambora y clarinete." In *A tambora batiente*, edited by Carlos Jesús Gómez Flores, 23–26. Monterrey: Dirección General de Culturas Populares, 1997.

———. "La música tradicional del noreste de México." In *El noreste: reflexiones*, edited by Isabel Ortega Ridaura, 233–239. Monterrey: Fondo Editorial de Nuevo León, 2006.

Garizurieta, Cesar. "Catarsis del mexicano." In *El hijo pródigo, antología*, edited by Francisco Caudet, 164–188. México: Siglo XXI, 1979.

Garza Guajardo, Celso. *Tanguma: Una tradición de más de un siglo de tres generaciones.* Monterrey: UANL, 2015.

Garza Gutiérrez, Luis Martín. *Raíces de la música regional de Nuevo León.* Monterrey: Consejo para la Cultura y las Artes de Nuevo León, 2006.

Garza Sada, Roberto. *Ensayos sobre la historia de una industria.* Monterrey: Litográfica Monterrey, 1981.

Garza Torres, Luis Antonio. *Los Rancheritos del Topo Chico de Catarino Leos Rodríguez, vida y obra.* Monterrey: UANL, 2013.

Geertz, Clifford. *La interpretación de las culturas.* Barcelona: Editorial Gedisa, 2001.

Gerhard, Peter. *La frontera norte de la Nueva España.* México: UNAM, 1996.

Giménez, Gilberto. "La frontera norte como representación y referente cultural en México." *Cultura y representaciones sociales* 2, no. 3 (Septiembre 2007): 28–31.

Gish, Erica, and Laurie E. Jasinski. "Goggan, Thomas." In *The Handbook of Texas Music second edition*, edited by Laurie E. Jasinski, 245–246. Denton: Texas State Historical Association, 2012.

Goodwyn, Wade. "Texas Gets the Accordion Bug and Never Looks Back." *Npr music*, June 3, 2011. http://www.npr.org/2011/06/03/136891051/texas-gets-the-accordion-bug-and-never-looks-back.
González, Verónica. "Templarios inspiran corridos del 'Movimiento Alterado.'" *Milenio*. March 13, 2014.
González, Víctor. "El renacimiento de una ciudad. Remembranzas de un pueblo 'calero'; La industria del algodón: desde la introducción de la electricidad y la red de agua potable." *El Mañana*, October 14, 2012.
González Ramírez, Eulalio. *Autobiogr . . . ajúa! Y anecdo . . . taconario*. México: Editorial Diana, 1999.
Govenar, Alan. *Everyday Music*. College Station: Texas A&M University Press, 2012.
Greb, Gordon, and Mike Adams. *Charles Herrold, Inventor of Radio Broadcasting*. Jefferson: McFarland Publishers, 2003.
Grebler, Leo, Joan W. Moore and Ralph C. Guzman. *The Mexican-American People: The Nation's Second Largest Minority*. New York: Free Press, 1970.
Gronow, Pekka and IlpoSaunio. *An International History of the Recording Industry*. London: Biddles Ltd., 1998.
Guidicelli, Christophe. "¿'Naciones' de enemigos? La identificación de los indios rebeldes en la Nueva Vizcaya (siglo XVII)." In *El gran norte mexicano: indios, misioneros y pobladores entre el mito y la historia*, edited by Salvador Bernabé Albert, 27–57. Madrid: CSIC, 2009.
Gurza, Agustín, Jonathan Clark and Chris Strachwitz. *The Arhoolie Foundation's Strachwitz Frontera Collection of Mexican and Mexican American Recordings*. Los Angeles: UCLA Chicano Studies Research Center Press, 2012.
Halliday, M. A. K. *El lenguaje como semiótica social, La interpretación social del lenguaje y del significado*. Bogotá: FCE, 1998.
Hartman, Gary. *History of Texas Music*. College Station: Texas A&M University Press, 2008.
Hernández, José Ángel. *Mexican American Colonization During the Nineteenth Century, A History of the U.S.-México Borderlands*. New York: Cambridge University Press, 2012.
Hernández Azuara, Cesar. *Huapango. El son huasteco y sus instrumentos en los siglos XIX y XX*. México: CIESAS-COLSAN-Programa de Desarrollo Cultural de la Huasteca, 2003.
Herrera-Sobek, María. *Chicano Folklore: A Handbook*. Westport: Greenwood Publishing Group, 2006.
Hewitt, Paul. G. *Física conceptual*. México: Pearson Educación, 2004.
Hickinbotham, Gary. S. "Recording Industry." In *The Handbook of Texas Music second edition*, edited by Laurie E. Jasinski, 497–507. Denton: Texas State Historical Association, 2012.
Hobsbawm, Eric. *Bandidos*. Barcelona: Crítica, 2003.
———, and Terence Ranger. *The Invention of Tradition*. Cambridge: Cambridge University Press, 2012.

Hoggart, Richard. *The Uses of Literacy, Aspects of Working-class Life with Special Reference to Publications and Entertainments*. Frome and London: Pelican Books, 1958.

Hutchinson, Sydney. "Becoming the Tíguera: The Female Accordionist in Dominican Merengue." *The World of Music* 50, no. 3 (2008): 37–56.

Jacobson, Marion. *Squeeze this! A Cultural History of the Accordion in America*. Champaign: University of Illinois Press, 2012.

Jáuregui, Jesús. *El mariachi. Símbolo musical de México*. México: INAH-CONACULTA-Santillana Ediciones Generales, 2007.

———. *El son mariachero de La Negra, de gusto regional independentista a aire nacional contemporáneo*. México: INAH/CONACULTA, 2012.

Jiménez Núñez, Alfredo. "El bravo en la mente y la voz del ilustrado: la frontera norte de Nueva España (s XVIII)." In *El gran norte mexicano: indios, misioneros y pobladores entre el mito y la historia*, edited by Salvador Bernabé Albert, 363–397. Madrid: CSIC, 2009.

———. *El gran norte de México: una frontera imperial en la Nueva España (1540-1820)*. Madrid: Editorial Tébar, 2006.

Johnson, Eric D. "Crossover Narratives: Intersections of Race, Genre, and Authenticity in Unpopular Popular Music." PhD diss., University of Iowa, 2012.

Katz, Mark. *Capturing Sound: How Technology has Changed Music*. Berkeley and Los Angeles: University of California Press, 2010.

———. "Sound Recording. Introduction" In *Music, Sound, and Technology in America: A Documentary History of Early Phonograph, Cinema, and Radio*, edited by Timothy D. Taylor, Mark Katz and Tony Grajeda, 11–28. Durham: Duke University Press, 2012.

Kirchhoff, Paul. "Los recolectores-cazadores del norte de México." In *El norte de México y el sur de los Estados Unidos*, edited by Sociedad Mexicana de Antropología, 133–144. México: Editorial Stylo, 1943.

Klooster, John W. *Icons of Invention: The Makers of the Modern World from Gutenberg to Gates*. Santa Barbara: ABC-CLIO, 2009.

Kotraba, Joseph A., and Phillip Vannini. *Understanding Society Through Popular Music*. New York: Routledge, 2009.

La Rue, Hélène. "Music, Literature and Etiquette: Musical Instruments and Social Identity from Castiglione to Austen." In *Ethnicity, Identity and Music, the Musical Construction of Place*, edited by Martin Stokes, 189–205. New York: Berg Publishers, 1997.

Lara, Eric. "'Salieron de San Isidro . . .' El corrido, el narcocorrido y tres de sus categorías de análisis: El hombre, la mujer y el soplón. Un acercamiento etnográfico." *Revista De Humanidades: Tecnologico de Monterrey*, no. 15, (2003): 209–230.

Lena, Jennifer C. *Banding Together: How Communities Create Genres in Popular Music*. Princeton: Princeton University Press, 2012.

Limón, José E. "'This is Our Música Guy!': Tejanos and Ethno/regional Musical Nationalist." In *Transnational Encounters, Music and Performance at the U.S.-Mexico Border*, edited by Alejandro L. Madrid, 111–126. New York: Oxford University Press, 2011.

López Castro, Gustavo. *El río Bravo es charco*. Zamora: El Colegio de Michoacán, 1995.

Loza, Steven. "Músicos chicanos y la experiencia de transetnicidad." In . . . *Y nos volvemos a encontrar: migración, identidad, y tradición cultural*, edited bv Álvaro Ochoa, 53–62. Zamora: El Colegio de Michoacán, 2001.

Madrid, Alejandro L. *Music in Mexico, Experiencing Music, Expressing Culture*. New York: Oxford University Press, 2013b.

———. "Música y nacionalismos en Latinoamérica." In *A tres bandas: mestizaje, sincretismo e hibridación en el espacio sonoro latinoamericano*, edited by Albert Recasens Barberà, 227–236. Madrid: Ediciones Akal, 2010.

———. *Nor-tec Rifa! Electronic Dance Music from Tijuana to the World*. New York: Oxford University Press, 2008.

———. "Rigo Tovar, Cumbia and the Transnational *Grupero* Boom." In *Cumbia! Scenes of a Migrant Latin American Music Genre*, edited by Héctor Fernández L'Hoeste and Pablo Vila, 105–118. Durham: Duke University Press, 2013.

Manuel, Peter. In *Creolizing Contradance in the Caribbean*. Philadelphia: Temple University Press, 2009.

Martínez, Glenn A. "Mojados, Malinches, and the Dismantling of the United States/México Border in Contemporary Mexican Cinema." *Latin American Issues* 14, no. 2 (1998): 31–50.

Martínez, Andrés. "Life Stories of Four Conjunto Musicians: Adding to the Culturally Relevant Curriculum of the Rio Grande Valley Schools." PhD diss., University of Texas Pan American, 2011.

McKenzie, Phyllis. *The Mexican Texans*. College Station: Texas A&M University Press, 2004.

Medina Montelongo, Filiberto, and Guadalupe Quezada. "Nuevo León y su música de acordeón." In *Tradiciones y costumbres de Nuevo León*, edited by Rogelio Velázquez de León and Francisco Javier Alvarado Segovia, 97–104. Monterrey: Gobierno del Estado de Nuevo León, 1995.

Mendívil, Julio. *En contra de la música: herramientas para pensar, comprender y vivir las músicas*. Buenos Aires: Gourmet Musical Ediciones, 2016.

Mendoza, Vicente T. *El corrido mexicano*. México: FCE, 1996.

———. *La canción mexicana, ensayo de clasificación y antología*. México: FCE, 1998.

Meyer, Jean. *Esperando a Lozada*. Guadalajara: COLMICH-CONACYT, 1984.

Miller, Karl Hagstrom. *Segregating Sounds. Inventing Folk and Pop Music in the Age of Jim Crow*. Durham & London: Duke University Press, 2010.

Miranda, Marcos, and Elinet Medina. "La radio hispana en los Estados Unidos." In *Enciclopedia del español en los Estados Unidos*, edited by Humberto López Morales, 482–496. Madrid: Instituto Cervantes, 2008.

Monsiváis, Carlos. "Las tradiciones que se van, las tradiciones que se quedan." In . . . *Y nos volvemos a encontrar: migración, identidad, y tradición cultural*, edited by Álvaro Ochoa, 199–212. Zamora: El Colegio de Michoacán, 2001.

Montejano, David. *Anglos and Mexicans in the Making of Texas, 1836-1986*. Austin: The University of Texas Press, 2010.

Montoya Arias, Luis. "El bajo sexto es del Bajío mexicano." In *¡Arriba el Norte . . . ! Música de acordeón y bajo sexto*, vol. 1, edited by Luis Montoya Arias, 191–208. México: INAH/CONACULTA, 2013.

———. "Músicas mexicanas en Bogotá. De la región a la internacionalización." In *Músicas migrantes, La movilidad artística en la era global*, edited by Miguel Olmos Aguilera, 169–213. México: El Colegio de la Frontera Norte/UAS/UANL/Bonilla Artigas Editores, 2012

Mora-Torres, Juan. *The Making of the Mexican Border, the State, Capitalism and Society in Nuevo León, 1848-1910*. Austin: The University of Texas Press, 2001.

Moreno Rivas, Yolanda. *Historia de la música popular mexicana*. México: Alianza Editorial Mexicana-CONACULTA, 1989a.

———. *Rostros del nacionalismo en la música mexicana, un ensayo de interpretación*. México: FCE. 1989b.

Morgenthaler, George J. *The River has Never Divided Us: A Border History of La Junta de Los Rios*. Austin: University of Texas Press, 2004.

Morton, David. *Off the Record: The Technology and Culture of Sound Recording in America*. Piscataway: Rutgers University Press, 2000.

Nettl, Bruno. *The Study of Ethnomusicology, Thirty-one Issues and Concepts*. Urbana and Chicago: The University of Illinois Press, 2005.

Nuñez Arellano, Gerardo. "Framing Illegality in the United States: Sonic Culture, Power and the Politics of Representation." PhD diss., University of California, 2010.

Ochoa Serrano, Álvaro. *Mitote, fandango y mariacheros*. Morelia: Centro Universitario de la Ciénega, Universidad de Guadalajara-Fondo Editorial Morevallado-Casa de la Cultura del Valle de Zamora, 2008.

Ogilvie, Sheilagh. *Social Capital, Social Networks, and History*. Cambridge: University of Cambridge, 2000.

Olavarría y Ferrari, Enrique. *Reseña histórica del teatro en México, 1538–1911*, vol. 1. México: Porrúa, 1961.

Olvera Gudiño, José Juan. *Colombianos en Monterrey, Origen de un gusto musical y su papel social en la construcción de una identidad social*. Monterrey: Consejo para la Cultura y las Artes de Nuevo León/CONACULTA, 2005.

———. "Cumbia in Mexico's Northeastern Region." In *Cumbia! Scenes of a Migrant Latin American Music Genre*, edited by Héctor Fernández L'Hoeste and Pablo Vila, 87–104. Durham: Duke University Press, 2013.

Ordaz, David. "Narcomúsica, otro trazo del crimen organizado." *El Economista*, December 16, 2009. http://eleconomista.com.mx/seguridad-publica/2009/12/16/narcomusica-otrobrazo-crimen-organizado.

Orozco Linares, Fernando. *Grandes personajes de México*. México: Panorama, 2005.

Orta Velázquez, Guillermo. *Breve historia de la música en México*. México: Joaquín Porrúa Editores, 1985.

Ortega Ridaura, Isabel, and María Gabriela Márquez Rodríguez. *Génesis y evolución de la administración pública de Nuevo León*. Monterrey: Fondo Editorial Nuevo León, 2005.

Ortiz, Fernando. *Contrapunteo cubano del tabaco y el azúcar.* Caracas: Biblioteca Ayacucho, 1987.

Pacini Hernandez, Deborah. *Oye Como Va! Hybridity and Identity in Latino Popular Music.* Philadelphia: Temple University Press, 2010.

Paredes, Americo. *Folklore and Culture on the Texas-Mexican Border.* Austin: CMAS Books, The University of Texas at Austin, 1995.

———. *With His Pistol in His Hand: A Border Ballad and its Hero.* Austin: The University of Texas Press, 2008.

Paredez, Deborah. *Selenidad: Selena, Latinos, and the Performance of Memory,* Durham: Duke University Press, 2009.

Parga, Pablo. *Cuerpo vestido de nación, Danza folklórica y nacionalismo mexicano, (1921-1939).* Puebla: CONACULTA-FONCA, 2004.

Peña, Manuel. *Música Tejana: The Cultural Economy of Artistic Transformation.* College Station: Texas A&M University Press, 1999a.

———. *The Mexican American Orquesta: Music, Culture, and the Dialectic of Conflict.* Austin: The University of Texas Press, 1999b.

———. *The Texas-Mexican Conjunto: History of a Working-class Music.* Austin: The University of Texas Press, 1985.

Pérez Montfort, Ricardo. *Estampas del nacionalismo popular mexicano.* CIESAS-CIDEHM, 2003.

Plesch, Melanie, Alejandra Cragnolini, and María Leonor Ilarraza. "Polka [polca]." In *Diccionario de la música española e hispanoamericana,* vol. 8, edited by Emilio Casares Rodicio, 869–872. Madrid: Sociedad General de Autores y Editores, 1999.

"Polka, roots of accordion playing in South Texas part 4 of 7." (n.d.). Retrieved from http://www.youtube.com/watch?v=-2hoixBAoJ4.

Pople, Anthony. "Styles and Languages Around the Turn of the Century." In *Cambridge History of Nineteenth-century Music,* edited by Jim Samson, 601–619. Cambridge: Cambridge University Press, 2002.

Powell, Philip Wayne. *Capitán Mestizo: Miguel Caldera y la frontera norteña, la pacificación de los chichimecas, 1548-1597.* México: FCE, 1997.

Prieto, Guillermo. *Memorias de mis tiempos.* México: Porrúa, 1996.

Quirarte, Jacinto. *The Art and Architecture of the Texas Missions.* Austin: University of Texas Press, 2002.

Quiroz Zamora, Mario. *Historia de México.* México: Pearson Educación, 1997.

Ragland, Catherine. "From Pistol-packing Pelado to Border Crossing Mojado: El Piporro and the Making of a 'Mexican' Border Space." In *Transnational Encounters, Music and Performance at the U.S.-Mexico Border,* edited by Alejandro L. Madrid, 341–372. New York: Oxford University Press, 2011.

———. *Música norteña: Mexican Migrants Creating a Nation Between Nations.* Philadelphia: Temple University Press, 2009.

———. "'Tejano and Proud': Regional Accordion Traditions of South Texas and the Border Region." In *The accordion in the Americas, Klezmer, Polka, Tango, Zydeco, and More!,* edited by Helena Simonett, 87–111. Urbana, Chicago and Springfield: University of Illinois Press, 2012.

Ramírez Almaraz, Jesús G. *Monterrey, origen y destino, Los grupos indígenas en Monterrey*. Monterrey: Museo Metropolitano de Monterrey, 2009.

Ramírez-Pimienta, Juan Carlos. *Cantar a los narcos, voces y versos del narcocorrido*. México: Editorial Planeta Mexicana, 2011.

———. "De torturaciones, balas y explosiones: Narcocultura. Movimiento Alterado e hiperrealismo en el sexenio de Felipe Calderón." *A contra corriente. Revista de historia social y literatura en América Latina* vol. 10, no. 3. (Spring 2013): 302–334.

Ramos Aguirre, Francisco. *Los Alegres de Terán, vida y canciones*. México: CONACULTA, 2006.

Ramos Sánchez, Daniel. *La ilusión del crecimiento de la economía mexicana*. México: UNAM, 2000.

Rey, Juan José, and Antonio Navarro. *Los instrumentos de púa en España, Bandurria, cítola y "laúdes españoles."* Madrid: Alianza Editorial, 1993.

Rivard, John, and Laurie E. Jasinski. (2012). "Polka Music." In *The Handbook of Texas Music second edition*, edited by Laurie E. Jasinski, 479–481. Denton: Texas State Historical Association, 2012.

Robles, Sonia. "Shaping México Lindo: Radio, Music, and Gender in Greater Mexico, 1923-1946." PhD diss., Michigan State University, 2012.

Roca, Ana. "El español en los Estados Unidos a principios del siglo XXI: apuntes relativos a la investigación sobre la variedad de la lengua y la coexistencia con el inglés en las comunidades bilingües." In *Teoría y práctica del contacto: el español en América en el candelero*, edited by Julio Calvo Pérez, 193–211. Frankfurt: Vervuert-Iberoamericana, 2000.

Roel, Santiago. *Nuevo León, Apuntes históricos*. Monterrey: Gobierno del Estado de Nuevo León, 1948.

Rojas Sandoval, Javier. *Fábricas pioneras de la industria en Nuevo León*. Monterrey: UANL-Consejo para la Cultura de Nuevo León-Pulsar Internacional, 1997.

Saldívar, Gabriel. *Historia de la música en México (épocas precortesiana y colonial)*. México: SEP, 1934.

Sammartino, Federico. "Estética, teoría crítica y estudios etnográficos de la música popular: algunas propuestas." In *Música popular y juicios de valor: una reflexión desde América Latina*, edited by Juan Francisco Sans and Rubén López Cano, 65–70. Caracas: Fundación CELARG, 2011.

Sánchez, George J. *Becoming Mexican American: Ethnicity, Culture, and Identity in Chicano Los Angeles, 1900-1945*. New York: Oxford University Press, 1995.

San Miguel Jr., Guadalupe. *Tejano Proud, Tex-mex Music in the Twentieth Century*. College Station: Texas A&M University Press, 2002.

Sevilla, Amparo. *Danza cultura y clases sociales*. México: INBA, 1990.

Shorkey, Clayton T. "Bruno Villarreal." In *Puro Conjunto, an Album in Words & Pictures*, edited by Juan Tejeda and Avelardo Valdez, 301–307. Austin: University of Texas Press, 2001.

———. "Cantú, Camilo." In *The Handbook of Texas Music second edition*, edited by Laurie E. Jasinski, 98–99. Denton: Texas State Historical Association, 2012.

Shuker, Roy. *Popular Music: The Key Concepts*. New York: Routledge, 2005.

Simonett, Helena. *Banda, Mexican Musical Life Across Borders*. Middletown: Wesleyan University Press, 2001.

Slobin, Mark. *Folk Music, a Very Short Introduction.* New York: Oxford University Press, 2011.

Smith, Justin Harvey. *The War with Mexico*, vol. 2. New York: The Macmillan Company, 1919.

Sobrino, Ramón. "Schotis." In *Diccionario de la música española e hispanoamericana*, vol. 9, edited by Emilio Casares Rodicio, 868–871. Madrid: Sociedad General de Autores y Editores, 1999.

Stokes, Martin. "Introduction: Ethnicity, Identity and Music." In *Ethnicity, Identity and Music, the Musical Construction of Place*, edited by Martin Stokes, 1–28. New York: Berg Publishers, 1997.

Strachwitz, Chris. "Notes to disc *Texas-Czech, Bohemian & Moravian Bands, Historic Recordings 1929-1959.*" El Cerrito: Arhoolie Records, 1993.

———. "Notes to disc *Mexican-American Border Music, pioneer recording artists, 1928-1958.*" El Cerrito: Arhoolie Records, 1994a.

———. "Notes to disc *Corridos & tragedias de la frontera, first recordings of historic Mexican-American ballads (1928-37).*" El Cerrito: Arhoolie Records, 1994b.

———. "Notes to disc *Norteño & Tejano accordion pioneers, 1929-1939.*" El Cerrito: Arhoolie Records, 1995.

———. "Notes to disc *Maya y Cantú, El primer conjunto norteño famoso, 1946-1949.*" El Cerrito: Arhoolie Records, 1999.

———. *They All Played for Us, Arhoolie Records 50th anniversary celebration.* Arhoolie Productions: El Cerrito, 2012.

Suisman, David. *Selling Sounds, the Commercial Revolution in American Music*. Cambridge: President and fellows of Harvard College, 2009.

Taibo I, Paco Ignacio. *Gloria y achaques del espectáculo en México, 1900-1929.* México: Ediciones Leega/Júcar, 1988.

Taylor, Timothy D. "General Introduction." In *Music, Sound, and Technology in America: A Documentary History of Early Phonograph, Cinema, and Radio*, edited by Timothy D. Taylor, Mark Katz and Tony Grajeda, 1–8. Durham: Duke University Press, 2012.

Tejeda, Juan. "¡Conjunto! Estilo y Clase: Narciso Martínez, Valerio Longoria, Tony de la Rosa, Paulino Bernal, Flaco Jiménez y Esteban Jordán." In *Puro Conjunto, an Album in Words & Pictures*, edited by Juan Tejeda and Avelardo Valdez, 315–351. Austin: University of Texas Press, 2001a.

———. "Eva Ybarra." In *Puro Conjunto, an Album in Words & Pictures*, edited by Juan Tejeda and Avelardo Valdez, 295–297. Austin: University of Texas Press, 2001b.

———. "Santiago Jiménez Sr." In *Puro Conjunto, an Album in Words & Pictures*, edited by Juan Tejeda and Avelardo Valdez, 255–278. Austin: University of Texas Press, 2001c.

Tilmouth, Michael, and Andrew Lamb. "Schottische." In *The New Grove Dictionary of Music and Musicians*, vol. 22, Stanley Sadie, 635. London: Macmillan, 1980.

Tinajero Medina, Rubén and María Hernández Iznaga. *El narcocorrido, ¿Tradición o mercado?* Chihuahua, México: UACH/SPAUACH, 2004.
Titus, Joan. "*Waila* as Transnational Practice." In *Transnational Encounters, Music and Performance at the U.S -Mexico Border*, edited by Alejandro L. Madrid, 149–167. New York: Oxford University Press, 2011.
Torres, Augusto M. *720 directores de cine*. Barcelona: Editorial Ariel, 2008.
Turino, Thomas. "The Urban-Mestizo Charango Tradition in Southern Peru. A Statement of Shifting Identity." *Ethnomusicology* 28, no. 2 (May 1984): 253–270.
Tyrrell, John. "Redowa." In *New Grove Dictionary of Music and Musicians,* vol. 21, edited by Stanley Sadie, 58–59. London: Macmillan, 1980.
Valenzuela, José Manuel. *Jefe de jefes, corridos y narcocultura en México*, México: Plaza y Janés, 2002.
Valerio-Jiménez, Omar S. *River of Hope: Forging Identity and Nation in the Rio Grande Borderlands.* Durham Duke University Press, 2013.
Van Wagenen, Michael. *The Texas Republic and the Mormon Kingdom of God.* Kingsville: Texas A&M University Press, 2002.
Vázquez, Josefina Zorada. "Los primeros tropiezos." In *Historia General de México versión 2000*, 525–582. México: Colmex, 2002.
Vizcaya Canales, Isidro. *Los orígenes de la industrialización en Monterrey, una historia económica y social desde la caída del segundo imperio hasta el fin de la revolución (1867-1920).* Monterrey, México: Fondo Editorial Nuevo León, ITESM, 2006.
Wald, Elijah. *Narcocorrido, A Journey Into the Music of Drugs, Guns and Guerrillas.* New York: Harper Collins Publishers, 2001.
Weber, David J. *La frontera española en América del Norte*. México: FCE, 2000.
———. *La frontera norte de México, 1821-1846*. México: FCE, 2005.
Weber, William. *Music and the Middle Class: The Social Structure of Concert Life in London, Paris and Vienna Between 1830 and 1848*. London: Croom Helm, 1975.
Weigand, Phil C. *Estudio histórico y cultural sobre los huicholes*. Colotlán: Universidad de Guadalajara, Campus Universitario del Norte, 2002.
Yépez, Benjamín. "Redova." In *Diccionario de la música española e hispanoamericana*, vol. 9, edited by Emilio Casares Rodicio, 73. Madrid: Sociedad General de Autores y Editores, 1999.
Zalpa, Genaro. *Cultura y acción social. Teoría(s) de la cultura*. México: UAA-Plaza y Valdés, 2011.
Zapata Vázquez, Dinorah. *Génesis y desarrollo de la radio y la televisión en Nuevo León*. Monterrey: UANL, 1990.
———. *La radio de Tárnava*. Monterrey, México: UANL, 2002.

Index

accordion, 3, 5-7, 13, 17, 19, 46, 53, 60, 62-65, 69-72, 75, 77, 78, 85-94, 96, 97, 99, 104, 106-108, 110, 120, 124-126, 128
Los Alegres de Terán, 7, 83, 86, 88, 89, 91, 93, 99, 104, 106, 112, 124
Alice, 71, 93, 127
Almeida, Santiago, 72, 78, 97
Anderson, Benedict, 39
audience, 10, 11, 31, 32, 49, 70, 72, 82, 89, 91, 94, 99, 103-105, 113, 121, 126, 127
Austin, 30, 50, 72, 80, 102, 124, 127
authenticity, 73, 85, 106
Avanzada Regia, 126
Ayala, Pedro, 8, 71, 75, 124
Ayala, Ramón, 8, 10, 75, 83, 90, 91, 98, 103, 104, 117

bajo sexto, 5-7, 10, 12, 13, 17, 50, 52, 62-69, 71, 72, 78, 86-90, 92, 94, 96, 106, 110, 120, 124-126, 128
ballads, 98, 110, 112, 118
ballroom, 16, 58, 60, 82, 98, 106, 115
banda, 48, 85, 116, 126
bandolón, 49, 50
Berger, Peter, and Thomas Luckman, 5,
Berlanga, Andrés, 72
Bernal, Paulino, 75, 89, 90, 107, 112

Beto Villa y los Populares de Nueva Rosita, 110
blues, 58, 98, 127
bolero, 3, 87, 89, 90, 107, 108,
border, 1, 4, 5, 7-11, 13, 18, 21-23, 28, 32, 35-37, 41, 42, 44, 45, 48, 49, 51, 53, 55, 57, 62, 63, 65, 66, 68, 71-74, 78, 81, 83, 86, 89, 91, 93, 96, 97, 100, 101, 104-106, 109, 113, 114, 116, 123, 127
Bronco, 111
Los Broncos de Reynosa, 104, 105
Buchanan, Patrick J., 101, 102

Los Cadetes de Linares, 104
Campos, Rubén M., 16, 48, 65
canción, 2, 17, 106
Canetti, Elias, 103
"Cantinflas" (Mario Moreno), 99
Cantú, Camilo, 72, 75, 124
Carlos y José, 124
Cavazos, Lolo, 71, 124
Cavazos, Ramiro, 50, 70, 74, 83, 86, 90, 106, 117
center-periphery conflict, 8, 13, 42, 80, 117
Chamorro Escalante, Arturo, 67
Chapa, Valentín, 71
"El Chapo" Guzmán (Joaquín Guzmán Loera), 118, 119

157

chotis, 48, 52, 60, 62, 97
cinema, 15, 35, 44, 70, 79, 81, 101, 103-105, 109
Conjunto Bernal, 12, 89, 90, 98, 112
Corpus Christi, 12, 72, 78, 121, 125, 127
Los Corraleros del Majagual, 109, 110
corrido, 2, 10, 11, 41, 42, 51, 52, 54, 71, 73, 90, 91, 95, 96, 98, 103, 105, 107, 112-122, 126
corridos por encargo, 118
couple dance, 60
crossover, 86, 90
cumbia, 3, 90, 94, 107-112, 126
Curti, Carlos, 49, 62, 67

diaspora, 13, 74, 89, 100, 122
Díaz, Porfirio, 1, 37, 50, 114
Los Donneños, 82, 83, 86, 87, 124
drum (s). *See* tambora and tarola

Edberg, Mark, 119
Escobar, Eligio, 93, 95
Escobar, Linda, 93, 109
ethnomusicology, 77

fandango, 43, 44, 49, 96, 108
Fernández, Rosita, 92
folklore, 4, 42, 52, 65, 97
Frankfurt School, 98
Frith, Simon, 2, 16

Geertz, Clifford, 14
globalization, 76, 84
González, Eulalio, 4, 35, 36, 45, 81, 91, 98-101, 104, 125
Los Gorriones del Topo Chico, 91
Grammy Awards, 4,
grupero/a, 2, 103, 110, 111
guitar, 5, 6, 40, 50, 51, 53, 61, 64-68, 72, 77, 86-89, 92, 96, 99, 104, 105, 110, 114, 125, 126
guitarrón, 65, 66

harmonic, 13, 62, 64
hegemony, 13, 42

heritage, 14, 15, 35, 73, 88, 94, 97, 107, 126-128
hip hop, 120
historiography, 11, 31, 32, 48
Hobsbawm, Eric, 44, 118, 119
Hoggart, Richard, 19, 124
The Hurricane of the Valley. *See* Martínez, Narciso
Hutchinson, Sydney, 94

identity, 2-5, 13, 18, 21, 32, 39, 41-44, 49, 53, 57, 69, 72, 75, 81, 82, 85, 87, 96, 109, 111, 124-126, 128
ideology, 7, 47, 74
imagined political community, 39
intertextuality, 124

jarabe, 40, 43, 44, 94
jarana/jaranita, 49, 67, 116
Jiménez, José Alfredo, 89, 100, 106, 127
Jiménez, Leonardo, 4, 12, 93, 97
Jiménez, Santiago, 4, 74, 75, 92, 103, 106
Jiménez, Santiago Jr., 97, 103
Jordan, Esteban "Steve," 107, 108
Juan Gabriel, 127

Laredo, 9, 19, 22, 34, 41
Lena, Jennifer, 82
Linares, 51, 69, 70
Longoria, Valerio, 97, 106, 107
Loza, Steve, 7
Luis y Julián, 91

Madrid, Alejandro L., 11, 22, 42
mandolin, 40, 66, 67, 86
marginal, 6, 85, 98, 112
marginalized, 2, 13, 40, 41, 51, 65, 108, 112, 113, 118, 119, 123, 125, 126
mariachi, 2, 13, 17, 42-44, 65, 90, 91, 93, 105, 119, 123, 127
Martínez, Narciso, 8, 12, 69, 72-75, 78, 92, 97, 106, 124, 127
Martínez, Reynaldo, 88
mazurka, 45, 59, 61, 62, 73
Mendoza, Lydia, 51, 52, 78, 92, 97

Index

Mendoza, Vicente T., 113, 118
mestizo, 44, 62, 63
Mexican-Americans, 22, 36, 53, 54, 57, 70, 78, 81, 88, 84, 96, 100, 101, 102, 128
mexican revolution, 1, 43, 52, 66, 70, 122
migration, 1-3, 5-8, 11-13, 18, 37, 39, 45, 57, 70, 72, 101-103, 105, 114, 121, 124, 125
modernity, 6, 40, 79, 126
Monsiváis, Carlos, 128
Los Montañeses del Álamo, 10, 51-53, 69, 94, 99
Monterrey, 5, 6, 10-12, 18, 24, 28, 36, 37, 41, 45-48, 51, 52, 59, 62, 64, 67, 68, 70-73, 78-81, 83, 88, 92, 96, 103, 105, 109-111, 125
multicultural, 96, 108
music industry, 85, 93, 110, 111

narcocorrido, 2, 18, 98, 112, 113, 115-122
National Endowment for the Arts, 97
Nor-tec, 126
Las Norteñitas, 93

Olvera Gudiño, José Juan, 109
onda grupera. *See* grupero/a
orquesta típica, 43, 47, 49, 50, 52, 62, 63, 65-69, 86, 87
otherness, 17

El Palomo y el Gorrión, 10, 89, 91, 107, 125
Paredes, Américo, 4, 41, 42, 114, 124
Peña, Manuel, 10, 11, 17, 59, 65, 70, 74, 89, 98, 124
Piporro. *See* González, Eulalio.
polka, 2, 7, 19, 45, 48, 51-53, 58-62, 69, 72-74, 78, 89, 97, 98, 107, 109, 126
Ponce, Manuel M., 16, 17, 44
Poniatowska, Elena, 101
popular culture, 2, 14, 15, 18, 26, 65, 85, 105, 113, 117

popular music, 2, 7, 10, 13-17, 40, 42, 60, 62, 76, 77, 80, 85, 98, 100, 106, 107, 110, 111
porfiriato. *See* Díaz, Porfirio
porro, 108, 109

radio, 6, 13, 15, 52, 55, 57, 70, 75, 78-82, 84, 85, 91, 92, 98, 102, 110-112, 121
Ragland, Cathy, 44, 65, 74, 90, 99, 124
ranchera, 44, 51, 90, 93, 95, 107
Los Rancheritos del Topo Chico, 89, 91
rap, 2, 120, 126
rascuache, 99
redova, 60, 97, 107
Reynosa, 12, 22, 35, 36, 71, 72, 83, 87, 90, 125
rock, 2, 4, 18, 19, 55, 58, 90, 103, 104, 107, 108, 111, 118, 126, 127

Saldívar, Mingo, 53, 97
salsa, 107, 108
salterio, 49
Saltillo, 34, 48
San Antonio, 4, 12, 25, 26, 28, 30, 33, 36, 37, 41, 45, 49, 54, 65, 68, 69, 72, 74, 75, 78, 81, 92, 93, 97, 102, 121-125, 127
Sánchez, Rosalino "Chalino," 116
saxophone, 5, 19, 53, 69, 94, 110
Selena, 96, 112
Simonett, Helena, 118
social dance, 60
Stokes, Martin, 62
Strachwitz, Chris, 12, 52, 102, 106, 108
Strachwitz Frontera Collection, 88

tambora, 6, 43, 51, 63, 69, 72
Tanguma, Antonio, 6, 59, 70, 71, 81, 83, 97, 126
tarola, 87
Los Temerarios, 111
Los Tigres del Norte, 5, 8, 75, 82, 89, 93, 103, 105, 112, 113, 115, 117, 118, 121, 122, 124, 126
tololoche, 5, 65, 75, 87, 94, 126

Tovar, Rigo, 111
transnational, 2, 8, 13, 37, 93, 99-111, 125, 126, 128
tropical, 2, 109, 111
Los Tucanes de Tijuana, 112, 120, 122
typical orchestra. *See* orquesta típica

upright bass. *See* tololoche

Verheyden, Dwayne, 54, 123
Villa, Beto (father of orquesta tejana), 52, 69
Villarreal, Bruno, 4, 70, 72, 78
Villarreal, Juan, 124
violin, 3, 49, 50, 52, 59, 60, 62, 67, 86, 94, 126

Wald, Elijah, 8
waltz, 45, 51, 52, 59-62, 90

Ybarra, Eva, 92, 93, 97

Zacatecas, 1, 17, 22, 24, 25, 27, 28, 30, 34, 41, 42, 46, 53, 62, 91, 94, 99, 118, 126
Zúñiga de la Garza, Agapito, 71, 124

About the Author

Luis Díaz-Santana Garza, PhD, is professor of music history and guitar in the Department of Arts at the Zacatecas Autonomous University in Zacatecas, Mexico, and member of the National System of Researchers

PREVIOUS PUBLICATIONS

Music Tradition in Zacatecas (1850–1930) (2009)
History of Mexican Norteño Music (2015)
Dictionary of Mexican Popular Music (2018)
Music Research in the Regions of Mexico editor (2018)
Music and regions in Mexico editor (2021)

www.ingramcontent.com/pod-product-compliance
Lightning Source LLC
Chambersburg PA
CBHW020124010526
44115CB00008B/959